CW01217216

The Battles of
BONNIE PRINCE CHARLIE

For
Fiona, Charlotte and Archer

The Battles of
BONNIE PRINCE CHARLIE
THE YOUNG CHEVALIER AT WAR

ARRAN JOHNSTON

PEN & SWORD
HISTORY

AN IMPRINT OF PEN & SWORD BOOKS LTD.
YORKSHIRE - PHILADELPHIA

First published in Great Britain in 2023 by
PEN AND SWORD HISTORY
An imprint of
Pen & Sword Books Ltd
Yorkshire – Philadelphia

Copyright © Arran Johnston, 2023

ISBN 978 1 39906 114 8

The right of Arran Johnston to be identified as Author of this work has been asserted by him in accordance with the Copyright, Designs and Patents Act 1988.

A CIP catalogue record for this book is available from the British Library.

All rights reserved. No part of this book may be reproduced or transmitted in any form or by any means, electronic or mechanical including photocopying, recording or by any information storage and retrieval system, without permission from the Publisher in writing.

Typeset in Times New Roman 11.5/14 by
SJmagic DESIGN SERVICES, India.
Printed and bound in the UK by CPI Group (UK) Ltd.

Pen & Sword Books Limited incorporates the imprints of Atlas, Archaeology, Aviation, Discovery, Family History, Fiction, History, Maritime, Military, After the Battle, Military Classics, Politics, Select, Transport, True Crime, Air World, Frontline Publishing, Leo Cooper, Remember When, Seaforth Publishing, The Praetorian Press, Wharncliffe Local History, Wharncliffe Transport, Wharncliffe True Crime and White Owl.

For a complete list of Pen & Sword titles please contact
PEN & SWORD BOOKS LIMITED
George House, Units 12 & 13, Beevor Street, Off Pontefract Road,
Barnsley, South Yorkshire, S71 1HN, England
E-mail: enquiries@pen-and-sword.co.uk
Website: www.pen-and-sword.co.uk

or
PEN AND SWORD BOOKS
1950 Lawrence Rd, Havertown, PA 19083, USA
E-mail: uspen-and-sword@casematepublishers.com
Website: www.penandswordbooks.com

Contents

Acknowledgements vi
List of Illustrations vii
Introduction ix

Chapter One	The Siege of Gaeta	1
Chapter Two	*Du Teillay*	21
Chapter Three	Holyroodhouse	39
Chapter Four	The Battle of Prestonpans	53
Chapter Five	The Retreat	82
Chapter Six	The Battle of Falkirk	105
Chapter Seven	Culloden	126
Epilogue		159

Bibliography 175
Notes 182
Index 203

Acknowledgements

I am grateful to all those who, over many years and in many places, have joined with me in countless discussions and debates about the life, cause and legacy of Charles Edward Stuart. Those countless conversations have been invaluable for the testing and re-articulating of my ideas and interpretations, and have helped me reason my way towards some conclusions over what sort of man Charles Edward really was.

I am indebted to Gordon Prestoungrange and our fellow trustees of The Battle of Prestonpans (1745) Heritage Trust for years of encouragement and opportunity.

For some specific insights, translations and permissions, I am also grateful to: the late Christopher Duffy, Deborah Dennison, Roddy Tulloch, Thierry Guiheneuf and Mike Nevin.

The National Library of Scotland maps service is an invaluable resource which makes the tracking of movements around historical landscapes a simple delight; I am grateful to the University of Edinburgh library service for its alumni access provision.

The Stuart Papers in the Royal Archive are quoted by gracious permission of His Majesty The King.

Most importantly of all, I owe unending thanks to my family for their continued patience and support, without which this work could not have been completed.

List of Illustrations

1. *Prince Charles Edward Stuart* by Louis-Gabriel Blanchet. Courtesy of the National Portrait Gallery, London.
2. *The Future Charles III of Spain at the Siege of Gaeta*, by Giovanni Luigi Rocco. Wikimedia Commons, Public Domain.
3. Panel 5 of *The Prestonpans Tapestry*, designed by Andrew Crummy and stitched by Elizabeth Duke and Lynne Schroder. By permission of the Battle of Prestonpans (1745) Heritage Trust.
4. The Glenfinnan Monument at the head of Loch Shiel. Author's collection.
5. The Palace of Holyroodhouse, from Frances Grose's *Antiquities of Scotland*. Wikimedia Commons, Public Domain.
6. Prince Charles Edward Stuart by Allan Ramsay. Courtesy of National Galleries Scotland.
7. David, Lord Elcho (1721–1787), by an unknown artist. Author's collection.
8. Lord George Murray (1694–1760), by Robert Strange. Creative Commons CC by NC.
9. Plan of the Battle of Prestonpans. Courtesy of the National Library of Scotland.
10. The Field of Preston Pans, after Sir William Allan. Courtesy of the National Army Museum.
11. Memorial Tables on Prestonpans Battlefield. Author's collection.
12. Gowan Hill from Stirling Castle. Author's collection.
13. Plan of the Battle of Falkirk, showing the British army's forced redeployment onto the moor. Reproduced with the permission of the National Library of Scotland.
14. The Prince's Stones on Falkirk Battlefield. Author's collection.
15. Falkirk Battlefield from near the Prince's Stones. Author's collection.

16. The monument on Falkirk Battlefield. Author's collection.
17. John Finlayson's map of the march on Nairn and the subsequent Battle of Culloden. Reproduced with the permission of the National Library of Scotland.
18. Plan of the Battle of Culloden by a French officer who was present. Reproduced with the permission of the National Library of Scotland.
19. Coloured engraving of the Battle of Culloden, by L. Sullivan after A. Heckel. Courtesy of the National Army Museum.
20. The clan graves at Culloden. Author's collection.
21. Halt of Prince Charles Edward at the banks of the Nairne, by Richard Beavis (1878).
22. The Prince's Cairn at Loch nan Uamh. Author's collection.
23. Prince Charles Edward Stuart by Cosmo Alexander. Courtesy of the Stirling Smith Art Gallery & Museum.
24. Prince Charles Edward Stuart by Anthony Stones. Author's collection.

Introduction

The Young Chevalier sits his horse with a straight back and firm shoulders, exuding both pride and resilience. Leaning just slightly forward in the saddle, he pushes his weight down through his booted legs and into his stirrups. A bonnet crowns his head, mounted with a cockade, covering his swept and powdered curls. Off the shoulder of the prince's frockcoat a plaid of tartan is draped, and on his chest glimmers the star of the Order of the Garter. The broadsword at his hip has a fine and elaborate hilt. The overall effect of the image is one of elegant simplicity, authority without ostentation. The prince's bearing is military, serious, but the hand-on-hip pose is not casual and his fist is clenched. Little emotion can be read on the soft features of his face, but the lips are pressed tight as if the expression is firmly controlled. The face looks to the south, large defiant eyes casting their gaze along the receding road. The horse, in contrast to its rider, displays a restless tension, its eyes wide and a hoof raised. Its head tugs to the north with an unheard jingle of bits.

This is how we encounter Prince Charles Edward Stuart today in the city of Derby, deep in the heart of England. The bronze figure gazes over our heads from its high stone plinth, capturing a critical moment in his story and in the city's: the Stuart prince is taking his last look towards London before his horse turns north towards Scotland. At the end of that road lies defeat, exile and a bitterly contested legacy. This impressive statue by Anthony Stones was erected in Derby for the 250th anniversary of the last Jacobite rising, and it is – for the time being at least – the world's only full statue of the famous 'Bonnie Prince Charlie'. The only other contender, the figure surmounting the Glenfinnan Monument, has an ambiguous identity and is probably best interpreted as an idealised Highland chieftain. The identity of a standing bronze in Edinburgh's City Chambers, recently theorised as being Charles Edward Stuart, remains unproven.

Charles Edward's war of 1745–6 was a failure. His army was defeated and dispersed, and he would never lead another. After his fourteen-month visit, he would also never return to Scotland. Viewed from this perspective, the fact that there are so few statues of him may not seem that surprising. And yet his is one of the most recognisable faces in Scottish public history, visible within most of the country's great galleries and museums, and used relentlessly for the promotion of tourism, tartan, shortbread and whisky. Artefacts connected to Charles Edward Stuart command consistently high prices in auction salerooms, and have the power to summon large and loyal audiences at exhibitions. For this, some of the credit must go to the royal Stuarts themselves as they understood the need to keep their faces familiar to their would-be subjects, even as they remained in distant exile. The portraits they commissioned, often by some of the greatest available talents, were copied, distributed and turned into more accessible engravings. Supporters had relics and likenesses worked into all manner of trinkets and talismans, creating the rich material culture that helps perpetuate so much interest in the Jacobite cause from behind so many glass cabinets today. But more than the fine and endearing character that was his father, or the crowned and anointed king that was his grandfather, it is Charles Edward Stuart who shines the brightest in our imaginations.

Of course, a large part of that is down to the inherent attraction of the story of The '45. The narrative reads today – as it ever has – like the most unlikely, desperate and high-spirited adventure. It has all the elements of the greatest heroic tales. From inauspicious beginnings, with intrigue and danger at every turn, the story develops against the stirring backdrop of the Scottish Highlands with a cast of big and contrasting personalities navigating unexpected successes and overcoming terrible obstacles, with ever-rising stakes. Even the final defeat of the Jacobites in the field does not end the tale, as it then becomes a romantic epilogue of loyalty in spite of all terrors, of a prince in the heather, and the bittersweet end of a beloved old song. And, as Sir Walter Scott acknowledged in his great nineteenth-century novel *Waverley*, it is a tale that took place in a world which was simultaneously both distant and near to us: in a bygone age, but one that is recognisable, only *just* beyond our reach.

The story of The '45 is also self-perpetuating. The more it is told, the more we want to tell it. To the contemporary portraits and battleplans we

Introduction

must add the grand tableaux of the Victorian artist; to the memoirs and news-sheets of the day, we must add *Waverley* and *Kidnapped*, Broster and Gabaldon. In their time came the silver-screen performances of Ivor Novello and then David Niven, contrasting in their romance with the bitter grit of Peter Watkins' *Culloden* (1964). And across the generations of cultural representations and re-interpretations, fresh pilgrims have sought the real or imagined relics of the story's heroes, walked the bitter ground of Culloden field, and nurtured the story as something they own and something that has made them.

The telling of the story has rarely been consistent. It has variously been understood as an Anglo-Scottish war, or as a Protestant-Catholic conflict: as a fight between modernity and feudalism, civilisation and savagery. Sometimes the redcoats are painted as a lesser enemy to the Highlanders than the callous aristos who led their brave but simple people to destruction for the cause of their own advancement, by order of their spoilt and petulant prince. The latter, for failing to lead the Highlanders to victory, is deemed as much at fault as those whose yoke he had promised to break. And it is always about the Highlanders, as the tale is far better told without the complexities of the Lowland Jacobites, or the Irish ones, and most certainly the English (who doomed their friends by their weakness and timidity). Red-coated soldiers have also been cast as the most despicable villains, regardless of their individual motives, gallantry or sympathies; pro-Union Scots have been damned as traitors for staying loyal to their own perceptions of their country's best interests. As ever, there are always germs of a foundation in all such tropes: some Jacobites were Catholic; some British soldiers committed appalling atrocities; some Jacobites were motivated by self-interest or intrigue; and the rising's failure became a catalyst (not a cause) of the collapse of the ancient clan system.

At the centre of this complex and shifting set of narrative fashions, enduring myths and simplified stereotypes is the persistently engaging figure of Charles Edward Stuart. Since the moment of his birth there have been two men of that name: the one who was reported by British agents as so weak and deformed that he would probably never walk; the other who was a strong and healthy boy whose arrival was celebrated by the appearance of a new star in the sky and a hurricane over Hanover. The two have remained largely apart ever since, and both have entered the popular imagination according to the recipients' own instincts, prejudice or politics. Some of the criticism and caricature is lifted straight from Hanoverian propaganda; some is kept alive by more contemporary attitudes. One persistent paradox is that some of those who profess to be ardent modern 'Jacobites' are amongst the most assertively hostile critics of the prince. If he left parts of Scotland worse than he found them, it was not for wont of effort or for selfishness of design. Nor is it persuasive that the feudal and economic systems of the Highlands would have remained static had the last rising never occurred, or even that it was desirable they should do so.

In contrast to the Charles Edward as the uninvited angel of destruction, there is the Peter Pan-like figure of the eternal boy prince with his pursed red lips and cream-white skin. Born from the popularity of his adolescent portraits – the ones most readily at hand when the prince suddenly burst onto his Scottish stage – this prince is set up as a symbol of youthful innocence which contrasts powerfully with the burly characters of the Highland warriors whose faithful adoration he sought to earn with his charm and courage. To complete the effect of the contrast, the tall and athletic Charles of history becomes diminutive; the gifted sportsman becomes soft, pampered and effeminate. To the eyes of the nineteenth-century romantic, this was in no way incompatible with bravery and endurance. Thus, we inherit another Charles Edward Stuart, or rather a 'Bonnie Prince Charlie', a contrasting figure who is just as unreal as the other.

As Michele de Vezzosi's translator remarked as early as 1748, 'to clear up and rescue the character of this remarkable youth, as well from the too fulsome flatteries of his friends as from the mean and contemptuous notions of his enemies, is an attempt which I apprehend is not unworthy of the regard of the public.' Alas Vezzosi, the prince's valet, was not averse to flattery or fabrication himself. He places the prince within the French ranks at Dettingen, for example, gaining himself an imagined degree of experience in the field. Nevertheless, he has the credit of being one of the earliest biographers of the prince with his *Young Juba, or the History of the Young Chevalier from his Birth to his Escape from Scotland*.

Many others have followed in the quest to 'clear up' the prince's true character. In the twentieth century the most important endeavours have come from: Andrew Lang (1903); Margaret Forster (1973); David Daiches (1973); Frank McLynn (1988); and the soldier and politician

Introduction

Fitzroy Maclean (1989). More recently, Hugh Douglas presented an analysis of the prince's relationships with women (2016), and Peter Pininski's *Bonnie Prince Charlie* (2010) has been revised and re-presented (2022). This list is not exclusive, nor does it include the great many more general texts on The '45 or the wider Jacobite context, or the more focused works exploring other personalities, themes, trends, events or material culture. So it is not for a lack of accessible research or engaging writing that misunderstandings continue to find currency (indeed, some older works that are still widely available have helped to sustain them). Nor do all the studies emphasise the same traits or present the same conclusions, meaning that two individuals' views of Charles Edward Stuart might be very different if they have met him through Forster, McLynn or Prebble.

The prince has always had his defenders as well as his critics. Some proclaimed his virtues from the scaffold before they made their final sacrifice for his cause; some had no love for his cause but felt obliged to concede that he was worthy of reluctant admiration. When British officers were merrily mocking the prince in Edinburgh, the Prince of Hesse-Kassel – George II's son-in-law, no less – rose to speak in defence of his character. In fact, the government struggled to find enough material to provide effective attack lines, and so stuck to the old but effective anti-Catholic and anti-Gaelic tropes, given colour by the occasional salacious fabrication. But the government did not entirely control the media space, however, and there was no shortage of eyewitness testimony being shared and reported during the 1745–6 conflict. Positive perceptions found voice throughout, and many of the prince's contemporaries did find it possible to both oppose *and* respect him simultaneously.

After the war, with the prince back in exile and living out of the public eye for extended periods, opinion comes to rely on gossip, speculation and the patchy evidence of brief encounters reported through a fog of distance, prejudice and disappointment. Getting a rounded picture of the later Charles becomes far more challenging, but the picture that emerges is of a man whose spirit had been broken by the events of 1746. Charles Edward's story becomes one of unfulfilled potential, felt most keenly by the man himself. His detractors often point to these long, depressing decades as if they show that he was never fit to rule. These days, such a lack of understanding is indefensible. To seek explanations for negative behaviours – alcohol dependency, paranoia, domestic abuse – is not the same as to excuse them. But they should be seen as what they were: symptoms rather than proofs.

There are inconsistencies in his behaviour which catch our attention even during The '45: he barely sleeps when things are going well, for example, but is dangerously lethargic in retreat. His fondness for alcohol, and his capacity to drink it, raised eyebrows even in an age accustomed to high consumption. He was persistently poor at managing relationships and controlling the expression of his emotions. During the conflict, it is possible to explain some of this as the result of the unprecedented pressures and stresses of a campaign for which he was physically but not mentally prepared. But the longer trends are more indicative. That the prince suffered post-traumatic stress as a result of the conflict is a real possibility, but he may already have been living with manic depression. This may have been an unhappy inheritance from his mother, Maria Clementina Sobieska. If this is the case, then we should assess Charles Edward differently. These days mental health is high in the public consciousness, but Charles is still commonly sneered at as a drunk rather than a man battling undiagnosed demons. If he were alive today, we might well feel uncomfortable with that attitude, and be more sympathetic in our treatment of such a man.

Other prejudices still creep into play as well, sometimes subconsciously. Sometimes it is shown by apparently innocent comments about accents and birthplace, a dislike of the prince's apparent foreign-ness. But Charles Edward was not cosplaying when he donned the Highland habit: it was an expression of his own personal identity. Today he would be considered a cosmopolitan celebrity of the Scottish diaspora, well-dressed, good-looking and media savvy; just as fascinating and engaging to journalists and tourists as he was in his own time, with readers just as desperate to hear the latest gossip, scandal or fake news about his family. The prince had a multi-dimensional personality that has the power to engage people and to keep them engaged, polarising people's opinions both politically and personally. It makes him a fascinating man to follow, especially during the course of the most famous incidents in his life.

Understanding Prince Charles is crucial to any understanding of what really happened in The '45, and why. While fashion has moved away

Introduction

from focusing historical study too greatly on privileged elites, military campaigns remain theatres in which individual players can demonstrably direct the course of great events. All the people named within this book are worthy of study and understanding, as are the thousands whose names pass unmentioned or unknown. But there is no escaping the fact that without Charles Edward Stuart's personal determination to make it happen, The '45 would not have taken place. There were opportunities for others to prevent it, and there were many who facilitated it, but he was its driver. Then, somewhere along the road, he lost control of it. Just as the prince is accused of doing lasting damage by his actions, so the experience inflicted lasting damage on him.

The Jacobite rising of 1745–6 was a military and political conflict, and, on behalf of his father, Charles Edward Stuart was the military and political head of his cause. Rarely, though, is he given due credit for the performance of the army he commanded. His achievements are often credited to others, and he is often blamed for the shortcomings of others. The prince was not a military genius, but nor was he inept. He repeatedly demonstrated personal courage, tactical competence and an ability to lead. Most of all, he showed himself to have a sound strategic understanding of the conflict and how it might be won, often more so than those around him. Very significantly, but often underappreciated, Charles Edward Stuart undertook his conflict with a humanity and sensitivity which bordered sometimes on the naïve, but stands in proud contrast to the tenor of some of his opponents. The prince understood the power of appearances, the importance of public relations, and how to earn the admiration of his men. He had an instinct for what they needed him to say or do, and was an effective political performer. But while he could generally control his emotions in public, in private he could be passionate to the point of volatility. Often, he needed the reassurance of trusted friendship, which encouraged him to rely on a close circle. Like his father, he could hold to those relationships even if they alienated or aggravated others.

All this is demonstrated by the study of the prince's military career, which, apart from a brief experience in his boyhood, was limited to the conflict of 1745–6. The purpose of this book, then, is to explore that career to gain a sense of who Charles Edward was and how substantial his contribution was to those great events. Its intention is not to provide a comprehensive narrative of the campaigns, for which there remains no greater volume than Christopher Duffy's *Fight for a Throne* (2015), a revised edition of his earlier *The '45* (2003). The focus is on the main military engagements at which the prince was present, mainly the Battles of Prestonpans, Falkirk and Culloden. Decisions have necessarily been taken as to which elements of the wider campaigns to include and in what detail, and the criteria are based mainly on whether incidents provide insights into the prince's own experience or others' perceptions of it.

This book does not pretend to offer a deep academic analysis of the composition, motivation or capacity of the Jacobite cause, political or military. There is much excellent work being done in these fields, showing an ever more nuanced picture that cannot be given due justice here. Nor do these pages seek to provide the most detailed topographical or archaeological analyses of the relevant battlefields, although the accounts within them are, of course, informed by careful study of all the available, ever-expanding research. Even aspects of a battle which could not be seen or understood by the prince will be presented in that context, which might leave some readers wanting more. The main battles are covered individually elsewhere, as are the sieges thanks to Jonathan Oates' recent work. Alas, our focus here does not help raise the profile of the smaller engagements of the conflict which deserve so much more attention: Highbridge, Clifton, Inverurie, Keith, Littleferry and the amphibious actions.

It is also important to accept before proceeding that the narrative in this book is deliberately presented solely from the Jacobite perspective. It seeks to understand the Jacobite army's experience of the conflict, or rather Charles Edward's, so the British army's activities are only related in the detail relevant to that context. This should not be interpreted as a judgemental bias, but a narrative one.

This book's presentation of Prince Charles Edward Stuart is the outcome of a persistent and protracted personal interest, and is distilled from a wide range of sources. In the main text, the most commonly cited are those whose accounts are considered the most revealing and reliable, or were at least written by those close enough to the events and characters to know of what they speak. None are without bias. John Sullivan's wonderful narrative of the campaign is the most openly favourable to the prince, reflecting the closeness of their relationship and the intended audience of the account, King James. Lord George Murray's main memoir is sometimes thorough, sometimes defensive, but always interesting. Both men occasionally offer contradictory evidence, and commonly gloss over less favourable incidents. This leaves an engaging challenge as we try to unpick the more probable truths, looking at what is left unsaid as well as what is revealed. John Murray of Broughton leaves us a detailed memoir of the campaign as far as Derby, and often provides valuable information. However, his reputation has never recovered from his actions after the conflict and, as with Sullivan, his evidence is occasionally neglected in favour of Murray's. Lord Elcho, who leaves us two accounts, was well placed to know a great deal, but was tainted by a bitterness against the prince which emerged early in his exile. James Johnstone and Maxwell of Kirkconnell both served as aides to senior officers during the campaign so were in a position to hear more than many. These are the voices we will hear most frequently within these pages, supplemented and corroborated by others.

There are other parameters which limit the scope of this book. The first is that if it lacks the space to provide a comprehensive narrative of the whole fourteen-month conflict, there is even less room to offer a full biography of the prince's sixty-eight-year life. While we will occasionally look both forward and back, our focus remains on the key military milestones of Charles Edward's life. The fullest biographies have already been named above, while Edward Corp's work on the Stuart court in exile provides an unrivalled understanding of the environment and community in which the prince and his family lived. There are a number of works devoted to the prince's famous adventures as a fugitive, although nothing compares to the chaotic experience of delving into *The Lyon in Mourning* for insights into those escapades. In the present volume, we will meet Prince Charles in his early adolescence, on the cusp of his first experience of war, and we will leave him after the destruction of the last army he would ever lead.

In short, then, the purpose of these pages is essentially biographical: to relate how Charles Edward Stuart influenced the military campaigns which defined his life, and how these events influenced him. The decisions he made, or did not make, had the potential to affect the lives of thousands of people. For that reason alone, he is a subject worthy of our study. That he was a real man, with all the innate human frailties and capacities we all share, means he is deserving of our understanding.

A note on dates, names and spellings

Until 1752, Britain used a different calendar to most European countries. The two calendars in use at that time are most commonly referred to as Old Style and New Style, and they were eleven days apart. The dates used within this book are those appropriate to the events being described, so an event taking place in Italy or France is dated in the New Style, and events in Britain according to the Old. This can cause confusion when, for example, a ship might leave France on a New Style date and arrive in Britain on an Old Style one. In such circumstances it should be clear within the text which is being used.

In this book, James Francis Stuart will be commonly referred to as King James. This should not be interpreted as a bias in sympathy by the author. Nor should any reference to King George.

Charles Edward Stuart will be variously referred to as Prince Charles, Charles Edward, the prince and the Young Chevalier.

John William Sullivan's name will be given as he himself writes it, although he is still frequently referred to elsewhere as O'Sullivan.

William Murray, Marquis of Tullibardine, will be referred to most commonly as Tullibardine, even though the Jacobites referred to him as the Duke of Atholl. This is to avoid any confusion with his brother, who was accepted by the Georgian government as Duke of Atholl. Titled lords will commonly be referred to by their territorial designation unless there is confusion with a geographic reference.

John Murray of Broughton, the prince's Secretary of State, will be referred to as either Secretary Murray or simply Broughton. This is to distinguish him from Lord George Murray.

King Charles VII of Naples (Charles V of Sicily) will be referred to as the King of Naples, or as Parma, the dukedom he held prior to securing the crown.

In direct quotations, the original spellings and punctuation have been maintained. It is hoped the reader will endure the vagaries of non-standardised spelling as the price of being able to read the words as they were written. This is particularly rewarding in the case of the prince's own words, and in the almost phonetic writing of Sullivan. Occasional interventions for clarity are made in parentheses.

Any direct quotations attributed to Sir John MacDonald are taken from the translation of his French account provided by A. & H. Taylor.

Chapter One

The Siege of Gaeta

On the evening of Tuesday 3 August 1734, two grandsons of a British king arrived at the headquarters of the Spanish king of Naples, who was besieging forces loyal to the Holy Roman Emperor within the fortified city of Gaeta, in central Italy, during the War of the Polish Succession. It was neither the first, last or bloodiest time that eighteenth-century Europe would be consumed by conflict due to a disputed royal succession; nor was it the last time that such a cause would be used as the pretext for settling older scores or seizing new advantages. It was an age of interconnected dynasties, multilateral alliances and global expansion.

The two men we are following – or rather, one man and one boy – passed out of the last warmth of the summer's evening and into a shaded portico; behind came a very modest entourage, just a few gentlemen and a pair of friars. In the cool hall within the building, the visitors were greeted formally by the Spanish guards and directed to the main interior stair. Their heeled shoes clipped on the polished steps as they ascended, a formal welcome awaiting them at the landing.

The older of the two men, aged 38, was James Francis FitzJames Stuart, 2nd Duke of Berwick. His father had been an illegitimate son of King James VII & II (who had been Duke of York at the time) and his mistress Arabella Churchill, the sister of the famous general who went on to become the 1st Duke of Marlborough. After serving in James' armies before the latter's overthrow and exile, Berwick's father had then entered French military service and emerged during the War of the Spanish Succession as one of the Bourbons' most capable commanders. The 1st Duke of Berwick had been slain by a cannonball while commanding at the Siege of Philippsburg in Germany, in June 1734. Our Berwick had therefore inherited his father's titles just a few weeks prior to us joining him here at the Siege of Gaeta.

The new duke, a naturalised Spaniard, had followed his father's example and established a reputation as a fine soldier in his own right. Now he was one of the senior commanders campaigning for the Bourbons' Spanish interests in southern Italy, and he was therefore a familiar face to the guards, aides and officials at this temporary residence of the King of Naples. The king was here to oversee his army's siege of the Hapsburg garrison of Gaeta, one of the last centres of resistance to his rule in Naples. But Berwick was not now arriving on military business: he was here to present his young guest to the court so that he might pay compliments to the newly proclaimed monarch. Berwick's guest was the son of his uncle, King James VIII & III of Scotland and England, a king who ruled only over his court in exile and reigned only in the aspirations of his supporters, the Jacobites. During his youth, Berwick's father had been an important influence in James' life as he grew up in exile to inherit the mission of restoring the family to the throne. But in later years it had been galling to James that one of Europe's foremost military commanders had not taken up arms in the family's cause. Despite that tension with his half-brother, King James had retained a fondness for his nephew. It was at least partly out of sympathy towards the bereaved duke that he had swallowed his own anxieties and allowed his eldest son to visit Berwick at Gaeta.

Prince Charles Edward Stuart was not yet 14 years old, still a child but tall and increasingly confident. Beautiful portrait drawings by Giles Hussey would capture his profile in the following year, showing soft, attractive features and large dark eyes. Charles still wore his own hair, though curled and powdered, and until now his life had been lived within the relatively narrow worlds of the *Palazzo del Re* in Rome and the family's holiday villa on Lake Albano.[1] It was a world he was starting to find suffocating, and he was desperately excited by this opportunity to broaden his horizons. Nevertheless, he kept his steps studiedly dignified, determined not to betray that excitement as he climbed the steps beside the Duke of Berwick. As well as hoping to offer some comfort to the duke, King James had agreed to this visit in order to give his son the 'opportunity of making his first appearance in the field,' a chance to gain some military experience and begin building a reputation of his own.[2] With the campaign so close to the exiled Stuart court in Rome and with a trusted relation in a senior post, here was an opportunity that the king could hardly have resisted. But he was nevertheless concerned that his son was too young for such an adventure, writing to Berwick with anxiety that, 'after all, he is very young and we cannot expect from him what we might do were he some years older.'[3] The prince was sure to be under public scrutiny like never before, and away from his father's guiding hand.

Before Prince Charles could experience war, however, he must experience diplomacy too. Ahead of his departure from Rome, his father had taken him to the Vatican to bid farewell to Pope Benedict XIV. The pontiff was, according to James, visibly moved at the occasion. James was an influential and highly visible figure in Roman society, and his two handsome boys were its darlings. Prince Charles had already shown his ability to win affection, and at public appearances beside his father he had never disappointed in his behaviour. But now he had a chance to step outside of his proud father's shadow, and show that he could also be trusted to perform independently of the king. Here, at the top of these stairs, he was being greeted by Manuel Domingo de Benavides y Aragón, Count of Santisteban del Puerto. Aged 52, Santisteban was the *mayordomo mayor* of the royal court in Naples, effectively the king's chief minister as well as the head of the royal household. Santisteban was also the source of a great deal of patronage, and a key link back to Spain where he was trusted greatly by the queen.

Elisabeth Farnese, Queen of Spain, was the second wife of King Philip V and a powerful influence in affairs of state. Their son, Don Carlos, was fourth in line to the throne behind three stepbrothers, but through his mother he had a claim to the independent Duchy of Parma in north-western Italy. Don Carlos had travelled to Italy to assert this claim at the end of 1731, when he was just 15 years old, and succeeded in being acknowledged as Duke of Parma. A few years later, the young duke was here leading an army into the south of Italy to claim the kingdom of Naples on behalf of his powerful Bourbon family. Santisteban travelled with him as his political mentor to smooth the transition of power if the Naples campaign proved successful. So far it had been very successful, with what remained of the enemy forces now bottled up in just a few remaining strongholds. And so here stood Santisteban, in the house commandeered for the royal court behind the lines at the Siege of Gaeta, ready to render honours to the Jacobite Prince of Wales at the top of the stairs.

Back at home, Charles Edward had been growing into what we might call a wilful child, confident in his sense of status and chafing under the authority of a governor he did not like and the attentions of a conscientious father. The prince was blessed with two parents who both loved him dearly and a caring younger brother who looked up to him. But despite this, family life had not been straightforward, with the diligent king's endless political correspondence and the increasing disappointment of continuing exile alienating James' sensitive young wife, Maria Clementina Sobieska. Paranoia and recrimination had followed, along with protracted periods of physical separation. The worst of these occurred in late 1725, while Prince Henry Benedict was still but a baby. The king had ordered Prince Charles to be 'breeched' years before the customary age, outraging Queen Clementina. Putting Charles into men's clothing also meant putting him into men's care, and to make matter worse for the distraught mother (who may have been suffering from depression, perhaps post-natal), James appointed a Protestant governor for the prince. The queen already despised the man, and the resulting arguments divided the Stuart court, the wider community of British exiles in Europe, and Roman society. It was a very public mess, and following the queen's eventual return to the Palazzo Muti she led an increasingly ascetic life devoted to her ever-deepening faith. Famously, Charles had written to his 'dear Papa' promising not to jump around too much near his mother.

Against this backdrop, the prince sought comfort in martial sports, growing ever more conscious of his ancestral rights and his responsibility to support his father in restoring them. His governor, James Murray (made Earl of Dunbar by King James), was finding it increasingly challenging to control Charles as he got older. This was perhaps unsurprising as Dunbar was a middle-aged bachelor with no children of his own and therefore no experience in this type of role. For a time he had served as a member of parliament for Dumfriesshire, and in exile he had gained the confidence of King James in the years following the failure of the 1715 uprising. He was the brother-in-law of James' favourite at court, the Earl of Inverness, although both proved adept at offending and alienating other Jacobites. Although Dunbar was ambitious, he was also loyal and conscientious. Despite being sent away for a period during the worst of the family crisis, he retained the confidence of the king and was later recalled and given the responsibility for the prince as intended. Perhaps no less sensitive to Dunbar's manners than other courtiers were, or perhaps conscious of his mother's feelings and Dunbar's part in the turbulent rift between his parents, Prince Charles showed no liking for his governor. He had, of course, no choice in the matter, and Dunbar was an essential companion on the trip to Gaeta. On arrival, the latter wrote that his charge was 'less fatigued than most of the company' from the journey down.[4]

But now that Prince Charles was under the eyes of seasoned diplomats and given, for the first time, a taste of independent manhood, he showed few of the traits which so exasperated Dunbar back at the palazzo. There was no lack of apparent maturity or self-control, and an easy confidence when engaging with men whose power and status might have intimidated less confident boys. He thanked Santisteban for the formality of the reception he had received and then, his voice gentle but steady, he said that no formal honours needed to be performed during his stay as he was travelling incognito. Charles was not appearing as the Prince of Wales, but under a name once used by his father in similar circumstances: the Chevalier de St George.[5] Shortly after his meeting with Santisteban, the Young Chevalier was shown into a salon and introduced to the Duke of Parma, who was now King of Naples. Charles, according to a satisfied Dunbar, 'made a compliment very prettily and without the least embarrass[ment]', after which they were invited through to a more intimate audience in an adjacent chamber.[6]

Parma had entered Naples in triumph on 10 May and been proclaimed king the following month. His campaign to date had been a spectacular success, and Charles Edward must have been following news of its progress with fascination from his father's palazzo in Rome. Naples had been controlled by the Spanish crown since it was wrested from France at the end of the fifteenth century. It was strategically situated in the heart of the Mediterranean, linking the Hapsburg powers of Spain and the Holy Roman Empire. But following the death of the childless Charles V and subsequent War of the Spanish Succession, the House of Bourbon had successfully secured the main prize of the Spanish throne but without the appendages of Naples and Sicily. These were retained by the Hapsburgs as part of the Empire.

King Philip was determined to recover the territories Spain had lost after that bloody conflict and, when Britain joined an alliance against them in 1718, it led to Spanish support for a Jacobite enterprise in Scotland.[7] Only a few years before, a major uprising in 1715 had demonstrated the scale of support that King James could call upon in Britain, although he himself had arrived too late on that occasion to influence the outcome of the conflict. In 1719, James had then put all his hopes into the Spanish alliance, only for a storm to disperse the planned invasion fleet. Only a vanguard of 300 Spanish soldiers actually reached Scotland, where they were defeated along with a small Jacobite army at the Battle of Glenshiel. On the ground in the Highlands, the Jacobite leaders of this military debacle were William Murray, Marquis of Tullibardine, and his younger brother, Lord George Murray. Quite aside from the failure of the planned Jacobite expedition, Spain found itself isolated against the major European powers, including the fellow Bourbon kingdom of France, and failed to secure its war aims in the Mediterranean. But the Queen of Spain was heir to the Italian Duchy of Parma, which would, in time, provide a valuable foothold on that peninsula. And so their teenage son Don Carlos had been sent to secure the duchy in 1731.

A few years later, another disputed succession – this time in Poland – had created the opportunity the Spanish crown was waiting for. As the European powers took rival sides in the conflict, Spain struck against the Hapsburgs in Italy. The Duke of Parma, now 18, marched the length of Italy to the kingdom of Naples. It was governed at the time by a Hapsburg viceroy, Giulio Visconti, who had little popular support. Parma's advance was preceded by proclamations from his father declaring that the ancient privileges of the kingdom would be restored, presenting Parma as a liberator who would set right the historical anomaly of Hapsburg rule in Naples. This did not lack appeal for the Neapolitans: as Parma had three older brothers, he was unlikely to ever become king of Spain, which meant that Naples and Sicily might at last be ruled directly by its own monarch rather than a despotic viceroy. The Pope had given his tacit approval to Parma's expedition by allowing his army to pass through papal territories. Although some Spanish soldiers appeared to desert at this point, it seems that most had gone sightseeing in Rome and soon returned!

Parma's army, although nominally under his command, was led by the veteran officer José Carrillo de Albornoz y Montiel, Count of Montemar. It faced its first major challenge when the Imperial forces attempted to block the road through the mountains at Mignano. Using local guides, a Spanish force outflanked the Imperial forces through terrain believed to be impassable. Alerted to the threat, the Imperial forces abandoned their artillery and baggage, and withdrew. Charles Edward Stuart would one day secure a battlefield victory using a similar tactic. Imperial strategy now rested on defending key cities, while awaiting sufficient reinforcements to turn the tide. Parma screened those strongpoints with troops, while he secured the capital and established himself in government. When the Imperial army eventually moved back into the field, Montemar defeated it decisively at the Battle of Bitonto.

It was after this victory that James began to seriously consider sending his son to gain some experience, as the Spanish seemed to be in control of much of the landscape so the risk of his travelling was slight. Britain had remained neutral in the conflict and France was allied with Spain, so there was little political risk for the Stuarts. On 18 June, Berwick had written to James that there was still plenty of time for the prince to come along, and that the Siege of Gaeta 'will be very well worth seeing.'[8] James, always anxious about his beloved Carluccio, told his son how he hoped to hear 'good accounts of you, which will be the greatest comfort I can have during your absence.' He asked Berwick and Dunbar not to sugarcoat their reports.

And so it was that Charles Edward Stuart, Jacobite Prince of Wales, now stood before Charles of Bourbon, Duke of Parma and King of Naples.[9] Both were teenagers, but to a boy of 13, someone of 18 is a grown man whose independence and experience are to be envied. Parma's campaign must have inspired Charles Edward's imagination: carrying his father's commission on a daring military campaign to liberate his people from a usurping power; a single decisive battle and a triumphant entrance into the capital; and establishing an apparently just and popular government. Casualties and collateral damage had been mercifully low on both sides, the Spanish suffering more from the sicknesses which always accompanied large armies than from the enemy's fire. The young Stuart prince must have weighed all this and imagined how he could replicate such feats himself, in his own family's ancestral kingdoms in Britain. Although Charles did not witness these events, they had been the talk of Rome all summer and here he was in the inner circle of those who had brought it all to pass. It simply must have made an impression.

Prince Charles, as was already becoming apparent, had a natural warmth and charisma which helped draw people to him and to build relationships quickly. Even as a boy he was comfortable conversing with his elders, drawing confidence from his self-belief and his awareness of his status, which he generally (if not exclusively) wore quite lightly.

Parma, although older, was cooler and more rigid, with Dunbar noticing 'the bashfulness of his temper'.[10] But Prince Charles had been prepared for this interview by his father on 29 July – 'remember and practice all I said to you yesterday,' the king had written – and so was ready to meet the king. He spoke to Parma with 'the same ease as he used to do to any of the Cardinals at Rome.'

Charles then presented both Dunbar and Sir Thomas Sheridan to the young king. Sheridan was his tutor and under-governor, an Irishman whose family had followed Charles' grandfather into exile in the 1690s. The relationship Charles had with him was very different to the one he had with Dunbar. Later, in August, Sheridan would write of his paternal feelings towards the prince, which is indicative of a genuine mutual affection.[11] But on the present occasion the prince did his duty to Dunbar too, presenting both to the King of Naples as men to whom he owed a great deal. This generous humility, as Dunbar told his master in Rome, was reported around the Neapolitan court to the prince's credit. Parma enquired after the health of Charles' parents, on which the prince offered Parma the compliments of King James. Dunbar felt that this short audience was a little awkward, due to Parma's shyness, but he was keen to emphasise in his report to King James that it had been a genuine welcome. The Duke of Berwick wrote hurriedly to Rome that 'the reception was better than I expected,' which suggests Dunbar's reading of the situation was quite correct. The prince, Berwick said, was 'in perfect health and is now asleep.'[12]

The following morning, Charles was introduced to Count Montemar, overall commander of the Spanish forces and the victor of Bitonto. The general apologised for not having met the prince the previous night, and after the customary formal exchanges the pair moved out onto a balcony. Here Montemar, presumably after consultation with Santiesteban, asked Charles specifically 'in what manner he would be pleased to be treated,' as the King of Spain had given him 'precise orders' to render all the honours due to the Prince of Wales if that was his wish.[13] The prince again confirmed his father's wish that he remain incognito. This was, of course, a diplomatic mask, for there was little doubt around the court as to who the prince might be. In the coming days, Charles drew much attention and the courtiers were much taken with his lively and charming manner.[14] A group of visiting French officers delayed their departure home in order to spend more time with him. The prince was

The Siege of Gaeta

also no longer a mere visiting observer: he was given an honorific rank as General of Artillery, complete with expenses.[15]

Around 10.00 am on Wednesday, the Young Chevalier attended the headquarters again and received an invitation to dine with the king, his governors accompanying him. Afterwards, and presumably much to Charles' satisfaction, he was invited to view the siege more closely. To do so, they boarded a Spanish galley and headed a short distance towards the peninsula city of Gaeta. At the tip of a long shallow bay, Gaeta licks out into the sea like a curling tongue. It is dominated by a massive hill, crowned with the large cylindrical mausoleum of Lucius Munatius Plancus (87–15 BC). The old town is squeezed into the spaces on the northern and eastern sides of the hill, the latter possessing a large stone castle which is still an operational military facility today. Both the seaward side and the landward approach from the west were protected by stout stone bastions. The very geography of the city forced these defences into angular shapes which created crossing fields of fire and made taking the city by storm a costly undertaking. The Spanish had therefore invested Gaeta with batteries and trenches.

After the short voyage Charles and Parma disembarked close to the main Spanish camp, which may have been near Porto Salvo as the best illustration of the siege shows the batteries based around a war-damaged coastal village with a hill rising sharply to the right. A house overlooking the siegeworks had been set aside for the king's use. The king had been told, according to Dunbar, that this was the military headquarters for the siege, which was why he headed there on his visits to the front to be met by the general officers overseeing the action. In reality, this property had been chosen because of the safety of its location and the officers contrived to be there ahead of the king; the well-intentioned deception was apparently 'a joke to the whole army' which Dunbar felt reflected poorly upon him. The King of Naples was in fact far less animated by military life than his recent experiences would suggest, rarely appearing in uniform and preferring to leave the implementation of military plans to his trusted – and perfectly capable – subordinates, Berwick and Montemar. Charles would learn little about actual warfare from here, however, and it suited his own spirit far less to simply observe the action from a distance. But for the moment, the dull thump of the guns and the drifting smoke shrouding the distant bastions served as the Young Chevalier's first introduction to war. The Duke of Berwick, tactfully waiting until they were away from the king, promised to take him down to the Spanish batteries at 11.00 am the following morning when, according to the normal pattern of events, the enemy's fire was generally quietest.

After viewing the siegeworks from a suitably safe distance, the king then decided to return to Naples; he suggested to Berwick that the prince would enjoy time to do some sightseeing there. Michele Vezzosi, a servant in the Stuart household who wrote his account many years later, reports that Parma was 'mightily pleased' with Charles and enjoyed his company.[16] It is easy for us to forget that the King of Naples was still himself a teenager, and he perhaps found some comfort in the presence of a younger boy amidst the politics and warfare. Indeed, Count Santiesteban told Dunbar that Prince Charles was welcome to dine with the king every day should he wish it, but the diplomatic response was that the prince would not wish to abuse such a favour and would therefore aim to do so around twice a week.

The prince lodged at the home of Cardinal Camillo Cibo at Castellone, Formia. This picturesque medieval harbour town, with its old stone towers, tomb of Cicero and hilltop hermitage, afforded Charles an excellent view towards Gaeta and allowed him to see 'every bombe or cannon that is fired either by day or night.'[17] Despite the rumble of the guns, Dunbar was able to enjoy the fresh, healthy air and the cool sea breeze which blew in from around 10.00 am each day and danced through the open windows of the house.

But the prince was not here for a holiday, and he was teasing both Berwick and Dunbar for permission to get into the trenches and see some real soldiering. This was not without political risk as well as physical, for it would be awkward if the prince's military enthusiasm drew comparisons with the new king's relative disinterest. Dunbar was sure 'the Spaniards will be mortifyed extremely when they see the Prince do more than he [Parma] does.'[18] Berwick was alert to this too, but he was also keen to indulge his infectiously enthusiastic young relation who, after all, was here to gain some experience of war and, importantly, to be seen doing so. Parma, despite his youth, was titular head of a successful army undertaking a triumphant campaign; he had little need to prove himself in the way the Stuart prince did.

Berwick judged that the risk to the reputation or pride of the new King of Naples was in fact slight, as long as Charles' visits to the trenches happened when Parma was not present at the lines. But the plan to take the prince up to the batteries on Thursday 5 August had to be postponed for operational reasons. The siege was an active one and neither Berwick, who was well placed to judge it, or Dunbar, who was less so, expected it to be over any time soon. When the opportunity did arise for Charles to visit the lines, 'he showed not the least concern for the enemy's fire, even when the balls were hissing about his ears.'[19]

Giovanni Rocco's spectacular painting of the siege, showing a mounted Parma directing operations in his breastplate, depicts four Spanish batteries firing on the city. They are fronted by gabions, huge wicker baskets filled with earth which screened the cannon and protected them from the counterfire of the defenders. Two are placed right on the shore beside the water and two are further inland, firing across the narrow neck of the Gaeta peninsula. Stretching between the king's pavilions and the edge of no man's land are the battered shells of houses, all shown several storeys high. In one of the foremost of these houses, in amongst the bombarding batteries, Charles Edward Stuart had his first opportunity to show his physical courage.

The house was being used as a command post for the Duke of Berwick, but it was exposed to the fire of the Imperial bastions protecting Gaeta. Eventually, with the fire of five cannon concentrating on his walls, Berwick was compelled to abandon it. But as the duke was leaving, Charles Edward arrived to visit him. Seeing the evacuation in progress, the prince insisted on making a show of entering the property while it was under fire. Berwick, responsible for both the siege operations and the safety of the prince, was genuinely impressed when the youngster ignored his pleading and headed indoors. As cannonballs struck and 'pierced through' the walls of the house, Charles nonetheless remained within for 'a considerable time with an undisturbed countenance.' The duke confessed that the incident made him 'pass some uneasy moments,' but moments like this were turning a pre-existing affection for the boy prince into a genuine admiration. Berwick's famous conclusion was that 'in great Princes whom nature has marked out for heroes, valour does not wait for number of years.'

The next day, and apparently contrary to expectations, the Siege of Gaeta was suddenly over. The garrison was outnumbered and outgunned. A breach was beginning to open, and the Spanish fire was starting to impact the houses beyond the walls. Even though the governor was willing to fight on, it was clear that no relief was coming and the population had little stomach for further suffering. Gaeta therefore surrendered, leaving Capua as the only city still holding out against Parma's forces. While the siege in Capua ground on, attention now turned towards a Spanish landing in Sicily to complete Parma's conquest. As many of the Imperial troops from the island had previously left to join the Imperial army before its defeat at Bitonto, the resistance was not expected to be heavy. There was, of course, still much activity around Gaeta as the conquered city was secured and the siegeworks dismantled, through much of which Prince Charles remained at the front primarily in the company of soldiers. Not until 11 August did he embark upon a Spanish galley and sail southwards to Naples, where he had the opportunity to enjoy the hospitality of the victorious king.

The plan was for Charles to stay at a convent known to his father (probably St Maria Donnaregina, where he attended a mass). Berwick was, however, eager to have the prince at the house he had rented for himself, prompting Dunbar to write to Rome for King James' permission before accepting. The short voyage to Naples was obviously uncomfortable for the prince, who was struck with sea-sickness. The effect was perhaps compounded by tiredness and perhaps simply an adrenaline crash after the high excitements of the past week. Dunbar reported that the prince slept for ten uninterrupted hours before arising quite recovered.[20] Berwick also wrote on 12 August that the prince was back to full health, being 'very well and cheerful, and he is lodged in the best situation we could imagine in the town.'[21] The house Berwick had loaned was close to the sea and benefitted from the good air which Dunbar so enjoyed, and the prince was flattered with multiple invitations to dinner. When he travelled he was attended by a royal coach, and Sir Thomas Sheridan reported that he was 'very well diverted.'[22]

Both Sheridan and Dunbar also observed that Charles was putting on a little weight, particularly in his face, prompting King James to again write to both Charles and Berwick about his son's diet. This was precisely the sort of micromanagement that the prince found so chafing about his father's attention, and if it caused him to roll his eyes then the gently chiding tone of some of the other letters he received will have made him groan aloud. Of all things, during this heady adventure, Charles was reminded to be more attentive to his spelling.[23] The letters he wrote back to his father were short and probably teased out of him under duress at a time when he had countless other things he would rather be doing.²⁴ A letter of 13 August reveals both the intense love the king held for his son and the impossible pressure his ambitions placed upon the child: 'I pray God make you as perfect as I wish you, and to bless you my dear child whom I truly love.'²⁵

Undeterred by his previous sea-sickness, Charles enjoyed a supper aboard the flagship Spanish galley, and thereafter made several trips into the bay of Naples. On one such occasion – or so the story goes – the prince was admiring the magnificent view of the Neapolitan coastline as it shimmered in the summer sun. Suddenly a gust of wind blew the prince's hat into the glistening waters. 'Do not worry,' cried Charles, 'for the people of England can buy me another erelong!' This fun little anecdote was reported years later by Vezzosi, who we can speculate may have heard it from the prince himself. If it is true, it gives an insight into the spirit of a boy on the cusp of manhood, his head already filled with visions about how he might one day replicate these feats of arms and restore his family to its rights again. Even if it never happened, it is the type of gossipy tale around which a popular reputation could be built.

And, certainly, the prince's reputation was continuing to grow during his time in Naples. Berwick beamed that 'he is generally adored by every body.'²⁶ Both Sheridan and Murray confirmed Charles' consistently fine behaviour and warm reception, and Berwick was gracious in reporting to the king that the prince was a credit to the governors. But success did breed risk. King James was becoming anxious that his son's growing reputation was causing the French some discomfort. Although their ambassador in Naples had responded favourably to the prince himself, Louis XV was currently pursuing a friendly policy towards Hanoverian Britain. The French king's agent in Rome, who kept a close eye on the pulse surrounding the Stuart court, was concerned that Charles would become 'in time a far more dangerous enemy to the present establishment of the Government of England than ever his father was.'²⁷ King James wrote with satisfaction that his son's short campaign had 'alarmed' his opponents in England.²⁸

Dunbar also expressed his view that 'the Prince has in the eyes of the Publick has outshined the king [of Naples],' which was now beginning to make their Spanish hosts feel uncomfortable after all.²⁹ Sensitive to these considerations, Berwick concluded that Charles' mission would reach a natural conclusion once the Spanish expedition to Sicily set sail.³⁰ James had previously expressed a hope that Charles might continue his military education by following the campaign further, but he was also missing his son desperately and agreed that the prince should leave Naples on 12 September.

Charles had travelled to Gaeta as the Chevalier de St George, but he undoubtedly returned from Naples as the Prince of Wales. Parma had given him numerous gifts, including jewels and horses, and the Spanish provided him with a military escort back to Albano. Most valuably of all, the prince carried with him a considerably enhanced reputation. The courts of Naples, Spain, France and Britain were alert to his potential. His parents had gained the reassurance that, however challenging his behaviour might have been towards his governor at home, there was a maturity and capacity within their son which could justify their hopes for him as the future head of their cause.

What had the prince actually learned about war? His practical experience had been foreshortened by the sudden surrender of Gaeta, and by the potential diplomatic barriers to him remaining with the army for a further campaign. He was also still very young, and there was a risk of exhausting the boy prematurely. However, Prince Charles had gained first-hand experience of modern warfare. He had observed a large army engaged in complex military and logistical operations, viewed from the heights of the senior command posts and the depths of the trenches and batteries. He had spent time with highly capable and successful military commanders and political decision-makers, and in their unrecorded conversations we can imagine a great many useful maxims might have been shared. Charles had proven himself able to engage with, and win the admiration of, both courtiers and the more common soldiery. He had learned that he possessed the physical courage to stand firm under fire, and the value of *being seen* to possess it.

One other lesson which Charles had had the opportunity to learn, although it was perhaps too subtle to lodge as long in his mind as the more exciting episodes did, was the extent to which planning and resourcing had contributed to Parma's victories. His campaign in Italy was no popular uprising, but an invasion by superior forces from the outside. The unqualified successes of Parma's audacious campaign in 1734–5 were built as much on the resources, manpower and logistical capacity of the Spanish forces he had been provided with as they had on the dissatisfaction or indifference of much of the populace towards their existing rulers. The Imperial response to the invasion had also been undermined by military pressures on them elsewhere in Europe, giving Parma time to strike decisively before adequate forces could be assembled against him. This, at least, was something the prince would remember.

It is perhaps possible to overstate the significance of the Gaeta campaign in Charles' career, and as we lack his own thoughts on the subject, we are tempted to apply our advantage of hindsight in drawing comparisons between 1734 and 1745. We can see the lessons the young prince *might* have learned from the opportunities we know he had, but the extent to which they stayed with him cannot be honestly quantified. There is enough evidence, however, to suggest that Charles Edward Stuart had in fact learned a great deal at Gaeta, either deliberately or unconsciously, and that he had also shown to the world that he possessed a degree of innate capacity. At the very least he had demonstrated his own potential, as much to himself as to others. His expedition had therefore been a triumphal success, and even before it was over King James began looking for other opportunities for his son to join a campaign. In particular, he hoped that the French would permit him to join their army in Lombardy: if the prince had performed so well at 13, how much more might he learn in a year's time?[31]

Prince Charles was reunited with his father at the Palazzo Apostolico in Albano on the evening of Tuesday 14 September. This property had long been at the king's disposal as a summer residence away from the stifling summer heat of the capital. It is now the town hall of Albano Laziale. James had arrived the previous day.[32] He must have been delighted to see his son returning in such good health and spirits, accompanied by his fifty guardsmen and exhausted governors. Queen Clementina drove out to meet them on Thursday, and as Prince Henry was also present the family was reunited. The queen did not stay long, but the boys stayed at Albano with their father until the end of the weekend. They then returned to their mother in Rome, and Charles was welcomed back with a papal audience.[33] Thus did the Young Chevalier's first campaign come to its end.

If the summer of 1734 was a high point for the young prince, it masked the horror that was to come. James was already concerned about his wife's health at the time of his son's return, writing to the queen that he 'did not find you so well yesterday as I would have wished.'[34] After the trauma of the late 1720s, the relationship between James and

Clementina had stabilised. But the experience had driven her away from the material world and firmly into the arms of the church, living an increasingly ascetic life which had left her drawn and frail. The queen had long been battling to manage mental challenges which are hard to diagnose at this distance, and the depression led to an eating disorder which was severely and visibly destroying her health. Her decline continued steadily into the new year, casting a pall of fearful expectation over the court.

By 12 January the king was resigned to the worst. He wrote to Lord Inverness that Clementina was 'perfectly within her senses, and dies with a tranquility, a piety, and a peace which is, with reason, a great comfort to me.'[35] In fact, the queen did not pass away until the early evening of 18 January. She was just 32. The following day James wrote to Inverness in a shaky hand: 'I write that you may see I am alive... I have really had a terrible time of it.'[36] Despite her former animosity towards Inverness and his wife (Dunbar's sister), the queen had left them a gift in her will. Although he forced himself to continue his extensive correspondences, King James was heartbroken. His sons were utterly devastated, inconsolable in their grief.

The funeral of the Stuart queen was a deeply affecting spectacle for Prince Charles. The Pope ensured it was performed in the most lavish and moving style. Clementina's body was carried in solemn procession from the Palazzo del Re to the Church of Santi Apostoli, escorted by the Swiss Guard and thirty-two cardinals. After the service, Clementina was borne through the streets of Rome to the heart of the Vatican. King James and his sons looked on, as did thousands of others. A comparison could be made to a similar event in our lifetimes, as the Roman public joined in the princes' mourning for the loss of their young mother. Clementina's intense religious devotion cast her, in hindsight, as a saintly figure; as she was placed in her coffin the royal robes were removed, revealing a simple nun's habit. Although the queen was interred beneath St Peter's Basilica, her funerary monument was at Santi Apostoli. Her heart was kept at the chapel royal within the Palazzo del Re, where James could mourn her in private.[37] A few years later, a new and more magnificent monument to Queen Clementina was erected within St Peter's itself.

Sensitive, fragile and tortured, Queen Clementina achieved a peace in death which her spirit had not enjoyed in life. In Antonio David's portrait of 1730, the queen's serene beauty speaks to us from across the centuries.[38] In her features, with her large dark eyes, soft pale skin and delicate lips, we can also see her beloved elder son. The prince inherited more from Clementina than just her looks, however. She was the granddaughter of John III Sobieski, King of Poland from 1674–96, who had led the Christian coalition against the Ottomans at the Battle of Vienna. There was a fire in the Sobieskis which was already visible in Prince Charles. But he also inherited Clementina's fragility, perhaps bipolar disorder, which could both drive him to great heights and plunge him into the depths. In Clementina its most dangerous manifestation was her eating disorder, euphemistically labelled as fasting by those who sought a saintly rather than psychological understanding; in Charles it would be alcoholism, of which commentators were (and remain) far less forgiving.

Having been breached prematurely in 1725, and after tasting both war and independence at Gaeta in 1734, the prince's progression towards maturity now stuttered. The king was in less of a hurry for his boys to grow up. He had lost his wife and lacked the consolation of any other close family. James' two older half-sisters, Mary and Anne, had both usurped his place in the succession and had died without children decades before. His only younger sister, Louisa, with whom he had grown up in exile, had died of smallpox at the age of just 19. The king's nearest surviving relation was therefore the Duke of Berwick, but he himself died in Naples in 1738. James then wrote that 'he is really a loss to me, and I sensibly feel it.'[39] No doubt Charles also lamented the death of his older cousin, whose military exploits and genuine affection, especially evident during their time at Gaeta, must have made him something of a hero to the boy. Berwick's son, now the 3rd Duke and two years older than Charles Edward, was invited to join the Stuart court.

As a king there were few opportunities for James to replace the comforts of family with those of genuine friendships. Social class was a barrier of course, and since the court had been pushed out of France in the wake of The '15, there had been fewer high-ranking British exiles available at the court. James' fondness for Lord Inverness, often against the grain of opinion within the household, court and wider Jacobite community, led to the latter's brief return to Rome in April 1736. Inverness had been out of court since the turbulent split between the king and queen a decade before, his resignation being James' big concession to his wife. But by then Inverness' brother-in-law had become jealous of his own position, and Dunbar was not eager to renew their former alliance. Inverness withdrew permanently to Avignon. The king was far from isolated, with a busy correspondence and an active social network in Rome itself, but as time passed his circle became ever more Italian.

Meanwhile Dunbar was still struggling to manage Prince Charles, who had learned too soon what was expected of him. But after Gaeta he was provided with no opportunities to develop himself. To Charles, an energetic and assertive teenager filled with a sense of his own potential, his father's dreary routine and constant letter writing held little appeal. King James was a role model in terms of his devotion, diligence and dignity, but the prince needed something more than that. Dunbar could certainly not provide it, and Charles had still not warmed to him in the slightest. The dashing boy of Gaeta had turned into a sulky, ill-tempered teenager who resented the interference of both his father and his governor. But that is hardly an unusual pattern for any spirited child, although the comparison with the more reserved Prince Henry probably did not help.

Charles tackled his frustrations by throwing himself into sports and hunting, preparing himself physically for future action. If he preferred physical activity to academic pursuits, he is little different to many boys of his age except perhaps in the extent to which he was indulged. But this should not lead us to think of Charles as in any way unintelligent or uncultured. He was conversant in multiple languages, as had been amply proven at Gaeta and Naples, although English remained the first language of the court and the one in which he corresponded with his father. The exiled court was a polyglot environment, but the prince's most intimate circle comprised of natural English speakers and the Palazzo del Re had become a form of unofficial embassy in Rome for British travellers, which ensured that Charles was regularly exposed to his father's would-be subjects. It is certain that he was therefore not only fluently conversant in English, but that he did so without any remarkable 'foreign' accent.

In conversation with cardinals, courtiers and kings, his wit and intelligence were not found wanting. As well as literature, Charles had studied mathematics, geometry, astronomy and physics; although he was not inclined to academia, he could be philosophical and thoughtful. The prince's disinclination to lengthy correspondence and his often-erratic spelling (from which some have detected the possibility of dyslexia) are certainly not evidence of a lack of intelligence. The Palazzo del Re was also a house of music, hosting regular high-quality performances which the two princes would have enjoyed as much as their father. At other times, the salons were enlivened by Henry's sonorous voice, sometimes accompanied by his brother on the harpsichord. After a day of exertion in the saddle, Charles would often relax with his cello.[40] He was a prince well suited to the time in which he lived, which is why he drew such admiration from his contemporaries.

At last, in the early summer of 1737, the Young Chevalier had another opportunity to repeat the success of his Gaeta expedition. Although the relative peace in Europe and the diplomatic obstructions of the British government prevented the prince from taking up arms, the king was ready to give him another taste of independence. Charles undertook a tour of northern Italy, again travelling incognito and declining the honours of a formal reception. Regardless, he was fêted wherever he went with dinners, balls and receptions. In Parma, the guards saluted the prince when he passed, and he impressed Dunbar with his patience listening to the toothless whistling of the dowager duchess.[41] It was like history repeating itself, as the governor wrote back to the king that 'the prince has behaved himself wonderfully in all the places he has been, and that he has charmed everybody who has seen him.'[42] On another occasion Dunbar reported that he could not have expected more from the 16-year-old prince even if he had been 20.[43] British embassies applied diplomatic pressure but to little avail, alarmed less by the fact that the Stuart prince was so well received than by the fact that he performed his own part so well.

During his visit to Venice, Prince Charles sat for a portrait by the famous Rosalba Carriera. Recently rediscovered, the resulting pastel provides an exceptional insight into the prince on the cusp of manhood. His eyes are challenging and confident, full of self-assurance. As he had in Gaeta, Charles had gained a little weight during his tour, the long and joyful dancing failing to compensate for the sumptuous dinners. As a result, he looks healthy, happy and full of spirit. Dunbar could not persuade the prince to moderation, but could also hardly deny that for all the times he had seen Charles at his petulant worst, he was now seeing him at his dazzling best. At the end of the tour, he reported to James that Charles 'certainly left behind him in Venice a reputation which passes what can be imagined.'[44] The king was again trying to secure his son some more military experience, preferably beyond Italy, but the diplomatic climate was not right for it. 'It does my heart good to know the Prince behaves so well,' sighed the king, 'which makes me regret the more his missing of the Campaign, but all I hope in good time...'[45]

The prince's time was indeed coming. Later that summer he had his hair cut, the final symbol of the end of his childhood. His reputation was spreading, and he continued to draw attention at his public appearances. Charles was also beginning to associate more openly with Scotland. During the Italian tour, a display in the shape of the saltire had been presented for his pleasure. A few years later, James Drummond, 3rd Duke of Perth, sent the prince the magnificent gift of a martial panoply: a cuirass and helmet, and a set containing a Highland broadsword, targe and pistols. They were followed in 1740 by a splendid coat of scarlet tartan laced with gold and a matching plaid. In January 1741, the Young Chevalier appeared at a ball 'wearing the uniform of an officer of the Scottish Highlanders, with a multi-coloured checked costume.'[46] New portraits were commissioned by Blanchet and Mossman, the foundations of the image for which he would become forever remembered: boyishly young, regal and Scottish. Charles Edward Stuart was sure of his destiny; all he needed was his opportunity.

Chapter Two

Du Teillay

With the tortured groaning of the ship's timbers and the rising motion of the swell, Prince Charles Edward Stuart closed his eyes. He tried to let the motion roll through him, but he pressed his palm hard onto the table. The prince did not sail well and had to fight against the disorientating queasiness: 'I find the more I struggle against it, the better,' he wrote.[1] He was now 24 years old and in the prime of his physical fitness; at 5ft 11 he found little comfort below the decks of this 78ft ship.[2] The prince was dressed simply, in a plain suit of black cloth, the cuffs already stiffened from the salt spray. It was the costume of an *abbé* or novice from the Scots College, simple and common enough not to draw much attention. Charles' cheeks were uncharacteristically roughened with a heavy ruddy stubble, for he had deliberately avoided shaving since he had boarded three weeks before.[3] With the disguised prince sat his old tutor, Sir Thomas Sheridan, past 60 and no longer present to control Charles but simply to support him.

Another familiar face was Francis Strickland, a 54-year-old English exile with some military experience back in his youth. He had joined Charles' household as his equerry shortly before the death of the queen, leaving French military service to do so.[4] During the prince's Italian tour, Strickland had indulged the prince's habits by (supposedly deliberately) failing to have his writing desk at hand to facilitate tedious correspondence! Charles may have liked Strickland, but his father had dismissed him from service after discovering he had advised the prince that a Protestant conversion would aid his cause in Britain.[5] Despite his father's opposition – or perhaps precisely because he wanted a party of his own – Charles had taken Strickland on again. James also distrusted Reverend George Kelly, an Irish clergyman who had escaped from the Tower of London after his arrest during the Atterbury Plot in 1722. Perhaps for the same reasons, however, he too now accompanied Charles on the present voyage.

Here too was John Sullivan, a middle-aged Irishman from County Kerry.[6] In contrast to Sheridan, Sullivan was a newcomer to the prince's entourage. At a young age he had been sent away from Dunkerron by his parents in order to train for the priesthood in Paris. Following their deaths he briefly returned to Ireland, but understood that prospects for an ambitious Catholic were more promising in Europe than the home country. Like many men in his position, he became a tutor to the son of a French nobleman: in this case, the military Marquis de Maillebois. The marquis persuaded Sullivan, although he was by no means a youngster by this stage, to consider a career in the army rather than the church. Sullivan was commissioned as a captain and accompanied Maillebois on his 1739 campaign across Corsica. He proved to be an effective organiser and was kept on as a staff officer for subsequent expeditions in Italy and the Rhineland.

Although he must have encountered many Jacobites in his time, exactly how Sullivan came to the attention of the Stuart court is unclear. He does not appear to have been one of their veteran agents, although he had clearly visited the court in Rome on at least one occasion.[7] Sheridan had recommended him to the prince in January 1745, perhaps precisely because of his independence from the petty intrigues which bedevilled the existing Jacobite networks there. The prince immediately sought to protect Sullivan from such jealousies by asking his father to retrospectively approve his decision to employ him. The king was only too happy to consent: 'I'm very glad you are thinking of taking Mr O'Sullivan with you into the country, and you may say as much as you please that I put him about you, for it is true I think him a proper person to be with you.' Sullivan's role was to organise Charles' household affairs, but his recent military experiences were also an attraction to the prince and, once their own intrigues had bound them to spending ever more time together, they developed a strong rapport. Another Irish soldier was also accompanying them, Sir John MacDonald, an ageing cavalry officer who had served the Bourbons in Spain.

The Young Chevalier had travelled to France at the beginning of 1744, with all the drama which befitted both his character and his times. The War of the Austrian Succession had broken out in 1740 following the death of the Holy Roman Emperor. The great powers of Europe had divided between those who accepted his daughter Maria Theresa as his successor, and those who saw an opportunity to reduce the power of the Hapsburgs. Britain and France took opposing sides, but were not officially at war with one another. But as the conflict spread, and after the death of Louis XV's chief minister Cardinal Fleury, the slide towards an Anglo-French conflict accelerated. The Jacobite networks were hyperactive, the consensus being that only with the help of France's military power could a restoration be effected.

This turn of events also brought to an end the career of John Murray, Earl of Dunbar. His importance had already declined after the two princes had come of age, but it was his perceived antipathy towards the French which finally ended his influence now that they were once again the Stuarts' best hope. Dunbar still had a part to play, however, in the opening scene of Charles' defining period. Before dawn on 9 January 1744, Charles, his brother and his former governor had left Rome for a hunting expedition to Cisterna. They headed south, but on the road the prince declared he would rather ride than continue in the chaise as it would help him keep warm. At the appropriate moment, Dunbar provided the distraction of falling into a ditch which allowed Prince Charles to ride away from their group.

The prince had then turned off the road, put on the official badge of a Neapolitan courier and rode hell for leather towards the Tuscan border. There he assumed the identity of a Spanish officer, complete with pre-arranged passport, before continuing through heavy snow to the small port of Massa. Charles then took a bark to Genoa, where he could finally catch his breath. After a day's rest he travelled to Savona, where he seems to have briefly aroused some suspicion as Henry heard he had been 'locked up,' before eventually sailing through a British fleet and on to Antibes.[8] From there the prince rode hard for Paris, completing the whole journey in ten days. Although caught out by the initial ruse, Prince Henry obliged his brother by behaving at Albano as if Charles was still with him, going so far as to send trophies from the hunt back to Rome.

Thus had the prince entered Paris, with a small and exhausted retinue, after the kind of adventure which ought not to exist outside of a romantic novel. Despite the perils and fatigues of this long winter journey, Charles Edward was full of drive. He was, he said, immediately ready to face all such trials again if it were necessary; 'but that is not the case, for I have nothing but the approaching Campaign to undergo, which will be a great pleasure to me who have desired so long to see and understand Military matters.' The excitement is palpable in the prince's letters, the political and paternal anxiety just as clear in the king's replies. Charles, whose biographers have chided for not reciprocating the warmth of his father's letters, reassured the king: 'the small dangers I may have run are nothing when for the service and Glory of a father who is so tender and kind for me, and for the service of his Country who is so dire [dear] to him.'[9]

Versailles was a world away from the petty courts of Italy, and the reception in France was polite but hard-headed. It remains unclear to what extent the prince's arrival was expected, and there may have been a degree of embarrassment in case he began drawing attention as he had done in Italy. Charles was thus obliged to remain in close incognito in humble circumstances, for France and Britain were still not at war. Nevertheless, his presence was soon known and formally protested by the British. A French expedition was indeed being prepared, although the plan was far from universally popular at court, and it had been assigned no less a commander than the renowned Maurice de Saxe. Charles moved out to Gravelines so that he could be closer to the assembly port at Dunkirk, and although he was in correspondence with Saxe, he had no official role in the preparations. If the invasion went ahead then the prince would be a crucial figurehead around which support would be rallied in Britain, but there was no question of him actually *leading* the campaign.

How Prince Charles might have performed in that event, and how Britain might have reacted to the arrival of a large French army, can only be guessed. For it was at Gravelines that the prince was to face his first great disappointment, and get his first real taste of the nature of the French government's friendship. As Saxe's army was beginning to embark, it was struck by what Charles himself called 'a violent storm of wind'.[10] It was fortunate that Charles had not already gone aboard himself, for even if he had survived the storm in which a number of ships were lost, there was now also a powerful British squadron lying off Dunkirk. French enthusiasm for a Channel crossing then waned with great speed. Charles remained hopeful that the French navy might yet push Admiral Norris' ships aside and allow Saxe's invasion to go ahead, but he was being naïve and probably knew it. On 13 March he wrote to his father with a degree of reluctant resignation: 'I will apply myself to succeed in whatever may seem next best for your Majestie's service.'[11]

But the expedition was cancelled. Those who had already been opposed to the operation had been given ample cause to protest its difficulty and cost, and to present the case for using Saxe and his 10,000 men elsewhere. France finally declared war on Britain, then threw its armies eastwards into its traditional theatres of war: Flanders and Germany. Charles was left lingering in Gravelines, losing hope that France would prove to be the saviour he had hoped for. George Keith, the exiled Earl Marischal, wrote to dissuade the prince from doing anything reckless: 'to go single... would be forever the destruction of the cause, and fix perhaps forever the family of Hanover in Britain.'[12]

Despite Keith's warning, sixteen months later, Charles Edward Stuart's expedition was finally under way. The ship he had boarded was called *Du Teillay*, named after the 74-year-old superintendent of the port of Nantes in Brittany.[13] It was a new ship, commissioned the previous year, built as a fast corsair raider capable of preying on the merchant vessels of the king's enemies. She was privately owned, belonging to the prosperous maritime trader Antoine Walsh, whose father Philip had carried King James VII & II away from Ireland after his defeat beside the Boyne in 1690. Walsh was an influential figure amongst the Franco-Irish community in Brittany, making his fortune on the back of the Atlantic slave trade.

Walsh had retained his father's Jacobite sympathies; when he heard that the Stuart prince needed a ship, he was ready to place one at his disposal. Walsh had been introduced to Charles by Walter Rutledge, a wealthy Irish merchant based out of Dunkirk, who had himself been introduced by Charles O'Brien, Lord Clare, a senior French commander and a relation of the Dukes of Berwick. Rutledge had also helped arrange another, far larger vessel, *L'Elisabeth*, which had been hired from the French navy and now protected *Du Teillay* with her heavy guns. Given all these connections, and the presence aboard of Sheridan, Sullivan, Kelly and MacDonald, this expedition had a distinctly Irish character.

Not all the prince's co-travellers were Irishmen. Francis Strickland was English, of course, and Michele Vezzosi, the prince's *valet de chambre*, was Italian. There were also a few Scotsmen. The first of these was Aeneas MacDonald, a 30-year-old banker who lived mainly in Paris and had naturally assisted with Charles' financial arrangements over the past year. It is also said that he read to the prince the poetry of Alasdair mac Mhaighstir Alasdair, the Gaelic bard, whose longing lyrics summoned the prince to be the saviour of the land. Aeneas' brother was Donald MacDonald of Kinlochmoidart, whose support Charles would need when he landed close to that region. Travelling with Aeneas was his Scottish clerk, Duncan Buchanan.[14]

The highest-ranking Scotsman aboard *Du Teillay* was William Murray, Jacobite Duke of Atholl, commonly referred to as the Marquis of Tullibardine.[15] Only the Jacobites acknowledged his dukedom because he had been attainted after being out in the risings of 1715 and 1719. Tullibardine had escaped into exile along with his younger brother Lord George Murray, but remained there even after the latter was pardoned in 1725. Tullibardine had shown little aptitude for military command at Glenshiel, but the Atholl territory was strategically significant and potentially a good recruiting ground for the cause. His protracted exile in Paris had left Tullibardine short of money and in poor health, and although his loyalty to the cause was undiminished, he had retired from the frontline of Jacobite political intrigue. But, at 58, he sensed that in Charles Edward Stuart there was a new hope, and an opportunity in 1745 which might never come around again. And so, despite the discomfort of his gout, Tullibardine was here aboard *Du Teillay* as it carried him homeward.

The prince and his small party, cooped up and incognito, were prey to countless concerns and anxieties. After a fair wind away from Belle Isle, they had weathered 'a brisk gale' on one and then 'dead calm' the next.[16] It was now 20 July by the New Style calendar in use in France (9 July by the Old Style British one), and it was already three weeks since Charles had left the port of Nantes. He had travelled by river boat as far as Saint-Nazaire, while the Captain Claude Durbé had overseen the loading of '1500 fuses [muskets], eteen hundred [1800] broadswords mounted, a good quantity of powder, Balls, flints, Durks, Brandy etc, and some hundred more of the fuses and broad swoards of which I cannot at present tell the exact number.' There were also 4,000 Louis d'or, and 'twenty small field pieces tow of which a mule may carry'.[17] Sullivan had also arranged a travelling chest for the prince's personal belongings, a dinner set and even a bed.[18]

The following evening, with *Du Teillay* having caught up, the Young Chevalier had been collected from the beach in the bay of Bonne Anse. They had sailed to Belle Isle the following morning, where they had awaited the arrival of *L'Elisabeth* ten days later. With a constant fear that their expedition might be discovered – perhaps even by the French authorities, if word got out prematurely[19] – the atmosphere below decks was tense.[20] Durbé had even cleared for action once, and although it turned out to be a false alarm the threat of encountering the Royal Navy was very real even here: 'the enemy's vessels are daily cruising close in to Belle Isle, and one must keep a sharp lookout,' the captain recorded.[21] Even when the two ships were finally united and under sail, there was no reprieve for the anxious. Sails had crowded the horizon on several successive days, and the distant rumble of cannon-fire drifted across the waves from the north-east. Durbé suspected that they were being pursued by seven or eight ships, and although *Du Teillay* might be able to outrun them, *L'Elisabeth* was, according to Sullivan, 'a heavy log.'[22]

On the morning of 20 July, two ships were sighted by the small Jacobite flotilla. Sullivan recalled how 'when they reconnoitered us, one of them went back, I suppose to advertise the Squadron.'[23] Captain Durbé logged that there were eight sails in view, 'sailing free so as to run down on us from windward', one being considerably closer than the others and out to the east.[24] This was HMS *Lion*, a British warship which had originally been built in 1709 and then completely rebuilt in 1738. Sullivan considered her 'a fine light ship of 64-guns', and she was commanded by the highly capable Peircy Brett.[25] In terms of armament, *Du Teillay* was no match for her. *L'Elisabeth* was closer to the task and, if a fight became unavoidable, the combination of the two might prove sufficient so long as those other hostile vessels could not close up in time. But the risk to the mission was severe, and the dangers to which the passengers would be exposed were considerable. Captain Durbé had accordingly signalled to *L'Elisabeth* and now her captain, Pierre Dehau, was coming aboard.

At the council of war which took place aboard *Du Teillay* on the late morning of 20 July 1745, the Young Chevalier had little choice but to defer to the advice of the two captains and to Antoine Walsh. The strategic decision was straightforward enough: the optimal course would be to avoid contact, but if that proved impossible then the necessity was to deal with *Lion* before it found support, to allow the flotilla to continue its voyage. The tactical options for dealing with the latter scenario required greater consideration, and while Charles was there to give his approval, nobody but the two captains could determine how best to use their ships at sea. The decision was to clear both ships for action, and for *L'Elisabeth* to engage *Lion* at close range. She would weather the British ship's fire until she was able to present a full close broadside and then move swiftly to board. At this point, the nimbler *Du Teillay* could come around in support with both cannon and small arms while the enemy was locked in combat.

The intention of closing quickly to a boarding action was not just based on the need for a swift resolution due to the fear of additional British vessels. It also played to an advantage *L'Elisabeth* had, which its enemy would not have expected: an unusually high number of fighting men. In his letter to King James, which was deliberately held up to ensure it would reach Rome too late to prevent the expedition, Charles wrote that the ship had '700 men aboard as also a company of sixty volonteers, all gentlemen.'[26] He repeats the same figure in a letter to Edgar. On occasion this has been interpreted as meaning 700 French regulars, presumed to have been arranged by Lord Clare and accordingly recruited from amongst the Irish Brigade. In fact, a far more plausible explanation is provided via the Dutch ambassador at Versailles, who reported that there were 70 uniformed gentlemen and 300 locally recruited volunteers (which, along with a ship's crew of around 400 men, equates to the prince's figure).[27] The gentlemen wore blue coats with thin gold lace and plumed hats, 'a prety uniform' according to the prince.[28] These men had all been recruited for the same ostensible purpose as the hiring of *L'Elisabeth* and purchasing of arms: a privateering venture to the West Indies. Unbeknownst to them, these were the first soldiers to have been raised for the Jacobite army of 1745.

Charles' plan for this expedition was astonishingly audacious and starkly simple: he was sailing to Scotland with as many men and munitions as he had been able to privately arrange, and would land them in the western Highlands where he would be within the heartland of the most loyal Jacobite supporters and remote enough to disembark without interference. Once he was amongst his father's people, they would answer his call to arms. He had turned the old plan on its head: rather than waiting for the French to land to trigger an uprising, he would use an uprising to trigger French aid. As his father later acknowledged, the prince had been driven to this extreme by the combination of apparent French disinterest and his own assertive temperament: 'the usage he met with in France, and the dread of a peace, were, no doubt, strong motives to push him on a rash undertaking rather than to sit still, and who knows but what he has done may, in some measure, force the Court of France, out of shame, to support him.'[29]

Lord Sempill, who had been with the prince at Gravelines but had then been left out of the planning, was horrified and quick to distance himself from the expedition. 'I began to fear that the Prince's counsellors had something extraordinary in view,' he wrote to Rome, suggesting that 'Sir Thomas Sheridan and Kelly had taken advantage of the Prince's ardent and lively temper, and led him into a measure that might prove fatal.'[30] But Charles had repeatedly warned that he was prepared to make such an undertaking, not just to Keith but also to Sempill and Dunbar. In Paris he had then met privately with John Murray of Broughton, who had previously visited the court in Rome. While Murray, a Borders Jacobite who had invested his inheritance in ventures in the Highlands, had repeatedly expressed the need for several thousand French troops, he had also assured his prince that the Highlands would rise at his presence.[31] Charles had simply not been able to get the French to commit to another expedition, and so had decided to do their work for them. He could not raise the requisite thousands, but he was hardly sailing to Scotland empty-handed. As the king sighed, they all now had to make the most of the opportunity the prince was creating: 'the question now is to look forward, and not to blame what is past.'[32] His son, he acknowledged with an anxious pride, was putting himself in the greatest danger for the Stuart cause.

At midday on Tuesday 20 July 1745, both *Du Teillay* and *L'Elisabeth* cleared for action. The crews systematically removed, packed or lashed all moveable items, and the magazines were opened. Weapons were distributed, especially aboard the larger ship which, given its intention to board, would have given out short pikes, pistols and blades as well as muskets. The decks crowded with sailors and marines, while the gun crews ran out their cannon. Interior partitions were removed, and the whole vessel given over to the expectation of combat. The *Du Teillay* was a raider, built for preying on the weaker ships and outrunning the stronger. But *L'Elisabeth* was a true ship of war, a survivor of the storm which had ruined the prince's hopes the previous year; it had the men and guns to try to fight this out. The same process was taking place on HMS *Lion*, which was advancing steadily.

Around 1.00 pm, the two Jacobite ships drew up close and their captains again conferred. Durbé's log makes it clear that both Prince

Charles and Antoine Walsh were again engaged in the decision-making.[33] The plan was refined insofar as fifty men from *Du Teillay* would support the boarding action as soon as the *Lion* had been successfully grappled. The ships continued to run a little longer yet, but after another hour it was clear that the British ship was gaining too steadily, and it was now apparent that if the expedition was to proceed then they needed to stand and fight. Dehau dropped his longboat and hoisted his colours, the huge white field and glittering fleurs-de-lis billowing in the wind as the ship hove to. The first French gun boomed its defiance.

With one of its targets now standing firm, *Lion* was momentarily chastened. She also drew up, the vast ensign of the red squadron unfurling at her stern, which prompted Dehau to resume his voyage. But this only encouraged Captain Brett to renew his pursuit, cutting away his longboat to gain every possible advantage in speed. Shortly after 5.00 pm, *Lion* was close enough to open fire with some of its port guns. All three ships were now shortening sail, understanding that the chase was over and the battle on. Dehau and his men endured the first shots without response, sticking to the plan, until the wind brought the enemy closer in.

When the moment was right, *L'Elisabeth* unleashed a full broadside with her starboard guns. The massive sound shook the air, punching across the sea toward the ears of the Young Chevalier. Now was the moment to close, her waiting crews braced with desperate courage as the cacophony roared around them. But *Lion* pulled up her standing jib and lurched ahead, and the French ship was slow to react. Captain Durbé and Aeneas MacDonald, both watching intently from the deck of *Du Teillay*, each noticed how 'the English sailors worked her better than the Frenchmen did the *Elisabeth*.'[34] Soon Captain Brett had not only passed Dehau but began to turn around her, led by the flapping colours of the Union at the prow, bringing his ship between the two French vessels. In moments he would be in a position to rake the length of *L'Elisabeth* 'from stem to stern', but the latter was finally turning too.

Captivated by this tense nautical dance, the prince and his companions were willing their comrades to close, desperate to see the grapples cast so that they too could close in on the enemy. As if she had sensed their silent prayers, *Lion*'s starboard guns – now facing *Du Teillay* – blasted forth in challenge. The whistling whip of grapeshot filled the air above the deck, lead balls punching through the canvas of the sails. But Durbé would not be drawn, his light cannon incapable of facing *Lion*'s massive double bank of heavy guns. The British ship continued its arc, but *L'Elisabeth* had turned sufficiently now that the two ships were again parallel.

The two bigger ships were now locked in a deadly duel of heavy guns, and Dehau was forced into a battle of attrition rather than the rapid boarding for which he had hoped. The two ships were soon swathed in thick smoke, the sulphurous stench of powder filling the air which shivered with razor-sharp splinters and the ripping passage of musket balls. The ships pounded one another hard, with the crew of *L'Elisabeth* struggling to keep pace with the accomplished craft of the Royal Navy: 'the British sailors showed their superior skill and dexterity, which were highly praised by all on board the *Doutelle* [sic], as well French and Scotch men.'[35] The French appeared to be particularly targeting the enemy's rigging, while *Lion* was raking their deck with fire. Eventually, with a shuddering crack and a great tearing of sail, *Lion*'s mizzen mast came crashing down from above. Rigging ropes flailed in the air as the upper half of the mast plunged into the sea. Sailors scrambled to chop the wreckage free, and all the time the guns continued to thunder around them.

Now, sensing an opportunity, *Du Teillay* dared to draw closer. Easing her way around the stern of its larger comrade, her own guns now added to the roar. Prince Charles was now in far greater danger than he had ever faced in the siege lines of Gaeta, at the mercy of all the horrors of close-quarters naval combat in the age of sail. But the wounded *Lion* spat fire and defiance from her stern-chasers. Sullivan recalls 'the ardeur the Prince showed on yt [that] occasion; he'd absolutely have a share in the fight... but Wels, who knew the wakeness of his Ship & the little succor he'd be off, wou'd not obey.'[36] Walsh and Durbé knew better than to press too close and drew back off.[37] *Du Teillay* now followed cautiously as the duelling warships drifted towards the south-east. The captain could only pray that their course did not lead them closer towards even greater danger.

Now there was nothing for Charles and his companions to do but watch. MacDonald remembered how they were now granted 'the time and leisure to observe the management and behaviour of both ships.'[38] We can imagine them there upon the deck, looking on as the cannon pounded away. They saw the thick fog of powder smoke bloom with flashes of orange fire, like lightning raging within a cloud. The roaring of the cannon was softened by the distance into a rolling percussive rhythm, heavy and constant. Periodically the sea would leap upwards in a glistening spray, or its surface would shiver as it was shattered by showers of debris flung from the decks. The cries of men, orders and pain would occasionally pierce through the constant pounding, or a splintering crack as mighty timbers split like kindling. But as the light began to fade, imperceptively at first, the rate of the firing also began to tire.

After 9.00 pm the two duellists began drifting apart like two battered old prize-fighters who each refused to yield. The broadsides slackened and the guns were now firing in fits and starts. Both ships were badly damaged, but *Lion*'s sails and rigging were in a visibly worse state than her enemy's. According to Aeneas MacDonald, still watching from the *Du Teillay*, the British ship fired a final defiant blast before striking its colours.[39] If the prince saw it too, his heart must have soared with relief. But *L'Elisabeth* did not attempt to close in for the kill, badly wounded herself, and Captain Brett rallied his strength and unfurled the red ensign once more. As *Lion* limped away, *Du Teillay* closed up and hailed its bloodied champion.

For almost five hours the battle had raged, and now, as the night closed in and the lanterns were hung, it was time to count the cost. Captain Pierre Dehau and his brother Lieutenant Charles Dehau had both been mortally wounded during the action. Prince Charles had last seen him drawing his sword after their final conference before the bloody encounter had begun. Aeneas believed it was the *Lion*'s final shots which had killed the captain, although others suggest it was one of the earliest broadsides. Over 150 men had lost their lives aboard *L'Elisabeth*, and scores more were wounded.[40] Her decks were a carnage of debris and broken men. The survivors, many of whom had never faced action before, were haggard and drawn: wide eyes staring blankly from blackened faces. Screams rose from below.

Pierre-Jean Bart (Mr Barr) had assumed command of *L'Elisabeth* during the action and had fought resolutely, although Sir John MacDonald believed that had he been better informed as to the nature of the mission, then he would have disengaged sooner. But now he made it clear to Walsh and Durbé that his ship was in no position to continue. The council of war which followed was a critical one for Prince Charles.

His little expedition had been badly bloodied, and his largest ship was so battered that it was incapable of doing anything other than heading to Brest for repairs. In fact, Bart was asking for sailors to be transferred from the *Du Teillay* to help him achieve even that. All eyes turned to the prince. Some of his companions – Aeneas MacDonald is careful not to name them – advised that the expedition be postponed. They could wait either until *L'Elisabeth* had been refitted or another escort secured. But 'to this he would not consent.'[41]

Charles' decision was a huge gamble. He was already heading to Scotland with far less by way of an army than had been his original intention, far short of what Murray of Broughton had advised him was necessary to ensure the clans would rise. From the planned French invasion of Kent in 1744, Charles was now down to a single vessel with a handful of friends and a few crates of weapons. But now he also had to weigh up the losses that had already been suffered, the risks already run, and the scale of the prize if it worked. He was undaunted. Captain Durbé recorded the outcome of the meeting in his log: 'we determined, by order of the Prince, to continue our course for Scotland.'[42]

The Young Chevalier, his cheeks scraped clean of the ruddy blonde beard he had grown at sea, was once more upon the water. According to the calendar then used in Britain, it was 19 August 1745, and there was no risk of British warships here on the shimmering waters of Loch Shiel. Either side of the loch the mountains rose sharply towards the sky, guiding him like an arrow-straight funnel towards his destiny. It was already eleven days since *Du Teillay* had departed, after serving as a part-time headquarters since his arrival on the Scottish mainland on 25 July. The day before it sailed, Antoine Walsh and Claude Durbé had visited the prince at Borrodale House where they had wished him success. Ten years later, Walsh would hang a large painting of their parting above the mantelpiece of his grand new chateau. Some artistic licence was deployed in its composition – it is unlikely, for example, that the prince was yet wearing full Highland dress, and Walsh is shown wearing a medal he had not yet received – but the landscape is evocative of the true location and *Du Teillay* is shown upon the loch. Now that ship, as Prince Charles made his gentle progress up Loch Shiel, was approaching Amsterdam.[43]

The prince had sent *Du Teillay* away as soon as he could, as a symbol of his intention to remain in Britain. Ahead of him, like a line of ants along the loch-side tracks, a train of Highlanders had carried by hand all the military stores that the ship had landed. They should now be waiting for him at Glenfinnan, the rendezvous to which he had summoned his supposed supporters. Thus, Charles had cut off his best lifeline back to France *before* he had seen whether the clans would rise. It was another of his now characteristic gambles, a trait which inspired as much admiration as it would criticism. He knew the value of such gestures, and he needed to win people over to him quickly. Lacking even a regiment of French soldiers to deploy, Charles Edward Stuart needed to create his army from scratch.

The first signs had, admittedly, not been good. On 23 July, after an anxious voyage around the western side of Ireland, dodging British warships in busy waters, the prince had arrived on the tiny island of Eriskay. There he had disembarked with most of his companions, no doubt desperate to set foot on firm ground. Tullibardine's gout prevented him from alighting with them. A storm was blowing up and the group sought sanctuary at a nearby black house. There were too few beds to lodge them all, and probably as much because he was full of nervous energy as from simple gallantry, Charles insisted his older companions take their rest first. He also insisted on inspecting the bed which was assigned to Sir Thomas Sheridan, prompting the indignant landlord to scoff that the lodging was good enough for a prince. Charles drew his wrath a second time by repeatedly getting up from the fireside to take fresh air by the door, choking on the peaty smoke of the humble hearth. 'What a plague is the matter with that fellow,' asked Angus MacDonald, 'that he can neither sit nor stand still, and neither keep within nor without doors?'[44] At his first landing the prince was already sowing the seeds of the romantic legends.

The storm presaged ill tidings, it seemed. The prince had sent out messengers to advise of his coming and to seek out local support. Alexander MacDonald of Boisdale, uncle of Young Clanranald 'who commanded that clan', called upon Charles and entreated him to leave.[45] Famously, when Boisdale urged him to go back home, the prince replied, 'I am come home.' But as Boisdale painted a bleak picture of their prospects, 'every body was', according to Sullivan, 'strock as with a thunder boult.'[46] All but the prince himself, Walsh and Sullivan were now for turning back, but the latter pointed out that trying to leave now ran as great a risk to their lives as staying. Charles was able to put this disappointment behind him by sailing on to the mainland and hoping for better. Aeneas was sent off to Kinlochmoidart to widen the search for friends.

The stuttering start to the grand enterprise continued thereafter. Although a company of Clanranald men were assembled for the prince's protection, Young Clanranald was under pressure from other local leaders not to encourage Charles to hope for any better. The prince sent him to elicit the support of MacLeod of MacLeod, but the latter immediately informed Duncan Forbes, president of the Court of Session, that there was a Stuart prince in Scotland. Rumours were soon flying around the western Highlands, but Charles still had no momentum behind his rising. Donald Cameron of Lochiel had come to pay his respects, and, again, the prince found himself deploying all his charm and rhetoric to overcome the well-reasoned doubts of men who both loved his cause and feared its failure. The prince played on Cameron's pride, suggesting with a shrug of disappointment that the great Lochiel would have to be content to read of their success in the news-sheets. Cameron had been warned to expect no less: his brother, John Cameron of Fassefern, had advised that 'if this Prince once sets his eyes upon you, he will make you do whatever he pleases.'[47]

Eventually Charles knew that he had to force a shift from words and into action, for although his friends now knew where to find him, so did his enemies. He moved on from Borrodale into Kinlochmoidart, going around the coast by boat while Clanranald's company went by land. While the prince was there, the first blows on land had been struck in his name: first, a British officer had been captured as he travelled towards Fort William; then two companies of the Royal Scots had been attacked and forced to surrender near Highbridge. Charles met the captured officer, Captain John Sweetenham of Guise's Regiment, when he arrived at Glenaladale on the evening of 18 August. The prisoner was being entertained by John Gordon, Old Glenbucket, a veteran of both Killiecrankie and Sheriffmuir, who would be heading back to his native Aberdeenshire to raise a regiment as soon as he had seen the standard raised. There really was no going back now.

As his little boat finally approached the head of Loch Shiel, Charles Edward surveyed the scene. The Clanranald men were here as expected, about 150 of them idling around the supply crates and baggage – including a stock of cheese and butter – which were stacked beside a small cottage close to the shore. The prince's little flotilla disembarked the fifty who had stayed with him as a guard. This was a measly portion of the overall potential strength of the MacDonalds of Clanranald, but the influence of Boisdale and others had restricted the numbers Young Clanranald could call upon. As well as his other companions, Charles had now been joined by John Murray of Broughton – who had initially responded to the news of his landing by writing to Sheridan advising the rising be called off. Sullivan recalls the tenor of Sheridan's reply: 'it was upon the strength of his [Broughton's] promises yt the prince made such a Step as he did, & it wou'd ly at his door if he did not perform his word.'[48] Murray had then rushed north to play his part and encourage others to do theirs. Also present with them now was Alasdair mac Mhaighstir Alasdair, the renowned Gaelic bard who now found himself as the prince's tutor in the language of the Highlands. But the shore at Glenfinnan was hardly thronging.

The precise location of the subsequent events at Glenfinnan has long proved controversial. The most detailed eyewitness account is that found in the Murray-Threipland papers, which was possibly written by Young Clanranald or somebody close to him, although it was composed some years after the event.[49] The key point the author makes is that the standard was carried across the River Finnan before being set up; there are few other clues. It makes sense to assume the actual ceremony was performed on an eminence from which it was possible for most attendees to witness it. By long-standing tradition, this was the low hill behind the current visitor centre which overlooks the early nineteenth-century monument. This location makes sense if it is assumed that the standard was carried there from the east, for to cross the Finnan the prince must have landed in the vicinity of the later Glenfinnan House. General Roy's military map, surveyed within a few years of the rising, shows a small settlement here, which makes it a very plausible landing place.

An alternative location has been proposed, however, on a higher hill behind the modern village. Here some inscribed stones were discovered in the 1980s which claim to identify the exact spot, complete with carved footprints supposedly identifying where a number of individuals stood. But the carvings are undated and are something of an enigma, not appearing in the written record. The main Latin inscription uses the famous motto 'Tandem Triumphans', although those words did not appear on the flag when the standard was raised. It seems unlikely that the stones, had they existed at the time, would not have been known to the builders of the Glenfinnan Monument in 1815. If so, we might expect them to have influenced its location more. If the standard was indeed raised at this alternative spot, then the Finnan must have been crossed east-west, suggesting that the prince landed nearer the monument and between the mouths of two small rivers. This does seem a less natural course, but with the information currently available it is unlikely we can draw a firm conclusion.

After landing at 1.00 pm the prince withdrew to a small building beside the gentle waters as he waited to discover whether his efforts would come to naught after all.[50] Critically, would Cameron of Lochiel's ardour – aroused against his better judgement at his interview with the prince – have cooled in the subsequent days? The afternoon dragged on, with just a few curious spectators arriving in the meantime. Finally, sometime after 3.00 pm, the distant skirl of the bagpipes floated down the glen. In a short time, two dense snaking columns of Camerons appeared on the heights. 'Never have I seen anything so quaintly pleasing,' recalled Sir John MacDonald, 'as the march of this troop of Highlanders as they descended a steep mountain by a zigzag path.'[51] Lochiel had mobilised in strength, and in throwing in his lot with the prince he had given a lead to others who looked to his example.

Charles would wait no longer. An honour guard of Clanranald men carried the prince's standard across the insubstantial stream of the Finnan, and ceremonially handed it to Tullibardine. Despite his unsteadiness, this was a privilege owed to his rank and status as the Jacobite Duke of Atholl. The flag was carried to Prince Charles, who then formally handed it back to the duke and commanded it be raised. This was duly done, the large silken banner billowing on its eminence as the clansmen cheered with 'a general Housaw [sic]'.[52] The prince's commission of regency was read aloud, followed by a political manifesto drafted in Paris. Finally, the prince himself made what Broughton called 'a short but very Pathetick speech.'[53] The prince rose to the moment, firing the Highlanders to follow the 'noble example of their predecessors' by joining him in 'so glorious an enterprise'. Then he ordered casks of brandy to be opened and the health of his father was drunk.[54]

The famous 'Glenfinnan standard' of a white square in a red field, sometimes with a blue border and the Latin motto *tandem triumphans*, is hard to locate in the original sources. John Home, who was not there, reports that it was twice the size of a normal infantry colour, making it something like 12 feet square. He describes the flag as 'made of white, blue and red silk,' but does not provide his source.[55] But most subsequent references to the prince's standard described it as being entirely white. Aeneas MacDonald confirms that, by Glenfinnan at least, the flag bore 'no motto at all'.[56] *The Scots Magazine* was also vexed by the issue of the flag, concluding in relation to the motto that 'it is doubted if there ever was any such standard, though it was currently so reported.'[57] Some still favour the idea that the Royal Standard was precisely that, although there is a tradition that the flag was stitched by ladies at Dalilea, the intended standard having been left aboard *L'Elisabeth*.

About an hour after the formal ceremony, Alexander MacDonnell of Keppoch arrived with around 300 men, escorting the bewildered prisoners they had taken at Highbridge. Now the crowded head of the loch was an intimidating space, full of motion and noise. The prince now had around 1,200 men under his command. He set himself up in a barn, presumably because it was the largest structure, and the prisoners were moved into the nearby houses.[58] Arms were soon being issued to those who had not been able to supply their own, and Sullivan began attempting (in vain) to organise the clansmen into regularly sized companies; he was now appointed 'adjutant general and quarter master of the army.'[59] Captain Sweetenham, who was now released on the prince's orders. In return, that officer gave his colleagues 'the most favourable account yt cou'd be given of the Princes personne & activity.'[60] Amidst the romantic drama of the Glenfinnan scene, it is easy to forget that it had all happened within 15 miles of a permanent British garrison (Fort William). And on the very day that the Young Chevalier had raised his standard, Lieutenant General Sir John Cope marched his army northwards to stop him.

Chapter Three

Holyroodhouse

The castle guns fired, but the measured thunder of the three successive cannon bursts was distant. Nevertheless, some of the Highland soldiers, 'with their bagpipers and plaids,' slowed their pace, bringing the parts of the column to a staggered halt.[1] The officers barked and jeered, and the weary feet in their leather brogues were soon back in motion. For most of the soldiers of Prince Charles' new 'Highland army', Edinburgh Castle was not even in sight, let alone range. They were deliberately taking a circuitous route around the southern side of Scotland's capital, well beyond the reach of the guns of its most formidable fortress. But despite the defiance of the guns, the Jacobites had little to worry about for the moment. It was 17 September, just four weeks since Glenfinnan, and they had already taken Edinburgh.

The Young Chevalier was marching on foot with his men, as had become his deliberate habit. One aspect of campaigning for which he *had* been adequately able to prepare himself was its physicality; he was also fully aware of the power of gesture. The prince wanted to be seen amongst his men, leading them in person, winning their affection with his proximity and their respect from his fortitude. The newspapers carried word of the prince's behaviour ahead of his advance: a letter to the *York Courant* reported of Prince Charles that, 'every river they have to cross, he's the first man that leaps into it.'[2] A few days later, the *Caledonian Mercury* carried an account from a British officer, whose sergeant had managed to slip through the Jacobites' forces near Linlithgow. He saw the prince 'sitting along with the Men on the Grass,' where he had been eating 'a Crust of brown Bread.'[3] Both of these examples concluded by making a comparison with Charles XII of Sweden: 'this Charles bids fair to imitate the Royal Swede of that Name.'[4] Of course, that famous soldier-king had lost his life in battle, struck down in the trenches before Fredriksten in 1718. That knowledge would not have stopped the young prince from seeking to emulate him, but his developing leadership style was as much to do with his own character and inclination as it was deliberate public relations.

The same must be said of his choice of attire. The prince had worn full Highland dress on several occasions in Rome, but he adopted it with zeal now that he was in Scotland. Today he was observed by a Lothian farmer who reported that 'the Prince was in Higland [sic] dress, a velvet bonet with both gold lace ringed abowt.'[5] John Home saw Charles about an hour or so later and elaborated further on the description: 'he had a light coloured periwig with his own hair combed over the front: he wore the Highland dress, that is a tartan short coat without the plaid, a blue bonnet on his head, and on his breast the star of the order of St. Andrew.'[6] Further detail is provided by Andrew Henderson: 'he was in Highland habit, had a blue Sash wrought with Gold, that came over his Shoulder; red Velvet Breeches; a green Velvet Bonnet, with a white Cockade and Gold Lace about it.'[7] Elcho further confirms that the prince was wearing breeches rather than a plaid, but stated that he wore boots that day.[8]

The prince did not always wear Highland dress, however; a few weeks later Magdalen Pringle described seeing him in a blue frock coat, and he wore a silver-grey velvet frock coat for his sitting with Allan Ramsay. But his appearances then, as he prepared to lead his army on into England, were intended for an audience far beyond his rank-and-file supporters. Raised in a court which paid scrupulous attention to its portraiture, Charles Edward Stuart knew the value of image and self-projection.

He also knew that the same rules applied to the army as to himself, and as his areas of recruitment expanded beyond the western and central Highlands, the prince encouraged all men to adopt some form of Highland habit, both to build a sense of common identity and to exploit his opponents' perception that Highlanders made more formidable enemies. Home confirms this attitude was indeed the case: 'if clothed like Low-country men [they] would appear inferior to the King's troops; but the Highland garb favoured them much as it shewed their naked limbs, which were strong and muscular'. Thus, would the Jacobite army, even in the words of its own officers, remain 'the Highland army' long after the majority of men would not naturally be classed as Highlanders.[9]

For the moment, however, the army was indeed a Highland one. It had grown since Glenfinnan to around 2,500 men, the majority from amongst the Highland clans with whom the prince or his line of march had made direct contact. The speed of the Jacobite advance had prevented some supporters from raising their men in time to yet reach the main army. After witnessing the raising of the standard, Old Glenbucket had returned to north-eastern Scotland to begin levying his tenants. In Atholl, Tullibardine was doing the same after being restored to his ancestral seat at Blair Castle and was then left behind to act as the prince's nexus in the north.

The anti-Jacobite witness from Woodhouselee listed the weapons he saw the army's 'hillskipers' carrying: 'guns of different sizes... some had swords over ther showlder instead of guns, one or two had pitchforks, and some bits of sythes upon poles without a cleek, some old Lochaber axes.'[10] Home again corroborates him, reporting carefully to General Cope that '1400 or 1500 of them were armed with firelocks and broad-swords; that their firelocks were not similar nor uniform, but of all sorts and sizes, muskets, fusees and fowling-pieces; that some of the rest had firelocks but without swords, and some of them swords without firelocks...; that a company or two (about 100 men) had each of them in his hand the shaft of a pitchfork, with the blade of a scythe fastened to it.'[11] These latter were the MacGregors, who were attached to the Duke of Perth's Regiment, as confirmed by the Jacobite officer James Johnstone: 'with these [scythes] he armed his company, and they proved very destructive weapons.'[12] Home also confirms, it should be noted, that 'many of their swords were not Highland broad-swords, but French.'[13] Given that the prince had, by his own account, brought 1,500 muskets and 1,800 swords, securing additional weapons was an important military priority on the march to Edinburgh.

That march had been conducted with brilliant speed and directness, aided by Sir John Cope's inability to contain the Jacobites within the Highlands. The little army born at Glenfinnan had remained in the vicinity only a short time, to allow for the equipment and supplies to be moved up. The lack of baggage horses was an immediate problem, and the artillery pieces supplied from *Du Teillay* had to be buried for wont of a means for their carriage. Then the Jacobites had marched straight out to meet Cope's advancing forces. The British army's presence in Scotland was weak in number and widely dispersed, both due to the pressures of the ongoing war in Europe and the unexpected nature of the prince's expedition. The state had invested vast sums of money since the last Jacobite disturbances to create a series of modern forts and barracks, connected by an ambitious network of roads and bridges. Their purpose was both to prevent hostile clans from assembling in mutual support and to provide rapid troop concentrations at trouble-spots. But they were undermanned and poorly maintained – Captain Sweetenham had been rushing to Fort William in response to reports of problems with its gates.

The Jacobites had shrugged off any risk from these garrisons, bypassing Fort William and then marching towards Fort Augustus before turning into the Corrieyairack Pass on 28 August. When they made an attempt on Ruthven Barracks in Badenoch, the operation was carried out against the prince's personal judgement. He 'judged it more proper to let it alone as a place of no consequence,' reports Murray of Broughton, but the chiefs had pressed the issue and he had conceded.[14] Without artillery, the Jacobites were not yet in a position to threaten such a substantial position, protected as it was by flanking towers, and the resulting effort was unsuccessful. The fact that the prince had yielded to others in approving the scheme is, however, significant.

Apparently without discussion, Charles Edward Stuart had assumed personal command of the army which he had assembled. This he was perfectly entitled to do, bearing as he did the commission of regency granted by his father for the proposed 1744 expedition. But for all his innate potential, much of which would have been unknown to those around him, the prince had never commanded a regiment, let alone an army. He had been under fire at Gaeta and on *Du Teillay* and shown courage, and both before and after the naval battle with *Lion* he had at the very least approved of the proposed plans of action. In its aftermath, however, he had asserted himself in insisting the expedition continue. But it would be wrong to assume there was an expectation on any part (perhaps except for his own) that he should, or would, take actual command of the army in operation. But without French aid, Charles had been obliged to take full ownership of his actions. By virtue of the fact that he had called the men together for the mission, they now looked to him for strategic leadership. Nobody else had much experience in senior independent command either.

So the Young Chevalier had assumed the role of commander-in-chief, and the Glenfinnan army was directed by him following consultation with the chieftains who had joined him, and Sullivan as adjutant general.

Sir John MacDonald, as a cavalry officer, probably contributed little. John Murray of Broughton was appointed Secretary of State, a civilian post, but offered rather more. Tullibardine's contribution was mainly through his zeal and the authority inherent in his rank, connections and impeccable Jacobite credentials, but he was too unfit to be a campaigner himself. The senior chiefs, Lochiel and Keppoch in particular, will have carried considerable authority too (not least because they best knew the lay of the land) and the prince was open in his consultations with them for all the obvious and natural reasons. But ultimately the decisions were down to Charles Edward himself.

Initially it had seemed that a confrontation with Cope would come quickly, and that a decisive engagement would be fought in the Highlands as it had in the last rising, although hopefully with better results for the cause. There was a race between the two armies to reach the Corrieyairack, which the military road ascended from the east by a steep series of zig-zags. If the Highlanders could catch the red-coated regulars there, or at the second winding ascent of the road at Snugborough further west, they would have a serious advantage. After pausing at Invergarry Castle, where he had been joined by fresh troops despite the sudden heavy rain, the prince pushed the army hard to get it to Snugborough ahead of his enemy. A hot sun had beat down on their bonnets as the Highlanders marched up rough tracks into the hills to reach the military road's most vulnerable points. Finding nobody to meet them, the prince sent scouts ahead. When their reports proved inadequate, he sent a more senior team which included Secretary Broughton. Once it was clear that the enemy was not in the pass, the Jacobite army had moved further on and, by 2.00 pm on 28 August, it reached Garvamore.

This was the Young Chevalier's first victory at the head of his own army. His advance had been preceded by a fog of misinformation which had clouded his enemy's assessment of the risks and made them cautious: Cope was close enough to have secured the pass before the Jacobites, but did not know that and could not take the risk. He had doubled back along the road and then turned northwards towards Inverness. The senior officers were asked to sign their consent to this course of action, which was contrary to the political instructions to seek and destroy the prince's fledgling force.

The prince now had a significant decision to make at Garvamore, presumably at the King's House (sometimes known as Garva Barracks, although it was a way-station for both military and civilian travellers). While he made it, he ordered cattle to be slaughtered to provide food for men who had marched nearly 20 miles in intense summer heat.[15] A group of Highland loyalists, deserters from Cope's army, had lingered near the barracks and were gently handled. After speaking freely of the motions and mood of Cope's army, they received a guinea by the prince's order.[16] Those who did not then join would nevertheless have carried the right sort of accounts when they left. But many of the Highlanders, believing the redcoats were now on the run, raised 'a continued Cry to be march'd against the Enemy.'[17] They were ready, they insisted, to march all through the night if need be to catch up with Cope, or to try to overtake him in the mountains towards Slochd. When he heard of the commotion and the sentiment in the ranks, the prince postponed dinner and called a council of war.

Charles 'maid [sic] the map be laid before him' and gathered the chiefs to discuss all that they knew of Cope's likely movements. Believing it to be impossible to successfully continue the forced march and then fight an engagement, the prince asked for opinions. Broughton recalls that 'most of the gentlemen present seem to acquiesce in his opinion,' but the options were debated and Charles explained his own reasoning. Then 'he determined to lay all thoughts of it [the Slochd plan] aside and send the Chiefs, who were all satisfied with the force of his arguments, to quiet their people.'[18] Instead, the army was to continue the next day to Dalwhinnie, then strike southwards into Atholl and on to Perth. The gap between them and their enemy would then grow daily, while the prize of the Scottish capital grew closer.

The council of war at Garvamore was extremely significant, determining that the decisive battle of the opening campaign would now be fought outside of the Highlands. The Jacobites would now have a considerable freedom of movement until they reached Stirling, beyond which Cope had left two regiments of dragoons to screen the capital. Charles Edward had led his army to where it needed to be, achieving an impressive march over difficult terrain in challenging conditions, himself on foot at its head. Then he had resisted both his own natural instincts to seek action, and the clamour of his own men for the same course. He had ensured the discipline of his army was achieved through the chiefs, who were sent out to explain the reasons on which the decision had been based, while allowing them the opportunity to present alternatives. The prince had shown, under considerable pressure, significant leadership skills and strategic understanding. And now he was about to take the capital of Scotland without a fight.

As the Jacobite army turned its way northwards towards the city, the prince and his senior commanders decided to pause and take refreshment. It was their last opportunity to do so before the biggest public appearance of their lives. The prince passed through a wyvern-guarded gateway into the small park of Grange House. The house itself was of the old baronial style of the Jacobean age, and yet to reach the splendid turreted proportions it would enjoy in the following century before its decline and demolition in the 1930s. The army continued moving up towards Duddingston Loch, knocking breaches into the boundary of the King's Park (Holyrood Park) in preparation for their final approach. The city itself was already secured, the Netherbow Port having been seized from the surprised guards in the early hours of the morning by Sullivan and Lochiel. The successful detachment had then efficiently disarmed what remained of the City Guard, secured the town walls and ports from the inside, and taken control of the tolbooth and its arsenal. The citizens had woken up under new management.

With Lochiel and Sullivan in the city, Prince Charles arrived at Grange House 'supported by the titular Duke of Perth on his right hand, Lord Weems his sone Lord Elcho on his left.'[19] Both men had joined the army as it had progressed towards the capital, and they provided the prince with the companionship of men of high rank who were closer to his own age than many of the other leading figures of the campaign. James Drummond, 3rd Duke of Perth, was a 32-year-old Catholic nobleman whose father and grandfather had both been committed to the Stuart cause and suffered for it. Perth's father had signed their estates over to his son prior to the 1715 uprising, which had preserved the family's wealth and influence at least, but the government no longer recognised their title. Perth had been educated in France, spoke with a broad Scots accent, loved horse racing and was immensely likeable. Charles Edward was surely comfortable in Perth's company, and it is likely that the 'silver-hilted broad Sword' he was wearing that day had been presented to him by the duke.[20] Perth's value to the Jacobite cause was such that the government had made a clumsy attempt to arrest him before he had even joined with the prince's army; the duke had escaped through a window. When he joined the prince at Perth with a 200-man regiment, his reward was a rank more appropriate to his high social rank than his military experience: he was made lieutenant general.

The other companion walking with the prince was David Wemyss, Lord Elcho. The eldest son of the Earl of Wemyss, Elcho was a year younger than the prince and had visited him at the Palazzo del Re in 1740. His maternal grandfather was the notorious Francis Charteris, and following his education at Winchester College he was well connected across British society. The family was not known for its Jacobitism, and King James had been delighted to encourage this straight-talking and wealthy young nobleman as a leading light for a new generation of supporters. Elcho was naïve and entitled, brave and diligent. He had ridden out to join Prince Charles just the previous day, 16 September, bringing with him some much-needed cash to support the campaign. The prince was grateful, but the investment was a poor one: Elcho continued to harangue Charles for repayment long into their exiles, and the rift between them would never heal. But all that lay in the future. For now, all was excitement as they 'drunk some bottles wine' at Grange House.[21] When the prince was ready, he mounted a bay gelding for the final approach to the capital.[22]

The prince's pause had allowed for the breaches to be made in the park walls which encircled the mighty rump of Arthur's Seat and the Salisbury Crags, and for the citizens of Edinburgh to begin gathering in expectation. It was now late in the morning and the citizens, many relieved that the tense few days which had passed appeared to have come to a peaceful resolution, were eager to witness the coming procession. A Royal Stuart had not arrived in Edinburgh since 1679, when Charles' grandfather had come here for a three-year residency while he was Duke of York. A reigning monarch had not been to the city since 1650, when the young Charles II (the prince's great-uncle) had visited during his ill-fated campaign to retain the crown that Cromwell had removed from his father's head. Regardless of politics, the arrival of a Stuart prince in the Scottish capital would make hearts pang, either as a symbol of a bygone age or as the coming of a new one. Regardless of politics, people wanted to witness what was so obviously an historic event.

At the outer limits of the park, there were already clusters of spectators. The martial procession was led by the Perthshire Squadron, the only small unit of cavalry which the Jacobites yet possessed. The thirty-six gentlemen riders were un-uniformed but smartly turned out, accompanied by their servants and led by the 55-year-old William Drummond, Viscount Strathallan. The latter, a veteran of Sheriffmuir, was perhaps the only one amongst them who was not in Highland dress.[23] Presumably Strathallan was accompanied by Sir John MacDonald, the Irish cavalry officer who was commissioned by the prince to the largely honorary post of Inspector of Cavalry.

Prince Charles and his entourage rode directly behind the Perthshire Squadron, Perth on his right and Elcho on his left.[24] They crossed into the royal park and then, screened from the guns of Edinburgh Castle by the volcanic crags, marched on towards the picturesque little chapel of St Anthony. As they progressed, the crowds of spectators became denser: 'the roads were so crowded for near upon a mile.'[25] Hands reached out towards the prince in the hope that they might 'touch his boots or his horse furniture.'[26] Charles Edward Stuart was no stranger to being fêted and praised, but these scenes were beyond imagining. More than ever, he must have been sure of his role as the longed-for saviour of an unhappy people.

Marching behind the prince came the main column of infantry, minus the large detachment which was already in the city. They were under the direction of Lord George Murray, who had joined the army at Perth shortly after the duke who bore the town's title. Like the duke, the 51-year-old Murray had been appointed to the rank of lieutenant general. The younger brother of Tullibardine, after an unrewarding time at Glasgow University, Murray had joined the British army in Flanders as an ensign shortly before the War of the Spanish Succession came to an end. He was too late (and initially too sick) to learn much about warfare, and his two years in military service were spent in the drudgery of peace-time soldiering at a low level.[27]

In 1715, Murray broke his military oath and leapt up the ranks by joining his brother Tullibardine in Jacobite service. He was commanded a regiment in the Atholl Brigade, although he missed the battle at Sheriffmuir, and with Tullibardine he went into exile after the rising's failure. Another brother had died in captivity after the Battle of Preston, to the double distress of his father who had not approved of his sons' Jacobitism. In 1719 Murray had returned, officially holding the rank of major general in the tiny Jacobite army which was defeated at Glenshiel, although without gaining any more experience of commanding large forces. Back in exile, Murray failed to find a commission or patron overseas, and asked King James' permission to seek a pardon from George I. His younger brother James, now acknowledged in Britain as Duke of Atholl, helped secure one in 1725.

Thus, Lord George Murray had been living the peaceful life of the minor gentry for the past twenty years at Tullibardine in Perthshire. Always proud and stubborn, often haughty and derisive of those he considered less capable, Murray was nevertheless a devoted and humane character, well respected in his community. Sir John Cope had met him on the march north and appointed him as Sheriff Depute for Perthshire, responsible for supporting the redcoat army logistics during their progress.[28] Murray had paid lip service only, but to some Jacobites it appeared he had been, at best, hedging his bets at the beginning of the campaign. Suspicions were reported to the prince on his arrival at Perth, with several people openly advising that Murray 'cou'd not be trusted to.'[29] But the prince assessed, as Sullivan admits, that Murray was too respected a name not to accept into service and was to prove 'a very active sturring man, [who] knew the Country perfectly well, gave himself a great deal of peines [pains].'[30] As he had been a major general in 1719, it was only fitting that he received a promotion in 1745.

The character and actions of Lord George Murray lie at the heart of the story of Charles Edward's war. To some, such as James Johnstone, Murray had 'a natural genius for military operations' and should have been 'one of the greatest generals of the age.'[31] To others, 'his carracter was not of the best' and his attitude was dangerously disruptive and his loyalty potentially suspect.[32] Certainly he possessed considerable leadership skills and personal courage; but even his greatest admirers acknowledged he could be 'blunt and imperious... and, feeling his superiority, would listen to no advice.'[33] There seems to be no evidence to suggest Murray was acting as a saboteur or hostile agent, but nor is there any compelling evidence that he was an exceptional military mind.

Murray's rank in Jacobite armies was inflated by his status, and he had shown competence rather than brilliance. Murray had not served in an army for twenty-six years, and not in a professional one above subaltern rank. From a strictly military perspective, his experience was of less immediate use to the prince than Sullivan's, of which Murray was scathingly dismissive. Here was a potentially powerful triumvirate: Charles Edward had strategic and political instincts; Sullivan was an effective organiser and staff officer; and Murray was a tactical thinker and inspiring front-liner. Charles had paved the way for this by putting them all into their proper positions within the army, but Charles and Sullivan were already close and Murray was not interested in courting their favour.

This was the Lord George Murray, then, who led the Highland infantry column into the King's Park behind his commander. He was described by James Johnstone, the naïvely excitable young son of an Edinburgh merchant, as 'tall and robust, and brave in the highest degree.'[34] In his portrait at Blair Castle, we can still see him, hard-faced and rigid, with a practical no-nonsense look. Despite his full Highland dress there is no flamboyance or romance about his stance, just the drawn sword and narrow eyes of a man who will perform the responsibilities allotted to him with efficiency rather than pleasure. Since Perth he had been working hard to support the transition of the Glenfinnan army into a more regular force, building on work already begun by Sullivan. The army had swollen to around 2,000 men and more units were following in the wake of the main column to reach Edinburgh in the coming days. For now, it was Murray's task to lead those who had already arrived towards the palace and then encamp them in the park. But since the capture of the city had been achieved by others, especially Sullivan, it receives only the barest mention in Murray's own account of the rising.[35]

By now Prince Charles was reaching the small spring in the rocks beneath St Anthony's Chapel, where the path descended more steeply towards St Anne's Yards and the royal palace. From here, he had a spectacular view over the heads of the throning crowd and across the high tight-packed tenements of the capital. Just as it is today, the view was dominated by the vast bulk of the castle brooding at the west end of the Old Town, and the squat crown of St Giles' kirk. Closer at hand was the southern façade of the palace of Holyroodhouse, rebuilt in a formal style for his great-uncle to face inwards onto a private quadrangle. Between himself and the palace spread an enormous crowd, and as the prince came into their view they roared in salute: 'it was here the first general Huzza was raised,' reported Henderson disapprovingly.[36] The prince dismounted, partly from the steepness of the path down to the Duke's Walk and partly because he could hardly push his horse forward in the throng. But the crowd was too great, and 'the Mob, out of curiosity, and some out of fondness to touch him or kiss his hand, were like to throw him down.'[37] He pressed through, 'smiling all the time,' revelling in the sudden adoration and impervious to both the physical and psychological dangers it held.[38]

At the foot of the slope, after descending the same route followed by countless thousands of tourists today, the prince reached the road known as the Duke's Walk. Here the jostling crowd made it impossible for him to be seen, so he remounted his horse. He walked the gelding on towards the palace 'amidst the Cries of 60,000 people, who fill'd the Air with their Acclamations of joy.'[39] Elcho's account, written years after the event, is still charged with the excitement of those extraordinary scenes. Hostile reporters could not deny the scale of the crowds, so instead presented them as being composed mainly of fickle women. But Sullivan says the crowds came from both 'Town & Subborbs' and included 'both gentle and simple' folk.[40] Secretary Broughton, who frequently rebuts malicious criticism in his account, pointedly states there were 'vast numbers of people from both sexes' and 'people of the best fashion.' He would know: his own wife was among them.[41]

The prince's figure could not have been better crafted to please such a crowd in such a setting. He was described by Home as 'in the prime of youth, tall and handsome, of a fair complexion.'[42] Henderson says he was 'a tall Slender young Man, about five Feet ten Inches high, of a ruddy Complexion, high nosed, large rolling brown Eyes, long visaged, red-haired.'[43] Having overhead the prince speaking, this witness also reports that the prince's voice was soft ('sly') and that his accent seemed to hint towards Irish. With his tartan coat adorned with the Order of St Andrew and crossed with the sash of the Garter, his appearance excited Edinburgh's proud heritage as the seat of Scotland's kings.

Shortly before midday, the prince rode around to the front of the palace and dismounted a second time. He walked across the open piazza and 'when he was near the door, which stood open to receive him, a gentleman stepped out of the crowd, drew his sword, and raising his arm aloft,' led the prince inside.[44] Clearly little thought had been put into either the security or the ceremonial arrangements: when James Hepburn of Keith, an ardent anti-Union Jacobite escorted the prince into Holyrood, he did so on his own initiative. John Sullivan and Murray of Broughton were here to meet the prince, presumably at the door, having done what little they could to bring the underused residence back to life in the four or five hours since the seizure of the gates.

Charles passed through the front doorway and into the cool cloistered passage which surrounded the classical facades of the inner quadrangle. He was guided to the left, up a flight of stairs to the first floor and through into the Great Gallery. There beneath the ceiling's clean white plaster, a grand parade of his royal ancestors and predecessors stretched out before him. Some faces were imaginary, semi-mythical kings from forgotten ages; others bore the familiar features of Stuarts past. Among them, robed and armoured, was his great-grandfather, the martyr-king, whose silver image the prince carried on a snuff box. Then his great-uncle, Charles II, who had come out of exile and restored the Stuart monarchy. And here hung the prince's royal grandfather, King James VII & II, the last male Stuart to rule in Britain and the last to visit this palace. Looking at his face, one wonders whether Charles felt a pang for his father. Prince Charles had already visited the old royal landmarks of Scone and Linlithgow, but nowhere else was the right of his cause writ more clearly than in the faces of these 111 extraordinary portraits.

From the Great Gallery the prince was shown through to an adjacent suite of rooms, officially the Queen's Apartments, which today are known as the Lobby, Antechamber and Darnley Bedchamber. These rooms would become his official headquarters, where meetings were held and where the prince and his staff dined. When the prince approached one of the windows looking out of the tower, the crowd cheered.[45] Beyond these rooms, in a now-demolished projecting wing, were the apartments which were kept for the hereditary keeper of the palace, the Dukes of Hamilton. Here Charles would lodge, the King's Apartments being totally unprepared.

The huge crowds had now concentrated around the palace and up the broad length of the Royal Mile. Sullivan remembered how 'all the windows of that fine street were full at every story.'[46] The multitude was now drawn to the Mercat Cross, the civic heart of Edinburgh, which had been draped with a 'large fine Persian carpet' for the occasion.[47] Lochiel's Regiment, which had been billeted in the old Scottish parliament building behind St Giles', marched out at midday 'in rank and fyle' and formed a ring around the Cross.[48] Within the ring assembled Jacobite officers, 'special favowrits', and the beautiful Margaret Murray of Broughton who was also adorned in tartan. Bagpipes filled the air in anticipation of the coming ceremony.

Preceded by a single trumpeter, the heralds of Scotland processed to the Cross, entering its stout wooden door and climbing the steps within onto the raised platform. They wore their full heraldry and gave the occasion all the official status that could have been arranged at short notice. Once the heralds in their bright surcoats appeared on the parapet, a 'profowd silence' fell across the crowd. One David Beatt then read the official texts, which were repeated by the herald Roderick Chalmers 'with ane awdable strong voice.'[49] Patrick Crichton was able to hear the words distinctly from a window on the north side of the High Street, whereas Andrew Henderson down in the crowd could not hear 'a single sentence.'[50] Fortunately the texts 'were cairfully dispersed every where amongst the people,' which shows the extent to which the Jacobite commanders understood the importance of the public relations battle.[51]

King James' declaration of December 1743 was read, followed by the commission of regency he had granted to his 'dearest son', and then the prince's own manifesto which had been written in Paris back in May. Charles asserted his father's 'undoubted right to the Throne of His Ancestors,' confirmed full pardon for all previous transgressions against his family, and vowed that the Stuarts would rule 'by and with the Advice of a free parliament'.[52] Once the proclamations had been read, the pipes struck up and blended their tones with the chimes of St Giles' Cathedral. The Camerons marched off and the crowds began to disperse, many thronging back to the palace where they 'continued all that night in the outward court.'[53] Inside, Charles Edward Stuart, now proclaimed as Prince Regent of England, Scotland and Ireland, was planning his next move.

Chapter Four

The Battle of Prestonpans

In the early morning of Friday 20 September 1745, the Young Chevalier stepped down from the front doorway of a modest two-storey house in the quiet little village of Duddingston. He wore boots, a tartan jacket, a scarlet waistcoat and a blue bonnet. He had left off the insignia of his knightly orders, giving the appearance of a well-dressed Highland officer. Michele Vezzosi followed, buckling on the prince's broadsword now that they were free from the confines of the cottage. Sullivan was there too, in his long-skirted frockcoat and cocked hat. The deep blue air was cool, tinged with the faint hues which precede the coming of day; they spoke a few words in the hushed tones which seem to come most naturally at such an hour. Prince Charles flashed a smile at the small guard of Highlanders, who followed him westwards along the narrow lane. As they approached the village inn, occasional sounds from muffled voices cut over the still air; the night was stirring into morning, and an army was stirring into life.

At the inn, more officers greeted the prince. Bonnets were snatched from heads; throats cleared, and the voices now were louder, clearer, with a little nervous laughter. A distance away, a drum began to beat. On the prince's instruction an aide strode briskly away and, a few moments later, a piper's drones began to sound. The first notes split the morning, and in answer to them the gathering tunes of the clans soon struck up along the hard-packed road below Arthur's Seat. Along the sides of the road, countless shapeless mounds swelled into motion as the Highlanders rose from beneath their dewy plaids. The men had 'lay out in rank and file in one line.'[1] Their officers knew what to do, the orders having been issued the previous day after the council of war had concluded.

That council had been held here in Duddingston, after the army had been moved the short distance away from the capital in readiness for the march. Prince Charles had been preparing for the likelihood of battle since his arrival at Holyrood: when John Home observed that 'his countenance was languid and melancholy,' it was undoubtedly because he had been told – even at the moment of his triumphal arrival – that Sir John Cope was disembarking in Dunbar.[2] The prince's army was still small, still untested, and some regiments were indifferently armed; these issues were running through his mind even as the crowds cheered outside his windows at Holyrood.

Charles Edward could not allow the atmosphere of the occasion to divert him from business; nor did he, immediately ordering Sullivan to search Edinburgh for additional arms.[3] The next morning, the burgesses were instructed to arrange the supply of '1000 tents, 2000 targets, 6000 p^r of Shoes, and 6000 Cantines.'[4] A 'quantity of bread' was also secured for the army,[5] and the Woodhouselee manuscript adds 'stokings' to the list and groans that 'it is good plaids were not asked.'[6] The arrival of reinforcements was a comfort, especially the timely return of John Murray, Lord Nairne, with the men he had raised in Perthshire. It might not have been as many men as had been hoped, but the Atholl Brigade would grow when given time. The drums sought recruits for the Duke of Perth's Regiment on the streets of Edinburgh, but to turn sympathy here into support, the Jacobites needed to secure a victory in the field. When Cope's departure from Dunbar was confirmed on 19 September, Charles concentrated the army at Duddingston and summoned his council that evening.

The prince sought reassurance as to how, bravado aside, the clansmen could actually be expected to perform. Alexander MacDonald of Keppoch, due to his experience as a captain in French service during his exile after 1715, was nominated to speak on behalf of the other chiefs. Keppoch was a commanding character, tall and severe, who prided himself on sharing the privations of his clansmen on campaign. It was also reputed that he ruled them through fear as much as respect. According to Home, who was, of course, not there to hear it despite providing the best account of the meeting, Keppoch vouched for the performance of the Highlanders, despite the fact that 'few or none of the private men had ever seen a battle.'[7] Satisfied, both from his own inclination and a calculated wish to further encourage his men's valour, Prince Charles declared his intention to 'charge at their head.' The chiefs were appalled, acknowledging the truth so often forgotten by the prince's critics: that he was the glue that bound them all, and that 'if any accident befell him, a defeat or a victory was the same to them.'[8]

A more contentious issue was who would have the honour of forming on the right wing in the coming battle. At Perth, the prince had asked the chiefs to resolve the matter between themselves in advance, free from the threat of imminent action, and they had done so by drawing lots. These gave the van to Lochiel and the Camerons. But now battle seemed to be at hand, the MacDonalds (particularly the Glengarry Regiment) reprised their ancient claim to that position. The issue was only resolved 'after a very long dispute', in which Lochiel agreed that his men would lead as planned but would concede to the Clan Donald regiments on the following day.[9]

The council possessed clear information on Cope's movements, and Secretary Murray confirms that they already knew the general was to camp at Haddington that night (19 September).[10] Cautious, Cope had, in fact, stopped his march early that afternoon out of concern for the availability of water further along the road. This gave plenty of time for information to spread, and later in the evening several of his civilian scouts were captured near Musselburgh and interrogated. Cope's dragoons were shaken from their ingloriously rapid abandonment of Edinburgh, so he had allowed them the previous day to rest while he took his time disembarking his infantry, artillery and baggage. John Home had arrived and given a clear account of the Jacobite strength, but all the displaced leaders of the capital were also flooding his ears. There was an expectation of reinforcements – Dutch troops due to land at Berwick – but Cope decided to march east to recover the capital before things could get any worse. Broughton confirms that the prince was afraid Cope would indeed wait for support, and 'expressed a great deal of satisfaction' that his opponent was also now seeking a battle.[11] The council agreed that the only sensible course was to meet General Cope on the road, where he could not expect support from the garrison of Edinburgh Castle. With that decision made, the prince had 'employed yt night in visiting the postes' before snatching what little rest he could in the village.

And so it was that the morning of 20 September slowly began to lighten, with the Jacobite army rising out of the soft tones of the pre-dawn. The prince and his slender staff moved along the forming column, 'setting every Regimt in order, the joy yt he had painted in his face, & his talking some words of hers [Erse/Gaelic] to the mens.'[12] This was the Young Chevalier at his best, amongst his men and knowing exactly what they needed from him. His smile masked his own anxieties, confidence coming from good intelligence and careful planning as much as the reassurances of Keppoch. Exactly as arranged, Lord Nairne's pickets in the city – 100 at Holyrood, 50 around the Netherbow Port, 50 at the City Guard house before the Tron kirk, 100 watching the Castle from the Weigh House, and 25 down on the Grassmarket below – withdrew before the dawn and joined the army at Duddingston. Significantly, they brought with them surgeons, coaches and chaises for the service of the wounded.[13] They appear to have been held back in readiness, rather than being taken with the army, to be summoned forward when needed. This prior consideration for the wounded, often overlooked, undoubtedly saved lives.

Some Jacobites were left behind in Edinburgh. Elcho reports how one drunken clansman, having missed his comrades' departure, spread it about that there were 300 others still in the town. This report dissuaded the castle garrison from sallying out and, amongst any other mischief, disturbing the civilians who were preparing the new accoutrements ordered by the army.[14] Another Jacobite was still on the High Street the following day to make a bold attempt to arrest some fugitive dragoons riding to the castle. While these might be isolated individuals, it seems likely that a skeleton guard was indeed left in the capital to keep an eye on the garrison (now in the army's rear) and protect the baggage. The vast majority of the Jacobites were, however, forming on the road into a column 'whose front was very narrow, three in a rank.'[15] The narrowness of the column presumably reflects the influence of those trained in French practice. As the dawn broke, the Highlanders were eager and alert, formed and ready.

Once he was satisfied that all was in hand, Prince Charles 'came towards the Centre, & called for all the Chiefs.'[16] He reminded them that he wished their success as much for their own sakes as for his father's, and that the enemy were already half-beaten on account of fighting for an unjust cause. Charles then drew his sword with a flourish. Perhaps it was the same one he had worn on his arrival in Edinburgh, which is likely to have been the one that is now displayed in the National Museum of Scotland. On the latter's blade is etched the double motto *'ne me tire sans raison; ne me remette point sans honneur'* (draw me not without cause; sheath me not without honour), and although those words were not unique to this particular sword, they surely lie behind the prince's next words: 'Now Gents,', said he, 'the Sword is Drawn; it wont be my fault if I set it in the Scabert before yu be a free & happy people.'[17] Secretary Murray refines the speech: 'Gentlemen, I have flung away the Scabbard; with Gods assistance I dont doubt of making you a free and happy people; Mr Cope will not escape us as he did in the Highlands.'[18]

The prince then made sure his words were circulated amongst the men, as Sullivan makes clear from the order which followed them: 'I desire yu may retire to yr postes, inform yr men of what I said, & march.'[19] The speech was duly repeated, and the men threw their bonnets in the air and let out 'such a Cry, yt it wou'd be wherewithal to fighten any enemy'.[20] The prince's short speech would soon be printed too, as a pamphlet contrasting against a scurrilous fictitious speech attributed to Sir John Cope.[21] The news-sheets were a crucial front in this conflict, and both sides knew it. Charles then mounted his horse and at 9.00 am he waved his bonnet to set the army into motion.

First to move was Strathallan's Perthshire Squadron, who had camped beyond Duddingston in the area now occupied by the Holy Rood RC High School. These thirty-six gentlemen and their servants trotted eastwards towards the coast road, their task to precede the infantry as their scouts and screen. Behind them came the vanguard of the infantry, Lord George Murray's division. First came the largest single regiment of the army, the 600 men of Clan Cameron, marching behind Donald Cameron of Lochiel and bearing their red and yellow colours. Then followed the impressive Charles Stewart of Ardsheal, a famous swordsman and the uncle of the young chief of the Stewarts of Appin, whose regiment of 200 men he now led beneath a yellow saltire. Behind the Appin Regiment came the Duke of Perth's 200, which included a company of about 40 ill-armed MacGregors.

Following behind Murray's division came that of the Duke of Perth himself, tall and good-looking, resplendent in his rich tartan suit. Here were the Clan Donald regiments. Keppoch led his own 250 clansmen brigaded with the 100 men of Glencoe, with their chief and another detachment of MacGregors. The 20-year-old Aeneas MacDonnell, Young Glengarry, came next with his substantial regiment of almost 400 men. These would soon be reinforced with a company of Grants from Glenmoriston and Glen Urquhart, who had been marching in defiance of their own chief and would arrive just in the nick of time for the coming battle. Then came Young Clanranald, the first to rally to the cause, with his 200 MacDonalds. If any of the Clan Donald regiments yet carried colours, their appearance is not known. The Glencoe men certainly did not, for they followed a sprig of heather tied upon a pike.

The third division was granted to Lord Nairne, a staunchly loyal Jacobite who had committed to the cause at Blair and then spent time raising the Athollmen before catching up with the army. Of the latter there were around 250, marching beneath a red saltire in a white field just as previous Atholl regiments had done in times gone by. With them marched 100 men of Clan Donnachaidh and a further 100 MacLachlans. The latter had been forced into a long detour to reach the prince in order to avoid the hostile territory of Clan Campbell.

In total, the Young Chevalier was now at the head of just over 2,300 men. After such an unpromising beginning, this itself was no small achievement. Since its birth at Glenfinnan just four weeks before, this force had taken the offensive against all the resources of a modern state, marched unimpeded for 200 miles and captured the capital of Scotland. It had been forced to grow on the march, snatching what little opportunity there had been for training at Perth, with limited capital and no support network. It was bound together by a high-level cause which masked significant variations in personal motivations, political intentions and strategic expectations. Now it was time for this remarkable little army, and its completely unproven commander, to be tested in the heat of battle.

The Jacobite army advanced eastwards towards the coming enemy, the volcanic hump of Arthur's Seat shutting out any view of the closes and castle of the capital like a door which closed behind them. They crossed a small burn and followed a straight and easy minor road towards the sun-dappled waters of the Firth of Forth. The road they took (now Milton Road West-Milton Road East) crossed through a raised open and fertile plateau looking out along the Lothian coast, with freshly harvested fields to either side. The Jacobite army passed through the hamlet of Easter Duddingston. There they were observed by a young girl, who described the scene 82 years later to Robert Chambers. The prince, according to Mrs Handasyde, rode slowly over stubble with a small group of officers, while the main column of infantry trudged along the road itself. She remembered the glint of the St Andrew badge fixed to the green sash of the Order of the Thistle, revealed when the prince's coat tails blew back in the breeze.[22] It is the sort of detail a child might well remember for decades, long after the prince's army had passed by. From her fascinated gaze, the clansmen descended the gentle slope towards the main highway, which they joined just before it crossed the Brunstane Burn over the Magdalene Bridge.

Once across the little bridge, the Highlanders had the coast and its salt pans on their left, and the walls of Newhailes estate to their right. The Jacobites next reached Crystal's Inn. It was at this roadside hostelry that Francis Garden and Robert Cunninghame, two gentleman volunteers scouting ahead for Cope, had been spotted the previous night enjoying a supper of white wine and oysters. There they had inadvertently spoken with John Roy Stuart, an experienced soldier who had served as an officer in both the British and French armies. Stuart, still on active service for King Louis in Flanders, had returned to Scotland at the first opportunity and joined the prince at Blair. Out scouting for information with Captain George Hamilton, he had tricked Garden and Cunninghame into revealing they were performing the same duty for the other side. Waiting for them outside, the two Jacobites had seized their counterparts and taken them to Duddingston, where a show had been performed as to whether or not to hang them as spies. This performance – and it was certainly no more than that, designed to loosen their tongues – was so effective as to induce little short of panic in the prisoners, a humiliation which was never forgotten.[23] Then only 18, Cunninghame was so incensed that he would later fight at Culloden in Price's Regiment. He went on to become a Member of the Irish Parliament. A few years older, Francis Garden became a judge in the Court of Session. But on 20 September 1745, in fear for their lives, these two young gentlemen must have looked upon Crystal's Inn with bitter regret as they were marched past again under guard.

The two prisoners were marching in the care of the Atholl Brigade, towards the rear of the column, so they passed the inn while most of the army was marching through Fisherrow. Here, according to the folk-memory of later generations, a Highlander stole a broom and tied it to the end of a staff. A great cheer went up from his companions, who understood the declaration that they were marching to sweep away the enemy. Along Market Street, now an unpretentious backstreet but then the main road through the village, the townsfolk watched from their windows; the prince bowed his head to acknowledge the ladies. He was more comfortable with such distanced gestures than with direct engagement, being 'always embarrassed' in women's company.[24] Nevertheless, Charles knew the value of winning them over, as he had shown when he had given a snuff box and ring to Beatrix and Mary Jenkinson, two respectable Presbyterian sisters he had met in Duddingston the previous day.

Charles Edward and his army had now reached their first objective, the River Esk. Fisherrow and Musselburgh were connected here by the high but narrow arched bridge, so old that tradition claimed the Romans had built it. The nearest alternative bridge was over 4 miles upstream at Dalkeith, and the most fordable places in between were dominated by a steep-sided ridge on the western bank. This latter had been occupied by a Scottish army two centuries past, before it had crossed the river to its doom at the Battle of Pinkie. By reaching the river ahead of the enemy, the Jacobites had ensured that Cope could not get around them into Edinburgh. By crossing it safely, they would then prevent him from using it as a defensive line. Alexander Carlyle, another civilian volunteer supporting Cope's advance and son of the minister at Prestonpans, believed that this had been his general's precise intention, and perhaps the Jacobites had thought so too.[25] Without pause, the army crossed the Esk. It was travelling light, unencumbered by baggage or artillery, and the narrowness of the bridge posed no challenge to the slender column of clansmen. The crossing was performed 'in good order'.[26]

Hew Dalrymple, Lord Drummore, confirms that it was indeed Cope's intention to encamp his army that night beside Musselburgh, with the river as their protection. Although a civilian, he was showing his loyalty by supporting Sir John Cope as much as possible. Along with the Earls of Loudoun and Home, both serving officers, and Lieutenant Colonel Charles Whitefoord of the marines, Drummore had ridden west to scout a location for the camp. He knew the area intimately as his own estate lay between Musselburgh and Prestonpans. This high-status scouting party observed the Jacobite advance through their field-glasses, and the two military men rode back to inform the general. Drummore himself, being unarmed and out of uniform, felt safe enough to observe longer, waiting until the Highlanders were 'not above four hundred Yards' away.[27] By then the Jacobites were marching around the southern edge of the Pinkie estate, owned by John Hay, 4th Marquess of Tweeddale and Secretary of State for Scotland, who was busy trying to direct Cope's campaign from London.

Lord Drummore did well not to draw attention, as he might have found himself between the main Jacobite army and its forward scouts. For it was as the army skirted Pinkie – the location unanimously confirmed by Broughton, Lord George, Sullivan and Elcho – that troopers from Strathallan's squadron came in with information. They had ridden far enough forward to sight the enemy, identifying 'parties of the dragoons about Tranent'.[28] The significance of the moment is hinted by the fact that the senior Jacobite memoirs are in such concurrence over an apparently trivial detail: it was a moment which stuck in their heads. If the dragoons seen by Strathallan's men were the outriders of General Cope's army, then he must be marching on the post road which led through Tranent along the top of a long ridge of hills. The scouts of both armies had successfully identified and reported the location of the other, with an approximate distance of just 3.5 miles between them. A clash was becoming inevitable.

The Jacobite commanders now needed to respond to their intelligence, and it seems likely that a brief conference of the senior officers was convened. Secretary Murray reports that 'the Chevalier conjectured that he [Cope] would engage him on the muir to the west ward of that Village [Tranent].'[29] The only possible option was to seek advantage by securing Falside Hill (misidentified by Broughton and Elcho as Carberry, but correctly remembered by Murray); from here they could dominate Cope with the momentum of a controlled downhill charge. But any discussion between the prince and his commanders was short: Murray believed 'there was no time to deliberate, or wait for orders; I was very well acquainted with the ground and... I struck off to the right hand through the fields, without holding to any road.'[30] Murray's division therefore rushed across the battlefield of Pinkie and up the steep slope above St Clement's Wells. 'In less than half an hour, by marching quick,' Murray covered the 2 miles to secure the heights.

The army had now split into two columns, with Murray's surging ahead of the prince's and then slowing down as it reached the top of the ridge to allow the others to catch up. What Murray found at the top was not was he was expecting: Cope's army was not at Tranent, but in full view on the low plain beyond Preston, still a couple of miles off to the north-east. Word was sent back to the prince, presumably again by Strathallan's troopers: 'before he had reached the top of the hill he was told that Sir John had marched to the left, and posted himself in a low ground betwixt Preston and Seaton.'[31] Charles Edward urged his men on and once they reached the summit, the Jacobites formed a battle line which then advanced along the ridgeline in good order onto Birslie Brae, where they had expected Cope to be positioning. There they stopped at around 1.00 pm, with Tranent off to their right, while the rear of the army came up behind them. The Atholl Brigade's prisoners, Francis Garden and Robert Cunninghame, were released without conditions as they were now both a useless distraction and a potential security risk.

The Young Chevalier was now in front of his army on the lip of the ridge at Birslie Brae, from which he had a fine view of the landscape of the battlefield and his enemy below. In the far distance, muted by a soft haze into pastel shadow, was the imprecise form of the Fife coast. Beneath it, a broad belt of blue spread ever wider as it expanded eastwards towards the sea. Between the coast and the prince's ridge lay a wide and open landscape which seemed to slide gently towards the water. There were four main settlements resting on this plain, framing a broad expanse of yellow-brown stubble. The nearest was the village of Preston, where the blackened ruin of a medieval tower overlooked a cluster of substantial white-rendered houses and a fine mercat cross. The village was dominated by the stately Preston House, with two pavilion wings, a park to its north side and formal gardens on its south, the whole surrounded by a stone wall which the Jacobite James Johnstone recalled as being 'from six to seven feet high'.[32] Across the road from this wall was another, enclosing the smaller estate of the orange-harled Bankton House, the nearest property to the foot of the hills. Bankton's owner was also in view: James Gardiner was colonel of one of the regiments of dragoons deploying on the plain.

To the north of Preston and separated from it by a narrow stretch of open ground, the larger village of Prestonpans ran along the coast. Its only discernible landmarks at this distance were the squat tower of its church and the sails of its windmill. A mile further along the rocky shoreline, a cluster of tiled roofs identified the harbour village of Cockenzie, the view smudged by smoke from its salt pans. Slightly inland, a smaller and more rural settlement could just be discerned; rising from behind it was the indistinct form of the dilapidated Seton Palace. Out of sight behind it was Seton's fine old collegiate church. While the Forth coast connected Prestonpans with Cockenzie, so an ancient brown road connected Preston and Seton village, running roughly parallel with the short, about three-quarters of a mile inland. Running along the south side of that road, visible as a dark scar studded here and there with tufts of vegetation, was 'a deep ditch filled with water' which terminated in a small lochan beside Seton.[33] On the near side of that ditch were a number of small enclosures surrounded by the patchy greens of rough ground: the marshy belt of the Tranent Meadows.

Perhaps one of the prince's officers – Elcho, at least, would have known – pointed out to him that Preston House, built at the beginning of the century, belonged to James Erskine, Lord Grange, whose brother had raised the Jacobite Standard at Braemar in 1715 and subsequently mishandled all the opportunity he had unleashed. The Earl of Mar was long dead, ending his days distrusted by supporters of both James and George; his brother was a member of parliament and, despite writing encouragingly to King James as recently as June 1745, did not stir from London during the prince's expedition. He was not, therefore, at home. Nor was the 67-year-old Earl of Winton, who remained in exile following his forfeiture after Mar's rising failed. Winton's crumbling palace and large estate had been purchased by the York Buildings Company, including his coal mines near Tranent and the salt pans at Cockenzie which they fed. In 1722 the company had connected the two with a wooden-railed waggon-way, running straight across the stubble field from Tranent to the coast: the only viable firm route from south to north across the meadows and their ditch.

In the centre of this complex landscape, with its combination of both rural and industrial activity mixed with stately and ecclesiastical architecture, lay the army of Sir John Cope. It seems likely that the prince had made ample enquiries as to the character of his adversary, and at least will have known that he was an experienced veteran and a career soldier. Charles' fears that Cope would avoid battle will have been based as much on a cautious reputation as the general's performance in the Highland campaign. Cope was all too aware of the weaknesses in his forces – the lack of trained gunners to man his pieces, the variable state of his dragoon horses, and the lack of combat experience of his foot – but could rely on superior training and firepower. These factors inclined the general to act defensively, a posture which 'added so much courage to the Princes Army.'[34]

As the Jacobite army formed on the ridge, the British army formed to face them. The redcoats, marching onto the field past Seton village, had initially deployed to face west, expecting the Highlanders to approach along the low road via Preston. Now, at around 2.00 pm, they wheeled to make their line 'extend along the Ditch,' as Lord Drummore recalled it.[35] This new position fronted the road and the ditch, facing south across the meadows. Once the two forces were aligned facing one another, the Highlanders let out a raucous cheer. The redcoats responded with a huzzah, both sides releasing their tensions and showing their defiance, although more than half a mile of distance softened the effect of their bravado upon the enemy.

Sullivan cast an appreciative eye over the British army's deployment: 'their position was very good; they had their right wing to Gardners house, with inclosieurs surrounded wth Stone walls... a deep ditch morasses & inclosiers to their front, between us & them.'[36] Lord Elcho did likewise, observing: 'Gen. Cope's Army drawn up in Line of Battle in the plains below Tranent, his foot in the Centre and the Dragoons on the Wings with a small Corps of Reserve, Colonel Gardners park walls on his right, his bagadge on his lift, a broad ditch in his front and the town of Preston pans in his rear.'[37] Cope's two regiments of dragoons, the 13th and 14th, comprised 750 officers and troopers. Although they had damaged their reputations in the last two weeks by retreating – generally with indecent haste – ahead of the Jacobite advance, their mobility and strike power were a major threat to the prince's clansmen. By contrast, Strathallan's Horse were too few to provide any significant contribution to the main action when it came.

Cope also had six light cannon, details of which are provided in a subsequent inventory taken at Holyrood. The guns were 6 foot in length, and the barrels had a bore of 2.25 inches. Two had been cast in 1719, two in 1721 and the final two in 1741. They were supplied with both iron balls and grape shot. In addition, there were four small coehorn mortars '4 inches in the chamber', and two larger royal mortars of 5.75 inches.[38] To this modest artillery the Jacobites had no answer, having abandoned their own cannon at Glenfinnan for lack of transport. Unknown to the Highlanders, however, Cope's repeated requests for trained artillery crews had failed to secure them in time, and he was left with an inadequate collection of invalids, volunteers and sailors. The latter had been sent ashore from HMS *Fox*, a sixth-rate frigate which was hovering off the coast of Cockenzie. Given the weakness of the gun teams, it was not possible to disperse the artillery along the line as would have been usual. From the Jacobite position, however, this modest battery must still have looked formidable.

The British infantry formed the centre of Cope's army. There was only one complete regiment, Murray's, although Lascelles' Regiment was only two companies short. Both these regiments would have carried both their King's and Regimental Colours, the latter being white and yellow respectively. There were also two companies from Guise's Regiment and five from Lee's. These battalions were drawn up in a long thin line, three soldiers deep. Behind was a small reserve comprising one company of the Black Watch, three understrength companies of Loudoun's Highlanders, and a company of gentleman volunteers. Estimates of Cope's total strength vary, with the general himself using the fact that his papers were lost after the battle as a cover for understating it. A figure of around 2,500 officers and men is the most likely, allowing for some variation either way. John Murray of Broughton, with the best Jacobite intelligence at his disposal, reckoned his enemy's total to be 2,700.[39] Allowing for spaces between the battalions and guns, the army probably occupied a frontage of nearly half a mile.

Prince Charles understood that he needed to fight this battle, and was anxious that his opponent might not feel the same. The challenge was therefore twofold: how to force an engagement onto Cope, and how to win it. As the British army swung to face them, the Jacobite army shogged along the ridge to anchor its flank more closely on Tranent. The village lay upon the east-west post road, the most direct route from Haddington to Edinburgh, but its layout was skewed into a north-south axis by a steep-sided wooded ravine called the Heugh. This ravine now protected the Jacobite army's right flank. But across the eastern bank, Tranent's parish church arose from behind a strong stone-walled kirkyard. Sullivan quickly assessed this as a potential danger point, as the churchyard could be accessed by the waggon-way path which led directly up to it from General Cope's position. He therefore instructed Murray, as commander of the right wing, to secure the church.

According to Sir John MacDonald, however, 'in spite of what Sullivan urged him, he [Murray] would not search the village nor place men in the steeple and the cemetery, which is the usual practice of infantry.'[40] Surprised and no doubt irritated, Sullivan seems to have then ordered the move himself. Murray reports that 'Mr O'Sullivan came up and, after taking a look at the enemy, took fifty of Lochiel's people who had the van and placed them in a churchyard at the foot of the town of Tranent, for what reason I could not understand.'[41] This was just the first of several instances during the day which exposed the different operating styles of Sullivan, whose recent experience was as a regular staff officer, and Murray, whose own experiences were decades past and mainly with Highland irregulars. Prince Charles, meanwhile, 'behaved on this juncture as the most experienced General, in posting of his Guardes to cover his army.'[42] What Sullivan probably means here is that the prince agreed with his own assessment; both Elcho and Murray of Broughton suggest the order to occupy the churchyard came from the prince himself.[43]

The prince's army was now itself in a strong position, with a walled churchyard and wooded ravine on their right, and a steep slope to their front. They had the advantage of the high ground, meaning that anything the British army did would be in full view of the Jacobites. Although Lord Elcho, Andrew Henderson and others would criticise Cope for not acting offensively, any attack by the British army would have been obliged to cross the ditch and the marsh before advancing uphill under fire. The cavalry would be restricted to attacking up the steep road to the west of Bankton or up the line of the waggon-way, or undertaking wide flanking marches which left the infantry outnumbered and exposed. For all the apparent strength of Cope's position, the redcoats were boxed in and could only march out of the battlefield through a bottleneck. No wonder it seemed wise to force the Highlanders to attack first, facing those same obstacles but into the teeth of superior fire. The ditch, the marsh and the bottlenecks passing Preston thus became the prince's problems to solve, not Cope's. And the more the Jacobites considered those problems, 'the more our uneasiness and chagrin increased, as we saw no possibility of attacking it without exposing ourselves to be cut to pieces in a disgraceful manner.'[44]

Charles Edward understood that he absolutely needed to fight this battle, and that his enemy might not feel the same pressure. For Cope, there was the possibility of reinforcement both to the west (Edinburgh Castle's garrison) and to the east (the imminently expected Dutch). But it was clear there was no possibility of a head-on attack across the marshes. To confirm the unsuitability of the ground, Lord George Murray asked Henry Ker of Graden to reconnoitre more closely. In his mid-forties, Ker was a Borderer and an experienced former soldier. He had been raised a Catholic and subsequently served as an officer in the Spanish army. After joining with the prince shortly before he reached Edinburgh, Ker had been given the rank of colonel and, no doubt thanks to his military experience, attached to the staff as an aide.

Now 10,000 eyes were trained upon Ker as he led his 'little white poney' down the slope between the two armies.[45] We are fortunate in having corroborating testimony for his actions from both sides of the field, remarking how Ker performed his task 'very coolly' and professionally.[46] When he reached the meadows, Ker dismounted and took the time to open a breach in a drystone dyke before leading the horse through the gap to test the ground beyond. As he did so, 'several of their men got alongst the ditches and shot at him.'[47] Both Prince Charles and General Cope were almost certainly watching the scene unfold, uniting them briefly in their shared focus. Only one of them had cause to be pleased. The first shots of the Battle of Prestonpans had been fired. But despite Colonel Ker's morale-boosting courage, the message he brought back to Murray (and through him, the prince) was that the ground was utterly unsuitable for an attack.

The impasse lasted for several hours, with neither side making much more of a move. The prince's huge white standard stirred lazily on the ridge, where it drew sufficient attention for informants to ensure its inclusion in several subsequent plans of the battle. Through their spyglasses, the Jacobite officers would have discerned parties of redcoats making breaches in Lord Grange's estate walls, making the eastern side sufficiently porous for the grounds to be garrisoned if required. They could also observe the army's baggage being drawn up into a large, hedged enclosure towards Cockenzie, a warren park. Sometime after 4.00 pm the redcoats 'raised some Huzzas, which were not answered.'[48] But if the excitement of the Highland army had settled down, it was now about to be stirred once more. Prince Charles was now convinced that his opponent was thinking entirely defensively, and suspected Cope might be waiting for darkness before making a dash towards Edinburgh. To forestall this, he decided to move Lord Nairne's division, which was formed behind the front line, down towards Dolphinstone village. From this position, to the west of Preston, they could control the road westwards. The prince sent Sullivan to Nairne with the order. No sooner had he gone than, off to the extreme right, the sound of musketry suddenly split the air.

Walter Grosset was a customs officer from Alloa, far up the River Forth. Such men are rarely popular, and Grosset's career was not without accusation and controversy. As an employee of the state, he had placed himself at General Cope's disposal and now, in the late afternoon of 20 September, he found himself stalking cautiously up the waggon-way towards Tranent. Grosset was not Henry Ker of Graden, but nor was he any type of coward. He approached the Heugh, which he described as 'a hollow Way and a thicket of Wood', on a mission to assess the situation at the top of this important dry route between the armies.[49] He must have been tense. Then, suddenly and without warning, his world exploded into a fury of sound and smoke. Muskets flashed from both sides, as he had stumbled straight into the picket posted at the churchyard by Sullivan, men placed here for this very purpose. There were fifty of them, all Camerons, and they were dispersed around the churchyard walls and the adjacent wooded ravine. Grosset scarpered, lucky to escape with his life. So far, neither army had displayed any particular proficiency at marksmanship.

Cope now seized upon an opportunity to be proactive. Prince Charles watched as two of Cope's guns were detached from the battery and drawn forward of the main line. Once they were at the lip of the ditch, they were loaded and levelled. The flash and the plume of smoke came first, the retort then rolling over the meadows. An impromptu huzzah went up from the redcoat line. Moments later, the second gun fired. The Jacobite army was under fire and it had no response to the enemy's cannon. As the prince watched the gunners reloading, Sullivan came galloping back up from the second line.[50] He was immediately sent to assess the situation on the extreme right, even as the cannon 'fired briskly upon it.'[51] Each shot, the iron balls disappearing into the Heugh with a crash of branches, was followed by a cheer from the enemy.

Meanwhile, the officer commanding the picket at the churchyard had scrambled out of the ravine in search of his colonel, Donald Cameron of Lochiel. He protested that he 'did not see what good they could possibly do in that place' now that they were under fire, and Lochiel followed him back for a closer assessment.[52] They passed a couple of wounded men who were being brought back to the rear, one cradling a shattered arm.[53] This was probably enough for Lochiel to make his decision, who returned from the Heugh to confirm to Lord George Murray that his clansmen were exposed to a fire which they could not return. Murray ordered the position to be abandoned, satisfied that he had never approved of its occupation in the first place. Lochiel withdrew the picket into the village itself, and Murray began shifting his division that way in order to probe for opportunities in the east. 'Of this,' he later recalled, 'I sent word to His Royal Highness.'[54] This was the scene that Sullivan found on his arrival at the right: his picket abandoned and the division extending into the village. Cope's cannon ceased their fire, the British officers satisfied that they had dislodged the enemy.

Sullivan rode up to Prince Charles 'in great distress', protesting at Lord George Murray's presumption. His fellow Irishman Sir John MacDonald pulled him aside and 'begged him' to keep his cool.[55] The prince himself was now watching for movement of Lord Nairne's men. The arrival of either Sullivan or Murray's own messenger with the news that the Camerons were being moved through Tranent village was an unexpected problem. The Jacobite army was in danger of overextending to both east and west, obliging Charles to ride across towards the right to confer with Lord George in person.

Murray was as surprised to discover the left was in motion as the prince had been to learn the same of the right. But Charles Edward was the army's commander and Murray was not at liberty to redeploy his division without prior approval. Instead of accepting the prince's rebuke, which had surely come, Murray responded 'in a very high tone' and demanded to know why the Atholl Brigade, the backbone of Nairne's division, had been moved.[56] His pride pricked, Murray dug into the argument and, according to Sullivan's biased recollection, he 'threw his gun on the Ground in a great passion,' demanding that they be recalled.[57] The prince, perhaps overawed by this display, or as Sullivan would have it, willing to overlook the disrespect to avoid the consequences of a fall-out at this critical moment, conceded. Sullivan himself rode out to stop Nairne, but in his absence Lochiel succeeded in calming Murray down. The latter then accepted the sense of the prince's intention and urged him to forestall the recall. Nairne was already bringing his division back towards the main line by the time the final change reached them. It is perhaps unsurprising given the confusion that Sir John MacDonald recalled 'these people shouting all at the same time, could neither hear nor carry out an order.'[58]

Eventually, around 5.00 pm, Nairne's division could at last complete its move towards Dolphinstone, with part of the Atholl Brigade hovering threateningly close to the Bankton enclosures. It is possible that Prince Charles had ridden westwards with them, as Home specifically describes the redeployment as being performed by 'Charles, with a great part of his army'.[59] Certainly a large white standard was visible throughout the afternoon on the western side of Tranent, as it appears in contemporary plans of the battle informed by eyewitnesses. It might well have been used for deliberate misdirection, fixing the redcoat's attention to the intended spot. So despite the shambolic situation surrounding its execution, Nairne's move westward was a significant success. Clearly observable by Cope, even without the aid of Alexander Carlyle's report from the spire of Prestonpans Church, the British army responded to the change by wheeling its entire line to face south-west. This was, the redcoats assumed, the prelude to a general assault.

As Sullivan left Nairne and his men behind, he now observed Murray resuming his motion on the right. He cursed to see the latter's division, and formed into column and was moving into Tranent, 'in full march, in presence of the enemy, without any thing to cover his flanck, & yet daylight.'[60] Lord George presumably felt their position on the heights was sufficiently secure for him to march without precautions, but maintaining a picket in the churchyard – against the walls of which Cope's artillery could have made no real impression – would have guaranteed no sudden threat to the column could emerge from the south. MacDonald agreed that Murray's move east was a sound idea, but was poorly and dangerously executed. Sullivan complained to the prince but the latter 'wou'd not oppose Ld George, fearing least he shou'd forget himself again, or if affaires turned ill, yt the blame wou'd fall upon him.'[61] This is significant: Prince Charles had good military instincts, but lacked the experience to give him confidence in the face of personalities as assertive as Murray's. Eventually, the dwindling light came to Sullivan's aid. Bonfires flickered into life in the meadows, confirming that Cope was going nowhere suddenly.

Throughout the evening, the Jacobite front line redeployed through Tranent and formed on its eastern side. It was perhaps during this time that the prince rode back from the lines to visit the Andersons of Windygoul. The father, whose home was immediately south of Tranent, had been out in 1715; the son, who had a farm of his own further out at Whitburgh, had joined the Jacobites as a quarter-master. If the visit happened, and it is related only through tradition, it was presumably at Robert Anderson's suggestion. It is said that the prince was given a glass of wine and complimented Robert's sister with a kiss. If Charles really was shy around women, he knew when to put on the performance. The Jenkinson sisters, whom he had met in Duddingston the previous day, were currently inside the manse at Tranent in the care of the minister. Those musket and cannon shots must have felt terrifying close.

Cope moved his position yet again, this time to counter the Jacobite shift towards the east. He redeployed to face southward once again and once it fell fully dark, he sent out his night guards. Those posted into Colonel Gardiner's grounds at Bankton were soon exchanging shots with the Atholl Brigade, causing enough concern for the picket to be reinforced. There had been occasional sporadic gunshots all afternoon, which Elcho blamed on superstitious clansmen shooting any 'hogs or hares' that crossed their front, but everything seemed worse in the darkness.[62] Fortunately for the Jacobites, however, Cope's intention of shelling their position with his mortars was thwarted by the failure of the first few bombs to explode. The general did not want to reveal this newly discovered deficiency to his enemy, the fuses being spoilt by damp storage in Edinburgh Castle, so he soon ceased firing. Little did he know, one shot had been fired 'in a direct line where the Prince was.' Had it not fallen short, or had it exploded as intended, the rising would be over. No doubt Charles Edward shared a knowing look with Lord Elcho, a moment to acknowledge both their good fortune and their near disaster.[63]

Around 9.00 pm the Duke of Perth's division passed through Tranent, triggering all the dogs there to begin barking. The whole army moved with the exception of the Atholl Brigade, who again made their presence felt by firing 'a good deal' around Bankton at around 10.00 pm. Their presence served to fixate Cope on the threat from the south and the south-west, while the Jacobites themselves were shifting their minds to the east. The Highlanders 'lay all down in rank and file... a small rising in their front, just enough to cover them.'[64] The prince was restless with his own nervous excitement, and Sullivan describes him as being constantly in motion, speaking encouragingly to the men as they settled down beneath their plaids. He was always at his happiest amongst his men, where he could strengthen a soldier with an easy smile or a clumsy Gaelic phrase, and where their respect and affection fortified his own confidence. In telling the Highlanders that the enemy would not stand against them, he helped persuade *himself* that they would win. Several accounts emphasise the quiet stillness of the Jacobite line, brief little pricks of candlelight here and there as the only evidence of their presence. By contrast, MacDonald later recalled, the enemy 'had lighted fires and made a great deal of noise.' As he silently inspected the Jacobite lines, he could hear the redcoat sentries 'talking and swearing'.[65] The two armies were now tantalisingly close.

At midnight, the prince's senior officers gathered for a moonlit council of war. With most of the army now on the eastern side of Tranent in an area which later became known as Prince's Park, the Jacobites were committed to seeking to attack from that direction rather than the Preston approach. Earlier, Murray had asserted to Sullivan 'how easy it would be' to attack from the eastern fields compared to the west, but the ditch and the bog extended so far as to present no less of a challenge.[66] Fortunately, Robert Anderson proposed a solution to the problem. Not only did his father farm at Windygoul, but other relations from their extensive family farmed out at nearby Riggonhead, land which sloped down to the marshes on their eastern side. There was a track by Riggonhead which crossed the ditch near Seton village by means of a small wooden bridge. This route, although narrow and passing through a defile close to the farm, was dry and firm and led onto the open ground where Sir John Cope had first led his army onto the battlefield.[67] Anderson spoke of this to James Hepburn, the man who had drawn his sword to lead the prince into Holyroodhouse. They were neighbours, living within a couple of miles, and it is natural that young Anderson sounded Hepburn out before taking his suggestion higher. Hepburn, perhaps aware of Murray's temperament as much as his rank, advised that Anderson informed him of the path. This he did, and ahead of the midnight council the prince was briefed on the Riggonhead path.

Prince Charles at this point was 'lying on straw' amongst Lochiel's Regiment, perhaps as a gesture of support for the only part of his army to have taken casualties that day.[68] He could have retired to sleep elsewhere, of course, commandeering a house or even staying with the Andersons at Windygoul. But he knew where he was most needed this night, and he probably wanted it no other way. As soon as the prince was informed of the possible route over the marshes, he had it reconnoitred.[69] Murray was busy assuming the credit for Anderson's critical information: 'I knew the ground myself, and had a gentleman or two with me who knew every part thereabouts.'⁷⁰ Once 'the prince and his friends had viewed the ground from the height of Tranent, and got information of tis road, they had little left to deliberate upon.'⁷¹ The midnight council agreed, unanimously it seems from Elcho, that they would use this path the following morning to reach the plain. They would sacrifice the high ground in order to force a battle. They would be out in the open in front of an opponent with superior firepower, but the enemy would have no option but to stand and face them and that was the most important factor: a battle could at last be fought.

Once the decision had been made, the last remaining preparation was to withdraw the Atholl Brigade from the western side of Tranent. This was completed at around 2.30 am, and Murray of Broughton reflects on how anxious this final committal made his prince – and rightly so. Not only had the road to Edinburgh now been left clear, the Jacobites were planning a move which would place the enemy between them and their homes. The prince had much to reflect upon. It had been a long and trying day, moving from the certainties of the morning's march to action to the disconcerting impasse of the afternoon. The army command had been stress-tested and had shown faults. Murray was presumptuous to the point of disruption, even danger, preferring to inform the prince what he was already doing rather than to seek approval or await instruction. Sullivan had proved himself to be diligent but inclined to micromanagement, struggling to reconcile his professional expectations with the nature of this Highland army. His relationship with Murray was proving difficult, and both parties had required the intervention of their comrades to cool them down. Prince Charles himself had shown good instincts, but needed experienced counsel and was instead struggling to manage personalities. There was still much to prove.

Earlier that day, 1,500 miles away in Rome, the pen of King James had scratched a note to Prince Henry: 'I know nothing more of your Brother than the publick reports, but no doubt can be made of his being landed. My chief anxiety now is for what may follow.'⁷² Little could he have imagined that night that his son was lying under the stars on a bed of pease straw, waiting to lead an army into battle for the first time.

The Young Chevalier had little sleep, and it was he who 'rous'd up every body' ahead of the scheduled 4.00 am departure on the morning of 21 September.⁷³ He was probably not alone in his restlessness, although Sir John MacDonald marvelled at the capacity of the Highlanders to sleep so peacefully in such close proximity to the enemy. The air was cool and the atmosphere tense as the Jacobite army rose into silent life. As it had at Duddingston, the army had lain to rest in its lines so that there was a minimum of commotion or disorder. The prince spoke in warm terms with Lord George, setting aside any ill feeling from the previous day. Sullivan recalls that the chiefs now again reminded the prince of his agreement not to engage too closely in the coming action. Charles, he says, insisted that, 'yu all expose your selfs, for King and contry's cause, & I am as much obliged to it as any of yu.'[74] Nevertheless, he agreed not only to remain with the second line, Lord Nairne's division, but also that he would fight on foot. This, of course, made the prince far less of a target, but it also limited his – or indeed anyone's – ability to command the army as a whole once the battle was joined. It was an acknowledgement of the absolute simplicity of the tactical plan for the morning: gain the plain, then attack across the whole front as rapidly as possible. The prince took his position with Lord Nairne, and at the appointed time, 'an hour before day,' the march began.[75]

The army was led off by the Duke of Perth, the Clan Donald regiments being given the position of honour they had demanded. Robert Anderson was with him, guiding the army along the track which led behind Riggonhead farm. Compared to the openness of the vistas on the previous day, this narrow cutting must have seemed claustrophobic and forbidding; but the track soon emerged back into the open as it descended into the patchy marshes where Anderson and his family went shooting for snipe. The march was silent, or as near silent as 2,500 men can ever be when marching in the dark. Strathallan's squadron, accompanied by Sir John MacDonald, remained behind at Tranent to limit the noise of the march, and the officers' horses had been corralled in the churchyard at Tranent.[76]

For the prince, watching the front of his army disappear into the darkness without him must have stirred some anxiety. He could not influence what happened now, placing his trust in the Duke of Perth's enthusiastic but inexperienced hands. John Sullivan had gone with him in support. Then Murray left too, leaving only Nairne's division behind, which 'the Prince conducted in person.'[77] Charles led his column eastwards towards Riggonhead farm, following the track as it curled around into the defile. Beyond that he marched, Lord Nairne at his side, into the boggy ground beyond. Although the darkness was fading, the wisps of a thin mist hung over the meadows; through these emerged James Johnstone, scrambling back up the track towards the prince. This energetic young gentleman, a charming but dissolute Episcopalian from Edinburgh, was serving as an aide to Lord George Murray. He had been sent back from Murray's division to guide Nairne's division and ensure it continued 'without noise or confusion.'[78]

Then, suddenly, they heard the muffled thunder of a single cannon being fired.[79] The suddenness of this threatening boom, although distant, must have sent a shockwave of energy through the Jacobite columns. The march was no longer a secret; Cope knew they were coming. But two-thirds of the Jacobite army had already passed 'before their noses' of the enemy, as the prince himself would put it.[80] Now Charles urged his men forward with greater haste, the need for silence passed. They rushed on, reaching the drainage ditch. Rather than move further along to reach the bridge, the men leapt or scrambled across the 3- or 4-foot-wide obstacle. Johnstone crossed, then turned to support the prince. Charles Edward made his jump, but stumbled on the far bank onto his knees, his boots sliding in the mud. Johnstone 'laid hold of his arm and immediately raised him up.'[81] As he did, they locked eyes. Was this a bad omen? Then the moment was passed, and the column surged on.

The prince's column moved out into the firm and open ground beyond the ditch, crossing the road which ran along its north side. The lightening sky allowed the dark and eerie form of Seton Palace to emerge from the skyline on their right, hardly noticed as the Jacobites' attention was inclined to the west. There they could see Murray's division, halted in the stubble, the Highlanders turning to their right to transform the column into a line. That line had drifted around a hundred paces from the road and ditch which would otherwise protect their flank, and Lord George had judged to go no further, despite the rear of Perth's division still being some distance off to the north. The latter were also now turning to face west, so the front line had formed for battle with a gap in its centre. Some men pulled off their bonnets to snatch a quick prayer with their eyes turned to heaven.[82] Once the third division was in a position to cover that gap, the prince halted their march and faced them likewise to their left. Murray of Broughton puts the second line only eighty paces behind the position of the front, which Johnstone reduced to fifty.[83] But the prince and his men barely had time to pause and take in the scene before the whole army suddenly surged back into motion, almost as one. 'Just at the break of day,' remembered Lord Elcho, 'they sett up a hideous scream and run in as fast as they could.'[84]

The Jacobite advance had something like a third of a mile to cover before making contact. It began on the left, with Murray's division. As they moved forward, Lord George ordered the Camerons to incline towards their left to come closer to the ditch – which widened the gap in the centre and brought Lochiel's men directly in front of the British army's clustered artillery, which had been concentrated there by necessity. After the signal gun had fired, informed by the alertness of at least some of Cope's pickets, the entire army had wheeled around to face east. The Jacobites could see the long scarlet line ahead, the colours clear against the stubble field in the first light of the day. On the other end of the Jacobite front line, the Duke of Perth's men advanced neatly. Lord Drummore, watching from beyond the British left, described how 'though their Motion was very quick, it was uniform and orderly.'[85] But as they moved, Sullivan saw an opportunity, calling out 'let the MccDonels come to this hedge, we have out wing'd them.'[86] This hedge was, in fact, a slip of marshy ground where the field dips on its northern side towards Cockenzie, too soft for cavalry but no obstacle to the Clanranald men. But by extending the line to the north to threaten the flank of Hamilton's Dragoons, Perth's division was also further opening that gap in the centre. Fortunately, the second line was so close in behind the front that the gap must not have been discernible to the enemy, whose cavalry could undoubtedly exploit it if given the chance. It made the prince's position far more vulnerable than had been envisaged.

Prince Charles drew his sword and led forward the second line. They were not yet running, but the pace was quick. The sounds were swelling all around, men drawing courage from their collective voices, feet pounding the stubbled ground; pipes skirled and here and there a drumbeat. In the words of one MacDonald officer, 'all our instruments, tongues and hands were at work.'[87] Then came the unmistakable thump of a cannon, and a moment later, another. They 'fired very briskly,' recalled Lord George, who was unable to know that the gunners had already taken to their heels and left the linstocks in the hands of their officers.[88] Five times the cannon blasted, and Murray's division 'seemed to shake' under the impact of the fire.[89] The archaeology of the battlefield tells us what the accounts do not: that the guns were loaded with man-shredding canister shot. The Jacobite advance had shuddered, and this may have been one of the moments recorded by Maxwell when the lines paused to dress ranks which had become 'discomposed by marching too quickly.'[90]

The Jacobite front line erupted with an irregular musket volley, 'at too great a distance to do much execution,' but sufficient to fill the ground in front of them with sulphurous smoke. Behind it the clansmen concentrated into the 'five square Bodies or Columns' which were soon observed from across the field by the Earl of Loudoun.[91] Drummore, watching from the opposite end of the line, called them 'Columns, Clews or Clumps.'[92] The advance resumed with greater speed and ever greater noise. The redcoats returned fire with both their foot and horse. On the right Sullivan judged the firing from Hamilton's Dragoons to be 'very irregular,' but a ball thudded into Captain Archibald MacDonnell, Keppoch's brother, snatching him backwards through the surging ranks.[93] The chief had himself fallen behind, unable to charge due to an injured foot.[94] In the centre, Elcho found the volleys from the infantry more impressive, which Maxwell says was given 'from right to left' along Cope's line.[95] The Jacobites roared a defiant huzzah in the face of the volleys, even as men dropped to the ground around them. Those with empty muskets turned now to their swords and 'rushed in upon them like a torrent'.[96]

Then suddenly the sounds of the battle changed. The brief minutes dominated by the crashing thunder of volleys were over, and the sound was now a general roar of hoarse men pierced by shrill cries and whinnying horses. Still the pipes played. The 'whole first line broke through the enemy,' the dragoons breaking at both ends of the line and the abandoned and outnumbered redcoat infantry overwhelmed in an instant. Some of the British foot platoons had found no enemy in front of them after the Jacobites had condensed into their clusters, and as the line was pierced either side of them, they were cut off behind the tide. But Nairne's division was closing in, and rather than face an unequal fight they turned and ran.[97]

'Running always as fast as we could,' James Johnstone was still beside the prince and Lord Nairne.[98] They ran over the former position of Cope's battle line, passing the tideline of dead and dying men, then continued beyond into a scene Johnstone described as 'a spectacle of horror, being covered with heads, legs, arms and mutilated bodies'.[99] Muskets added to the litter of the landscape. Soon they reached the waggon-way, which slowed them down but a little as they leapt across its drain and then ran over its gentle hump. Most men barely even noticed it. It seems likely that the prince now stopped, surveying the carnage of the scene in front of him. Muskets and pistols still fired sporadically, but the pipes had stopped. There was still a savage, animal roar across the whole field, but it was less intense and more distant, rising and falling in waves as the patchy skirmishing flared and failed. The wave of fugitives had crashed onto the high park walls around Preston House, the Jacobites closing in on the helpless foe. There was a distinctive burst of musketry off to the forward left, where the road passed between the estates of Preston and Bankton, after which the yellow and gold of the Cameron colours could be seen being flourished. Once a body had formed, they were led off and the musketry ceased: a party of redcoats had made a stand in the ditch, but it was soon induced to surrender.

There was motion off to the left where the waggon-way crossed the meadows, and Lord George rushed a hundred Camerons towards the spot.[100] But this was no rallying of the enemy, but the servants and grooms of the Jacobite army coming down from the churchyard. A body of Strathallan's horse came with them to join the pursuit, Sir John MacDonald and a small group having ridden too fast for most of the squadron to keep up.[101] The grooms brought down the officers' horses, a critical and presumably pre-arranged decision which allowed the Jacobite commanders to begin recovering order in their army.

Without further hesitation Prince Charles mounted his horse, driving back his spurs and surging forwards towards the uneven melee spreading out along the park walls. As their horses reached them, other officers did likewise, following the prince's example to gain 'more honour by their humanity than even by their bravery.'[102] Charles Edward 'galloped all over the field, calling out to his men to spare the lives of his enemies, whom he no longer looked upon as such.'[103] Now, with senior officers riding amongst the Highlanders and demanding they give quarter, the pipes began to call the men back to order. Behind them, Murray rushed the Camerons he had with him down the waggon-way to Cockenzie where he was aided by the British officer he had taken prisoner in the ditch, Lieutenant Colonel Peter Halkett, in arranging the peaceful surrender of the remaining baggage guards at Cockenzie House. MacDonald of Glenaladale had already secured the warren parks, a task allotted to him at the outset.

The Battle of Prestonpans was over, the long build-up of the previous day giving way to a rapid, cacophonous and terrifying climax. As soon as it was clear that there was no further resistance, the prince 'gave

1. *Prince Charles Edward Stuart* by Blanchet. Here we see Charles in his late teens, painted in Rome and reflecting how his father wished him to be seen: royal, confident and ready to lead.

2. *The Future Charles III of Spain at the Siege of Gaeta*, by Giovanni Luigi Rocco (1734). The Spanish batteries lie around the battered shells of the coastal settlement, whilst the fortified town dominates the skyline.

3. Panel 5 of *The Prestonpans Tapestry*, stitched in 2010, showing the engagement of *Lion*, *Elisabeth* and *Du Teillay* (left). Based on sketches made by Captain Peircy Brett of *Lion*, subsequently turned into a series of paintings by Dominic Serres.

4. The Glenfinnan Monument at the head of Loch Shiel, viewed from one of the possible sites of the Raising of the Standard. The early nineteenth-century monument is now one of the most iconic landmarks in the Highlands.

5. The Palace of Holyroodhouse as it appeared in the second half of the eighteenth century. Today, thousands of visitors walk in the footsteps of Charles Edward Stuart as they pass through the rooms which he used. It remains the monarch's official royal residence in Scotland.

6. *Prince Charles Edward Stuart* by Allan Ramsay. The so-called 'lost portrait', the prince sat for Ramsay at Holyroodhouse shortly before leading the army into England.

7. *David, Lord Elcho* (1721–1787). Closer to the prince's own age than many of the senior officers, Elcho should have been a natural friend and confidant. But the two men were very different personalities, and Elcho's later hostility has helped colour perceptions of Charles Edward.

8. *Lord George Murray* (1694–1760), by the Jacobite artist Robert Strange. Portraits survive of Murray in both Highland and Lowland clothes. Brave but arrogant, Murray proved to be both a tactical asset and a strategic liability.

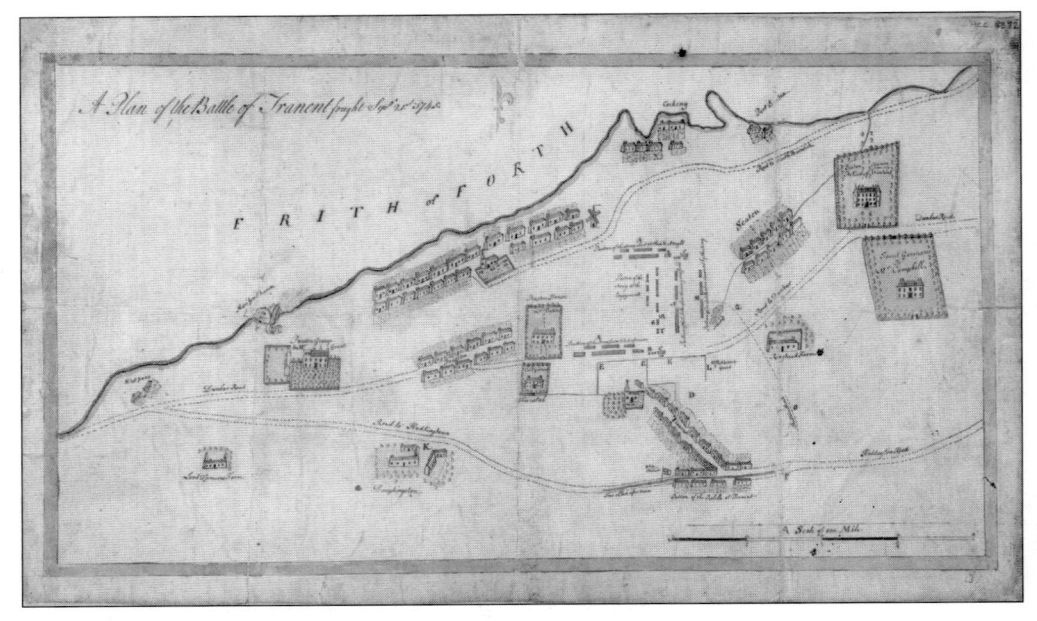

9. Plan of the Battle of Prestonpans, showing the various redeployments over 20 and 21 September. The final Jacobite attack came from the east (right) and drove the British army back towards Preston (centre).

10. *The Field of Preston Pans*, after Sir William Allan. Created a century after the event, this famous image focuses on the death of Colonel James Gardiner in the aftermath of the British army's rout. The prince is erroneously depicted on horseback in the background.

11. Memorial Tables on Prestonpans Battlefield. These stone monuments were erected in 2018 and dedicated to the fallen soldiers of the two armies. They lie to the rear of the British army's position and are now the focus for annual commemorations.

12. Gowan Hill, from Stirling Castle. The wall running across the picture is the outer wall of the castle. The Jacobites erected batteries on the low hill in the mid-ground, which were easily overwhelmed by the garrison's guns.

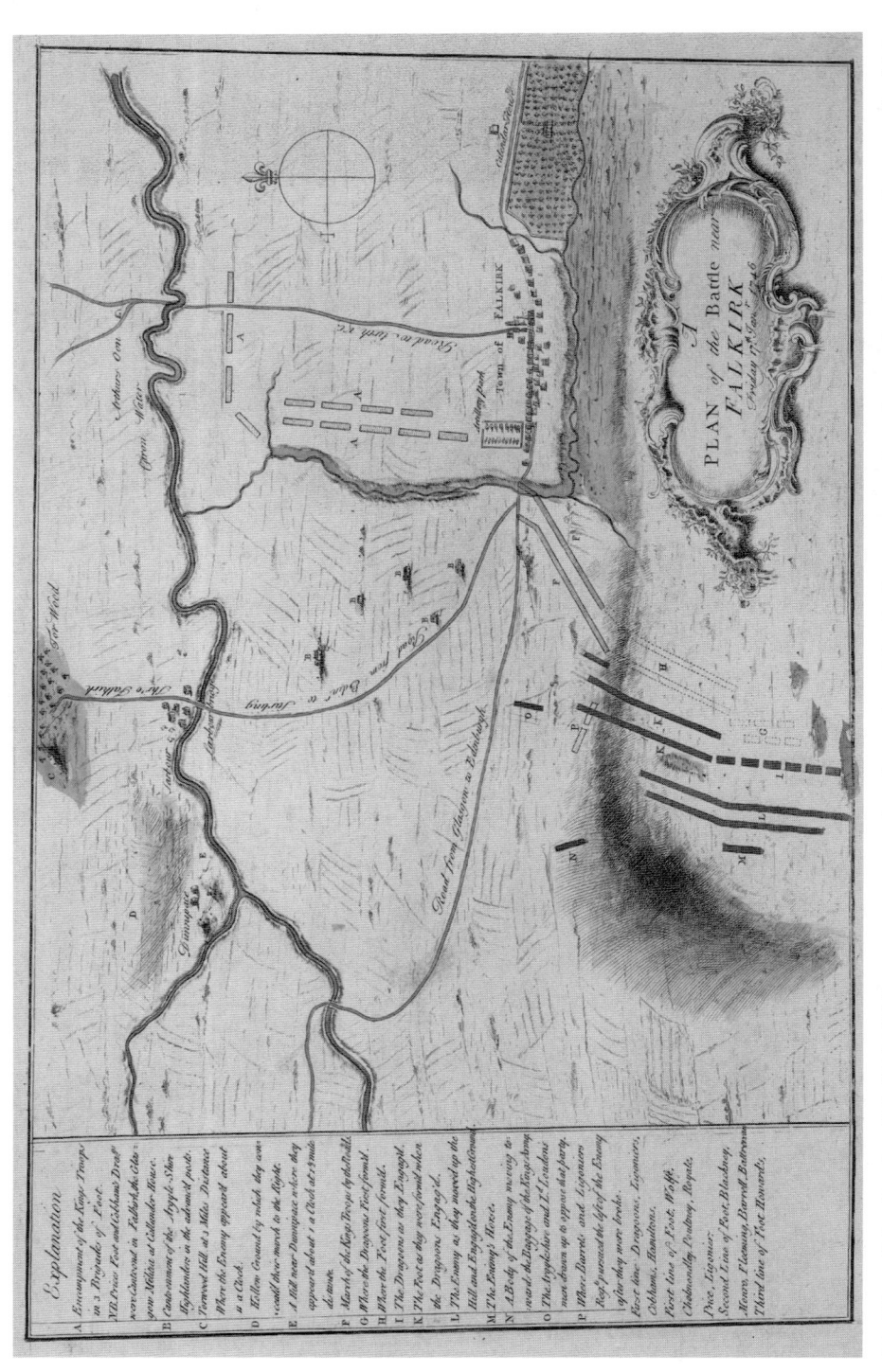

13. Plan of the Battle of Falkirk. This contemporary plan shows how Hawley's army was forced to rush up the step rise onto the high muir, with all its cavalry stacked on its left. The overlapping lines of battle reveal the dangers each army faced, and the potential for confusion once all was in motion.

14. The Prince's Stones, Falkirk Battlefield. These stones, placed here at an unknown date, are said to mark the prince's initial command position at the battle. They are accessible by an easy footpath and identified by a battlefield trail marker.

15. Falkirk Battlefield, from near the Prince's Stones. From this position the prince could look towards the crest of the muir (now tree-lined), where the Jacobite right received the charge of the British dragoons.

16. The monument on Falkirk Battlefield. The early twentieth-century obelisk stands on the Jacobite left. The trees behind it mark the line of the steep ravine blocking the Jacobite advance and protecting the enemy beyond.

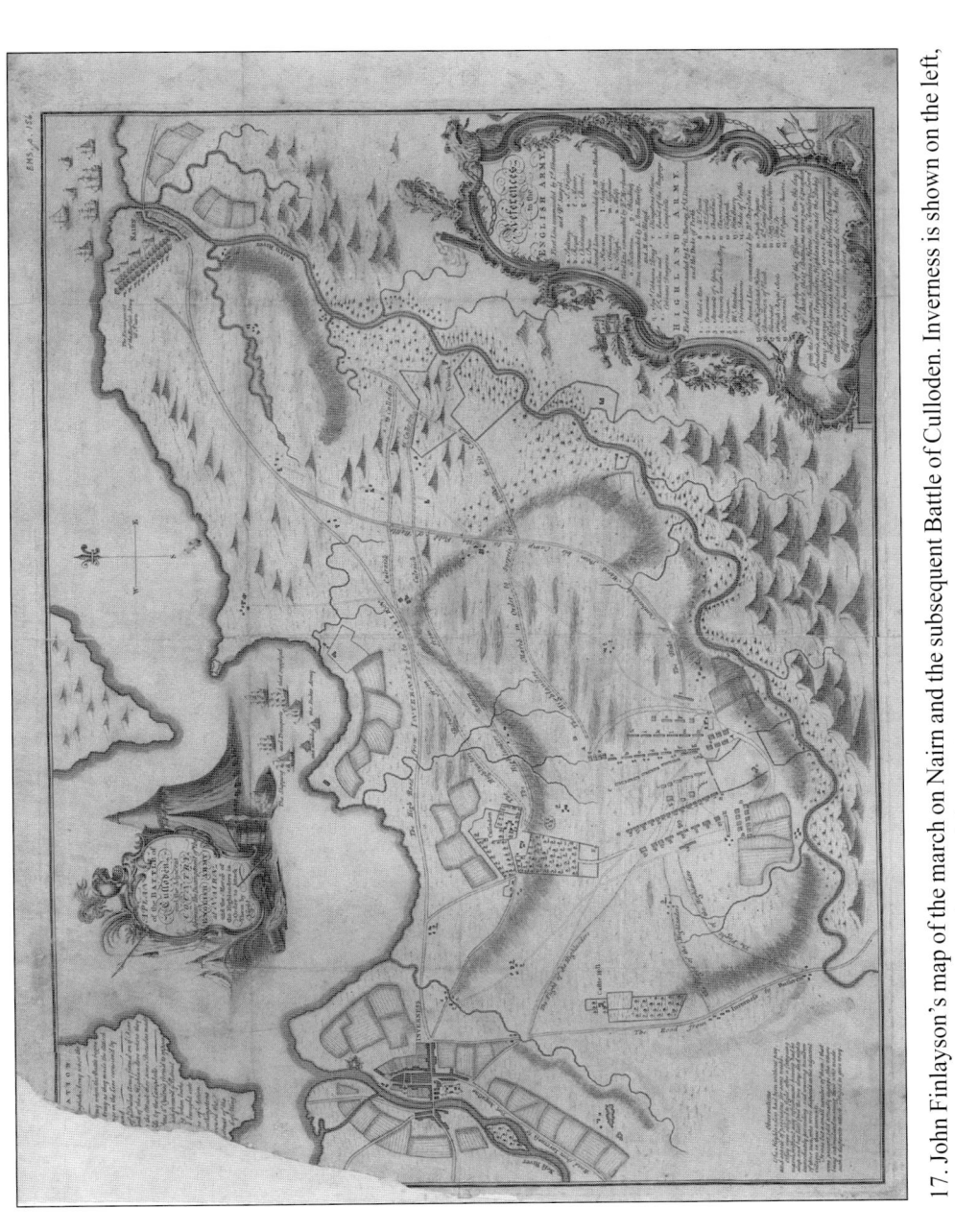

17. John Finlayson's map of the march on Nairn and the subsequent Battle of Culloden. Inverness is shown on the left, with Cumberland's camp at the top-right corner.

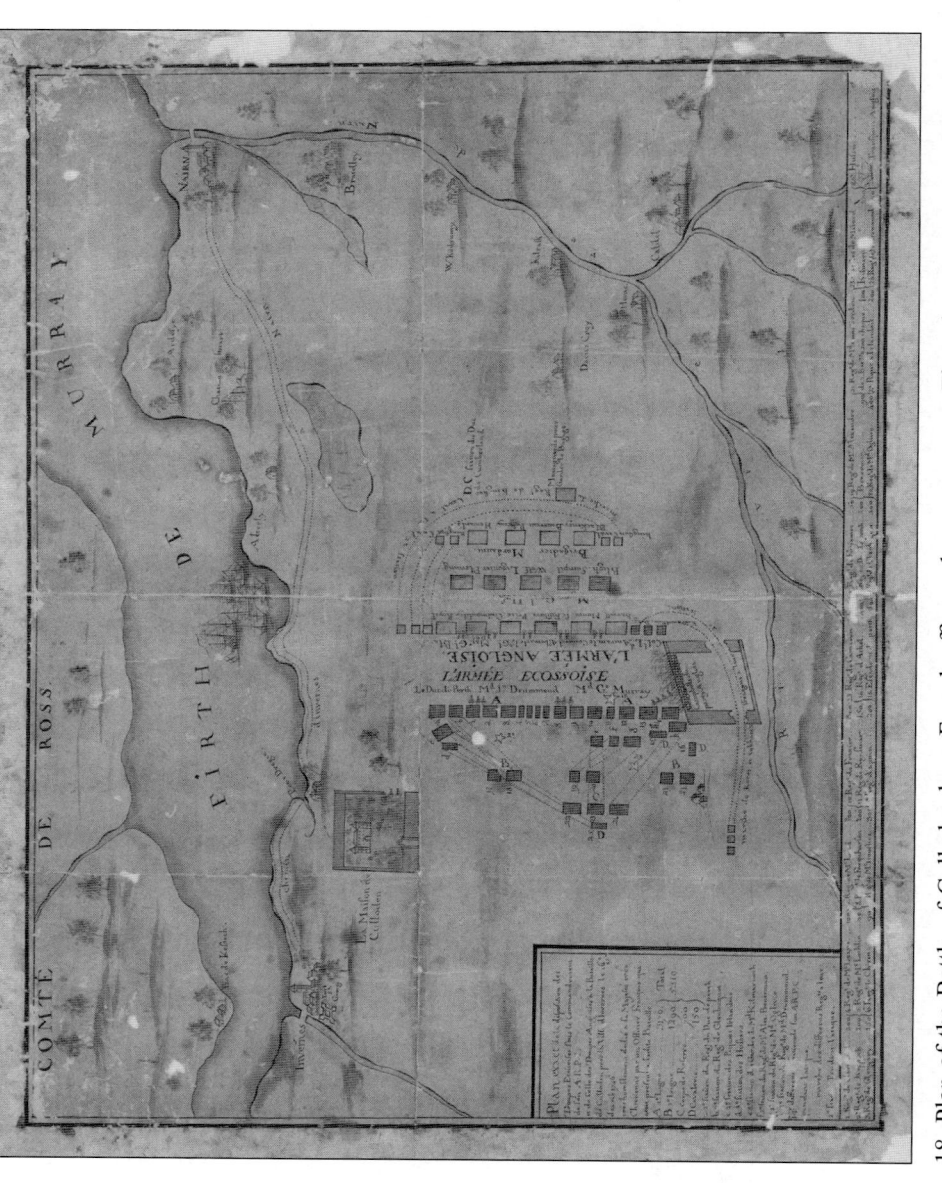

18. Plan of the Battle of Culloden by a French officer who was present. Three locations are marked as the successive locations for 'ARPC' during the battle (*son Altesse Royale Prince Charles*).

19. Coloured engraving of the Battle of Culloden, by L. Sullivan after A. Heckel. The central figure is the Duke of Cumberland, shown in an artificial location for the benefit of the composition.

20. The clan graves at Culloden, where nineteenth-century markers preserve the locations of mass burials. The battlefield is much larger than the area currently owned by the National Trust for Scotland, and these graves mark the high-water mark of the Jacobite attack towards Cumberland's left.

21. *Halt of Prince Charles Edward Stuart at the Banks of the Nairne*, by Richard Beavis (1878). This evocative and typically Victorian image shows the prince immediately after quitting the battlefield. Fugitives and casualties flow around him, as officers cluster around a map and debate where to go.

22. The Prince's Cairn at Loch nan Uamh, marking the traditional site of the prince's departure from Scotland in 1746. It was in this same area that Charles Edward had first landed on the mainland.

23. Prince Charles Edward Stuart in armour, by Cosmo Alexander. The artist was a veteran of the prince's campaign, surviving Culloden and escaping into exile. This later portrait emphasises Charles' status both as a royal and as a military commander. It shows a confidence that defies defeat, a self-belief the prince himself would never fully recover.

24. Prince Charles Edward Stuart by Anthony Stones. Standing on the Cathedral Green in the centre of Derby, this fine modern bronze was commissioned for the 250th anniversary of the Jacobite rising.

orders to have the wounded dressed and carriages provided to take them off the field.'[104] There were few surgeons with the Jacobite army at this point, but a number of British army surgeons had surrendered in order to aid their comrades. A search was soon undertaken to find their medical chests amongst the captured baggage. Alexander Carlyle, who had been awoken by the sounds of gunfire, stepped out of his house to find Lord Elcho glaring at him 'with an air of savage ferocity which disgusted and alarmed.' Elcho had ridden into Prestonpans in search of an inn with sufficient space to bring some of the wounded. Carlyle later saw the Duke of Perth making similar arrangements, who spoke to him 'in a very different tone' as befits his reputation.[105] As many as possible were taken to Colonel Gardiner's house at Bankton, close to the park walls around which so many had been hurt and the Edinburgh road down which further help would come once word had reached the city. Lord George Murray complained that some of the villagers refused to help move the wounded, although they had come out to survey the scene of their misery.[106] They were probably in shock; some would be hosting wounded men for days and weeks to come.

Once he was sure the wounded were being tended to, the prince 'breakfasted on the field.'[107] He had rested for less than a couple of hours out of more than twenty-four, and it is doubtful he slept much even in those. There is no reference at any point to him, or anyone else for that matter, eating during that time. At most he is said to have taken a glass of wine during that brief visit to Windygoul, if that tradition is true. But however understandable it was that the prince needed refreshment, it was a rare public relations misstep. Andrew Henderson saw him and gleefully wrote into his *History of the Rebellion* how the prince, 'with the utmost Composure ate a piece of cold Beef, and drank a Glass of Wine, amidst the deep and piercing Groans of the wounded and dying, who had fallen a Sacrifice to his Ambition.'[108] In retaliation, John Murray of Broughton's memoir calls Henderson a 'little ignorant Scholl master' for deliberately misrepresenting the scene.[109] Sullivan is also clear that Prince Charles refused to eat until it was clear that his orders with regard to the wounded had been undertaken. Home's assessment, and he was no friend of the Jacobites, was that the prince had shown, 'from temper or from judgement, every appearance of moderation and humanity.'[110]

The prince gave further instructions that the dead should be decently buried. Up until this point they had been guarded to prevent their being stripped, a sight which surprised Sir John MacDonald who goes on to say that the British army's women were the first to strip the bodies of the fallen. The villagers were ordered to bring their tools for digging the necessary trenches. There were some 400 British soldiers laid to rest in the coming hours, and around fifty Jacobites. The wounded and the prisoners – some 1,200 or more – required serious attention. So too did the management of the captured baggage, which included all the weapons, artillery, supplies and money which had accompanied the British army. It all had to be accounted, logged, secured and transported. Only once all of this was under way was there time for the magnitude of the victory to sink in.

Men began to crowd around the prince expressing their joy at so comprehensive a success. A teenage prodigy was presented to the prince, said to have struck down fourteen men.[111] The captured standards of the British army were also brought to him. Elcho says there were 'a great many,' which Henderson quantifies as seven. According to the latter, the very definition of a hostile witness, the prince was impressed by the haul of colours and simply replied, in French, 'we have missed some of them.'[112] The prince is also said to have been presented with Colonel Gardiner's horse. The colonel himself was then lying in the manse at Tranent in the care of the Jenkinson sisters. By 11.00 am he was dead, having been repeatedly wounded while trying to make a stand beneath a hawthorn tree. There were other spoils too, including all of Sir John Cope's personal belongings. Most of these were given to Alexander Robertson of Struan, as compensation for the prince's recommendation that he pursue the campaign no further in person. Struan was 76 and a veteran of both Sheriffmuir and Killiecrankie. Cope's travelling fiddle can still be seen in the Clan Donnachaidh Museum today.

Prince Charles eventually left the field at around midday, having done all that he could in the hours following the battle to ensure the best care would be taken of the dead and wounded, and that all the military necessities were being undertaken as well. The victory at Prestonpans was so comprehensive that his army was now better equipped and resourced than at any point yet in the rising, and surely those who doubted either his intent or his capacity must now take him seriously. Word spread quickly, sending shockwaves to London and reaching France through the mouths of Norman smugglers within days.[113] From there the first reports of victory were sent to King James in Rome.

The prince, meanwhile, spent the night of the battle at Pinkie House in Musselburgh, home of George II's Secretary of State for Scotland. Here it is said that he composed a long and detailed letter to his father, recounting his accomplishments thus far, detailing his victory and analysing the justice of the cause. Much within it surely reflects the prince's true feelings, but the letter is not genuine. Several copies survive, none in the prince's hand, and it was probably written as a propaganda piece. Not only was such a long letter completely out of character, but much of its content only makes sense if it was intended for domestic public consumption. At Pinkie House, however, it is far more likely that the prince was simply overwhelmed by exhaustion. In fact, it would not be until 7 October that he finally wrote a description of the battle for his father, which bears quoting in full:

> It is impossible for me to give you a distinct journal of my proceedings, because of my being so much hurried with business, which allows me no time; but notwithstanding, I cannot let slip this occasion of giving a short account of the battle of Gladsmuir [Prestonpans], fought on the 21st of September, which was one of the most surprising actions that ever was. We gained a complete victory over General Cope, who commanded 3000 foot, and two regiments of the best dragoons in the island, he being advantageously posted, with also batteries of cannon and mortars, we having neither horse nor artillery with us, and being to attack them in their post, and obliged to pass before their noses in a defile and bog. Only our first line had occasion to engage; for actually in five minutes the field was cleared of the enemies; all the foot killed, wounded, or taken prisoners; and of the horse only 200 escaped, like rabbits, one by one. On our side we only lost a hundred men, between killed and wounded; and the army afterwards had a fine plunder.[114]

In just two months, the Young Chevalier had raised the standard, assembled an army, secured the Scottish capital and triumphed in his first pitched battle.

Chapter Five

The Retreat

Charles Edward Stuart and his men were being lashed with 'the cruellest rain'.[1] All day it had poured from the black skies, gusting at them in icy sheets driven by a bitter wind. The Jacobites turned their faces away from the squalls, their cheeks red from long exposure, their plaids drawn up over their backs and pinned at the neck like cloaks. Their feet churned in the rocky sludge as they toiled down the treacherous slope, the surface of the road destroyed, despite the valiant efforts of the army's heroic pioneers, by the appalling weather and the passage of the preceding regiments. The rainwater flowed freely along the track, tumbling towards the dale below, but as other local routes had been broken up by the locals, this high track was the army's only option. The barren landscape to either side was shrouded in soaking cloud, obscuring all landmarks and denying any sense of progress. Forward the soldiers trudged, struggling to maintain their footing while clinging to their arms, the locks of their muskets wrapped with rags too sodden to serve their purpose. A sudden gust cleared the view ahead just for a moment, like the billow of a curtain, showing the road suddenly climbing steeply back up into the grey cloud beyond. If they had the energy these men might have groaned, looking across at the dark column of men preceding them up onto the fell.

At the foot of the slope, before the road turned upwards once more, a swollen burn rumbled noisily over the rocky bottom of the dale. Its surface seemed to boil with the constant rain as it rolled straight across the path of the weary marchers. There was the Young Chevalier, wading slowly and deliberately through the icy water as it splashed around his knees. His double-breasted coat was buttoned across his chest beneath the heavy folds of tartan thrown across his back and shoulders. His left arm held his buckled sword clear of the stream as he used his right to balance. The leather soles of his boots scrabbled on the slick stones of the burn's bed, and rain streamed off the brown of his dark sodden bonnet. Around the prince was a small cluster of aides, most leading their miserable horses as they followed the example of their leader. As they climbed out of the water, one officer called upon him, as they had all done countless times, to take his mount. Prince Charles shook his head ruefully, flashing a forced but encouraging smile at the watching clansmen toiling alongside. One called out that 'they wou'd follow him a' horse-back wth the same hart they did a foot.' The prince replied that 'he was more concern'd for what they suffer'd then for himself.' Besides, he added, he was young yet. Sullivan later reflected that 'if it was not for the way he acted yt day, I verily believe we cou'd not keep half our men together.'[2]

The prince's army was already over 8 miles into its march that day, and there were more than 15 to go if it was to reach its destination. But the progress had been slow even for the unencumbered. Lord George Murray cursed that the march had initially been delayed by Sullivan's tardy writing of the orders the night before, later sniping that the Irishman had seemed more interested in his wine.[3] Now the artillery and baggage were falling ever further behind on the terrible trackway. Charles Edward sent word back to Lord George, emphasising his orders that no matter the difficulties, nothing was to be left behind. Not so much as a cannonball was to be abandoned, 'for he would rather return himself than that there should be any thing left.'[4] Murray, labouring heroically at the rear with Keppoch's Regiment, replied bitterly that he had agreed to command the rearguard on the assurance that responsibility for the baggage train would not fall to him. Nevertheless, he obeyed the prince's orders to the letter, and when they came upon an abandoned ammunition cart, he offered a bounty to the clansmen if they would each carry a cannonball in the folds of their plaids.

As the day wore on beneath the relentless downpour, it became clear to the Stuart prince that his army would never reach its intended goal before nightfall. The target was Penrith, a town large enough to hold the promise of shelter and comfort, but they would not make it past the lesser village of Shap. The prince threw himself into the gestures of fording the streams and enduring the march on foot, not only to boost the morale of his men but also because there was little else he could do either to ease their suffering or encourage their pace. The physical trial of the march distracted him from his deepening anxieties. There was worrying news from the front: the Duke of Perth's attempt to return to Scotland and summon reinforcements had ended badly, with his squadron driven back by the hostile population the previous day.[5] Lives had been lost on both sides, and communication with the north was threatened. But the need to hurry forward must not leave the road strewn with abandoned guns and valuable supplies, as Prince Charles remained determined not to allow his enemies the moral victory of humiliating his army. It would be a shame, he had protested at Lancaster, 'to go so fast before the son of an Usurper.'[6] The man of whom he spoke was now Prince Charles' most dangerous concern – William Augustus, Duke of Cumberland, youngest son of King George II – and he was champing at his heels.

Charles Edward finally reached Shap at around 10.00 pm that night, 16 December, and lodged at the inn.[7] Already the village was overwhelmed by the numbers, and detachments had to be sent out to neighbouring settlements.[8] Lord George and the rearguard, struggling to keep the baggage train on the move, did not even make it that far. James Johnstone, now a captain in the Duke of Perth's Regiment, recalled spending 'the whole night on the high-road, exposed to a dreadful storm of wind and rain.'[9] Early the following morning, the prince prepared to move the main army on to Penrith, but lingered until he had confirmation as to the situation with the rearguard. Sullivan was ordered to make contact with Murray, in the hope that the whole army could be brought together again at Penrith.[10] Then eventually the prince felt able to commence his march – after paying over the odds for his accommodation – and he joined the column which was already snaking down into the broadening landscape.[11]

Compared to the previous day, the march from Shap to Penrith seemed straightforward for the main body. On the last miles towards the town, the prince's path passed through the village of Clifton. He looked upon its enclosures, hedges and dykes, and along the narrow street which led northwards to a modest church and the squat stone keep of Clifton Hall. Then he crossed the pink stone arches of the Lowther Bridge, passing a pair of massive prehistoric earthworks behind to his left, and traversed a second bridge over the Eamont. But by the time Prince Charles was within Penrith, his army's discipline was in danger of breaking. The men were incensed by the open hostility of the locals, who had been emboldened by news of the Jacobite retreat and an apparent turning of the tide, and had begun actively trying to hinder their progress.[12] Their attack on the Duke of Perth proved to have been particularly provocative, and now elements within the army wanted revenge: some began 'committing all the mitchchief they cou'd' within the town, abandoning the careful restraint which had marked the army's previous passage southwards.[13] Appalled, the prince ordered the army's pipers to play their assemblies, drawing the men to their regiments for an impromptu review. The whole Jacobite army was being tested, from the lowliest to the highest, both physically and mentally.

As Charles Edward Stuart mounted his horse, a wave of exhaustion rolled through him. He could feel his temper rising, his frustrations bubbling up in his stomach even as he forced to keep it down. Still the prince was under the eyes of his men, and if some of them had disappointed him with their behaviour at Penrith, he strove not to show them. It was not *their* fault that it had come to this; they had done everything that had been asked of them, and more. So how could it have come to this, this desperate march through the bitter winter in some of England's most inhospitable country, harried by an increasingly hostile population and the enemy closing in behind? How, barely three months since his victory at Prestonpans, was the Young Chevalier in retreat? And how, more to the point, could he turn their fortunes around?

Gladsmuir, the name by which most Jacobites knew their triumph over Sir John Cope, had brought all the moral and material advantages the prince could have hoped for. For almost six weeks Charles occupied the royal palace of Holyroodhouse, settling into a pattern of military briefings, public appearances and civil administration.[14] The army was subsidised mainly through the collection of existing tax obligations, striving for both legitimacy and efficiency without rousing public ire. But these sums could only be levied once, and unless the army kept moving it could not tap further resources.[15] When a delegation was sent to Glasgow to raise additional funds, it was deliberately unthreatening in its size and composition in order to show 'he did not come as a Conqueror to levey Contributions, but as their Master to desire a loan he soon hoped to repay'.[16] While the clansmen were threatened with dire consequences for 'any abuse in taking, pillaging or disturbing the good people' and instructed to make 'fair Bargain, and Payment,' a petition from Presbyterian ministers asking liberty to pray for King George II was told explicitly the prince would turn a blind eye.[17] Court martials sat every day to enforce army discipline.[18]

As the prince juggled the twin challenges of military command and civilian government over a country he only partially controlled, he was observed by a young lady called Magdalen Pringle. She wrote one of the most engaging eyewitness reports of him during this period after going to see the prince's pavilion in Holyrood Park. With the prince were Perth, Elcho, Sullivan and Henry Ker of Graden, the staff officer who had reconnoitred the Tranent Meadows so calmly under fire. Lord Pitsligo later joined the group, arriving at the head of his new cavalry regiment. The prince wore a blue frock coat trimmed with gold lace with a red waistcoat and breeches, a similarly gold-trimmed hat with white feather, and the familiar accessories of the Order of the Garter and the fine silver broadsword. Although no Jacobite, Magdalen Pringle was captivated by the prince himself: 'in all my Life I never saw so noble nor so Graceful an appearance as His Highness made, he was in great spirits and very cheerful.' Nor was it just his status and appearance which conjured the magic, but his natural manner and inclination towards accessibility: 'he came out of the Tent with a grace and Majesty that is inexpressible. He saluted all ye Circle with an air of grandeur and affability capable of Charming ye most obstinate Whig.'[19]

But even during this relatively sedate interlude in the conflict, the prince was barely snatching four hours of sleep.[20] He spent more time visiting the army's cantonments around Edinburgh than he did in the relative comforts of Holyroodhouse, and even the generally critical Elcho recalled that 'the Prince lay always in the Camp & never Strip'd.'[21] Regiments were regularly reviewed, sometimes on the links at Leith, but never the whole army in order to keep the enemy's agents in the dark as to their numbers. Keeping himself active also helped the prince to keep his army alert during long weeks of relative inactivity.

When a ball was held at Holyroodhouse, at which the ladies flashed their specially commissioned fans, Sullivan suggests it was as much out of concern for the prince's wellbeing as it was for the pleasure of the public, in the hope that it would allow him some brief distraction. The prince, although he famously enjoyed dancing, had retired early after complimenting the ladies. When pressed, he said, 'I like dancing, & am very glad to see the Lady's & yu divert yr selfs, but I have now another Air to dance; until that be finished I'l dance no other.'[22] This single-mindedness and self-denial created a real risk that the prince might burn out, and it is easy from the vantage point of history not to see the intensity of the mental strain this young man was under, pressure for which he had no preparation.

Edinburgh Castle was an aggressive neighbour, and without heavy artillery the prince was powerless to do anything about it. His efforts to blockade the garrison had been thwarted when the latter retaliated by making life both miserable and dangerous for the civilian population. Charles Edward was appalled by such callousness and ended the blockade.[23] The scenario in the capital therefore lacked appeal to those clansmen who considered their work complete after Prestonpans and found little attraction in idleness so far from home. Officers were sent north to secure the return of those who had headed home while drumming up fresh support.[24] There was a danger that the prince's campaign, so rapid and driven till now, would lose all the benefits of that momentum.

The army's early strategic goals had been achieved with the twin triumphs of the capture of Edinburgh and the defeat of Sir John Cope. There was less unanimity over what to do next. Some have argued that the prince should have followed through immediately and marched on Berwick-upon-Tweed in the wake of Prestonpans. To this, Murray of Broughton answers that 'he not only proposed it, but for some hours Considered seriously of it.'[25] But although Prince Charles might have been able to take the town while it was still panicked by Cope's defeat, it was a heavily fortified garrison and it might just have easily repulsed him. The Jacobite army was also still too small to simultaneously advance, maintain a line of communication and supply, and guard the prisoners and garrisons now in its rear. Instead, then, the army's position in Scotland would be consolidated first.

This approach was vindicated by the arrival – admittedly as a steady stream rather than a torrent – of fresh recruits. As they came, the general character of the army began to change as the recruits were no longer drawn only from the western and central Highlands. As Elcho put it, 'a great many people of fashion joined the army, particularly Lord Ogilvy and Glenbuckett with 300 men each.'[26] Lowland lords like Ogilvy could not hold a regiment together in the same manner as Keppoch or Lochiel did. Nevertheless, in the absence of uniform and in recognition of the power of imagery, even Lowland recruits were encouraged to adopt elements of Highland dress. The army's cavalry wing expanded too, including the uniformed Lifeguards squadrons. These fine-looking gentlemen wore blue coats faced with red and had been founded at

Prestonpans after protests that the prince's person had been too greatly exposed to danger during that battle. On the march these men would often provide a gallant first impression for communities warned to expect a horde of savage Gaels.

The pressure to get the army moving again grew even as the winter drew nearer. Arguments could always be found for remaining in Scotland: a nationalistic one-kingdom strategy, which was at odds with the prince's vow to restore the family's full inheritance; the lack of apparent overt support in England, where troop numbers were growing; the time needed to raise the full strength of potential support in Scotland; and the continuing presence of several small but entrenched British garrisons north of Edinburgh. But just as the Stuarts were disinclined to abandon the English portion of their claim, the Hanoverian monarch was unprepared to countenance the loss of the Scottish portion of his. So the longer the Jacobites waited, the more prepared England became to resist them, as regular forces continued to assemble in Newcastle and the south, with militias and volunteer regiments raising across the country. Time was also healing the panic triggered by Prestonpans. Finally, while the French had not yet put military boots on the ground for the cause, they had begun sending military supplies. The Marquis d'Éguilles also arrived as an envoy, with only vague terms of reference, to be Louis XV's eyes on the ground, and Prince Charles treated him as an official ambassador from Versailles.

The prince's council repeatedly deliberated upon all these considerations, and under needlessly strained circumstances. Fault lines had already been exposed at Prestonpans, particularly centring around Sullivan and Lord George Murray. The latter despised Sullivan and often treated him with barely concealed contempt, and while some of this was due to their different approaches as to how the army could, and should, be managed, a large part was simply down to personality. Lord George, as accepted even by his advocates, was haughty to the point of arrogance and was convinced that only *he* knew how to prosecute this war. The relationship was further poisoned by the general view amongst most of the Scottish commanders that the Irish officers had less stake in the outcome as they held formal commissions from France. It is a view often repeated even today, and one which utterly disregards the physical and mental hardships these men shared with their Scottish companions, and the services many had already rendered in the past. If some of the

Irish officers had less to lose in terms of estates and fortunes, they also had more to gain from success and so no less an incentive to make it happen.

But while Lord George focused his animosity on Sullivan, his namesake Murray of Broughton was actually his bigger problem. As the prince's Secretary of State, Broughton was accused of trying to control Prince Charles by surrounding him with his own 'tools and creatures.'[27] Some of these were Franco-Irish officers who had arrived with d'Éguilles, men for whom Jacobite service offered the prospect of promotion. Sir John MacDonald, on the Irish side of the racial divide, believed the Scottish officers wanted Charles in *their* hands alone, comparing them to the Covenanters who had attempted to control Charles II in 1650.[28]

Disentangling fact from prejudice within this fractious network – and such problems had long plagued the Jacobite cause – remains problematic. Accounts given by participants are often completely at odds, each masking their own errors to highlight those of others, and usually written after the event with a retrospective bitterness nurtured by the effects of defeat. Secretary Murray was thoughtful and diligent, assessments of him generally being coloured by the stigma of later events. It is likely that he disliked Lord George because of his overbearing manner and his frequent disregard for Prince Charles' authority, and if he really did believe him to be a danger at least to the army's cohesion, then it would have been natural to seek to limit his influence. According to Maxwell, the Duke of Perth 'entertained the highest opinion' of Secretary Murray, which helped consolidate the prince's confidence in him.[29]

The factionalism within the council really began during the sojourn in Edinburgh, in the absence of an immediate and pressing target for action and when its meetings became routine. It would take time before its full impacts were felt. It is worth acknowledging, however, that the council genuinely did serve as the army's decision-making body, and that the prince did not use his authority arbitrarily. He 'always consulted the principal people in his army upon every emergency, and nothing of consequence had been done but with their consent.'[30] It is not necessary, therefore, to dwell on Lord Elcho's later accusation that Charles was 'unable to tolerate any advice that did not coincide with his own opinion, and firmly convinced that the whole country belonged to him and that all the people in it were his slaves.'[31] This is at odds with all other evidence, including numerous occasions to come when the prince conceded his own opinions to those of the majority.[32] Indeed, the council gradually expanded to include almost all Jacobite officers ranked colonel and above. But Elcho might well have been truthful in reporting that the prince's habit at council meetings was to declare his own opinion first, which might naturally have hindered some weaker voices from speaking out to the contrary.[33]

When the moment finally came to decide upon the army's forward progress, the decision to march on England was, in fact, unanimous.[34] The disagreement was over which road to take, and how far to follow it. The options were, in short: to strike at Berwick-upon-Tweed and Newcastle in the south-east; or to dash towards Carlisle in the south-west. The prince was for the former course, that which had seemed initially most obvious in the wake of Prestonpans. The British army was concentrating at Newcastle, and Charles' instinct was to force another battle. Elcho believed he had become convinced 'regular troops would not fight against him, because of his being their natural Prince,' but Charles was not, in fact, guilty of such naïvety.[35] He did, however, believe that he could win, and a victory over Marshal Wade's army would prove that Prestonpans was no fluke and trigger the open support of the English Jacobites. But the counterargument, made principally by Lord George Murray, was that a battle should be avoided until the outcome was more or less certain: if the object of marching into England was to raise the prince's friends, then the army's mere presence should secure that. Sir John MacDonald scoffed that the Scottish Jacobites seemed to want to conquer England without having to contribute to the outcome themselves.[36]

Without being able to bring the consensus to his view, according to Elcho, the prince instead proposed a compromise measure by which the army would at least move into the Borders. This would be a challenge to Wade, threaten both Newcastle *and* Carlisle, and give the Jacobite army a chance to get back onto a proper war-footing away from Edinburgh.[37] Having at least secured the agreement to march south, the prince then approached Lord George Murray. He said that, 'as he found that most of the officers were for the Carlisle road... he agreed to it.'[38] Whether Charles Edward had been persuaded by the arguments or had simply conceded to the majority, he was at least able to move the army southwards with the full approval of his council. On 31 October the prince spent the night at Pinkie House as his army began to concentrate around Dalkeith. To hostile eyes it seemed the prince was leaning east. From Dalkeith, Prince Charles marched out, according to *The Scots Magazine*, 'with his target over his shoulder' towards Lauderdale. From Thirlestane Castle he continued at the head of a column of Highlanders to Kelso, where he and his army forded the Tweed. Fixated on the prince himself, his opponents still saw the main danger being to Newcastle.

Prince Charles Edward Stuart entered England for the first time on 8 November 1745. Between Jedburgh and the border, he had marched 'by terrible mountains, very bad roads, & worse quarters.'[39] Nevertheless, the march had proceeded without incident. The prince had again drawn admiration by marching on foot not just for a few token miles, but for whole days: 'in dirty lanes and deep snow he took his chance with the common men... It's not to be imagined how much this manner of bringing himself down to a level with the men, and his affable behaviour to the meanest of them, endeared him to the army.'[40] When a number of stragglers had fallen behind during the march out of Lauderdale, the prince had indeed mounted his horse, riding personally to the rear to rouse them onwards. Now his Highlanders had reached the River Esk, and by their own collective instinct they waded across with their swords drawn. On the far side – in England – they then turned to face their homeland once more before resuming their ranks and files.[41]

The following day, the prince's column made its planned rendezvous with that led by the Duke of Perth and the Marquis of Tullibardine. The latter had finally rejoined the army just before its march began, returning from his work in the north with a sizeable reinforcement for the Atholl Brigade. While his brother Lord George accompanied the prince, Tullibardine marched with Perth in command of the Lowland regiments, baggage and artillery. To ease the latter along the way, their column had taken a more westerly route than the prince's, whose march to Kelso had succeeded in misdirecting Marshal Wade's informants. Details of the rendezvous had been changed during the course of the march, making corrections according to the columns' progress, but the junction had been 'arranged and executed with such precision that there was not an interval of two hours between the arrival of the different columns.'[42] This was the result of highly competent planning and staff work, for which Sullivan surely deserves much of the credit. So much of the army's day-to-day operations, the tedious minutiae of campaigning, fell to Sullivan and the small staff of aides which buzzed between commanders. The only slight disappointment was that Perth had left part of the baggage behind on his way through Dumfries, the tents being set aside as a useless encumbrance.[43]

The Jacobite army now comprised around 5,500 men. Although a number had drifted away during the march south, disinclined to a winter campaign beyond the border, desertion would be too risky an option now the army was out of Scotland. Besides the fighting men there was also a large body of supporting civilian dependents, for whom the army took no formal responsibility but who did help mask its true number. This army was substantially larger than the Jacobite force in England had been in 1715, but the latter was not the principal army of the conflict. It was, however, half the size of the Scottish army which had entered England in 1648, and Charles II's army of 1651 had been bigger even than that. All of these forces had been destroyed, two of them after battles at Preston. Charles Edward's little army must have seemed small for the scale of its task. But then not everyone was clear what that task was: were they there, as Murray believed, simply to test the water and encourage the English Jacobites out into the open; to force Marshal Wade away from Newcastle and onto a battlefield of their choosing; to spur the French into a decisive intervention? Or were they now committed, as the prince desired, to making a dash for London which would surely result in at least two of these outcomes?

The Jacobites opened trenches before the medieval walls of Carlisle, formally investing the town and its castle. But when word arrived that Wade had marched westwards towards them, 'the Prince immediately resolved to go and meet him, and marched next day to Brampton.'[44] On 12 November the Jacobites selected a battlefield of 'Hillocks, morasses, & passes' within which Wade's regulars would be unable to deploy effectively against the Highlanders.[45] But eventually, with the skies growing heavy with snow, it became clear that Wade's army was unlikely to have progressed as far as first believed. Patrols were sent out to confirm Wade's true position, which was then rightly assessed as posing no immediate challenge. After a council of war that evening Charles Edward, displaying considerable confidence, divided his army. Half – the Atholl Brigade, Ogilvy's, John Roy Stuart's, Glenbucket's and Perth's regiments of foot, supported by Elcho's, Pitsligo's and Kilmarnock's Horse – went west to resume the Siege of Carlisle under the command of the Duke of Perth. The Highlanders remained with the prince at Brampton waiting for Wade to present himself. As James Maxwell put it, 'such was the reputation of the Prince's army and councils at that time, that it was enough for him to undertake a thing briskly to make every body believe he knew how to compass it.'[46]

The Siege of Carlisle was, in fact, brilliantly executed. The besieging force divided into three to cover the main approaches, after which trenches and batteries were opened on both the east and west sides of the town. The Jacobite artillery were all too small to have any hope of breaching the massive stone fortifications, but the sight of scaling ladders being crafted worked powerfully on the defenders' imaginations. The defenders 'kept a constant fire of Cannon and Small arms,' but the Jacobites were undeterred. The town offered to surrender separately, but Perth rejected this. Given time, the pressure within the walls secured its joint surrender with the castle on 15 November.

The siege had been conducted in freezing conditions, and the Jacobites had to be kept in the trenches by the example of their officers – most notably the Duke of Perth. But any satisfaction the prince could take from the performance of his lieutenant generals was marred by the petulance of Lord George Murray. Already chafing that the overall management of the siege had fallen to Perth, he was outraged when Murray of Broughton joined the duke for the negotiation. Lord George sent the prince 'a very high letter' resigning his commission and offering to stay on as a volunteer only. Maxwell comments with subtle inference, 'it would be rash in me to pretend to determine whether ambition or zeal for the Prince's service determined Lord George to take this step, or if both had a share in it, which was predominant.'[47] Charles Edward, as happy with Perth's loyal service and recent achievement as he was rankled by Murray's repeatedly objectionable attitude, accepted Murray's resignation 'with dignity.'[48] Sir John MacDonald was delighted, seeing an opportunity 'to get rid of this dangerous man.'

Murray himself wrote to his brother, 'I can be of more use charging in the first rank of your Atholl men than as a general, where I was constantly at a loss to know what was doing.'[49] But Tullibardine could not defend his younger brother's conduct, leaving the latter to write again the following day. By then he had been refused an interview with the prince, and through Sheridan he had tried to excuse any potential offence in his letter (in which he had expressed his attachment to the king, but not to the prince). Murray was clearly hurt that Tullibardine was willing to 'hearken to designing people' rather than his brother, although Sullivan was sure that the latter had, in fact, interceded on Lord George's behalf.[50] In the background, others were scrambling to gauge the temperature of their comrades' feelings. Sir John MacDonald reports that both Tullibardine and Glengarry had a low view of Murray's behaviour.[51] On the flip side, James Maxwell opined that Murray 'thought himself the fittest man in the army to be at the head of it; and he was not the only person who thought so.'[52] By this he meant not to usurp the prince's position, but to reduce the Duke of Perth's.

In the end it was the Duke of Perth who broke the deadlock. Buoyed by his success at Carlisle but fully aware of his lack of military credentials, he offered to resign in Lord George Murray's place. While he remained confident that he himself had committed no error or outrage, Perth's view was that anything he could do for the prince's service should be done. If that meant resigning, so be it.[53] His civil rank and his general popularity would ensure that he retained a degree of influence and the friendship of his prince, and Perth would continue to serve the cause loyally as a volunteer at the head of his regiment. The only mark that had been against him in many men's minds was his religion, and the wisdom of having a Catholic peer negotiate the surrender of Carlisle was criticised. But Carlisle was the Duke of Perth's victory and he deserves the credit. It had been a masterpiece of military intimidation, with the Jacobites showing all the appearance of professional competence which the defending militia had doubted in themselves. The whole exercise shows how the army's capacity had grown, how its opponents continued to underestimate it, and how its most dangerous flaws were the interpersonal politics of the high command.

In the end, Marshal Wade never made it to Brampton and the bloody battle Charles Edward had planned for him there. Poor roads and heavy snow had slowed his already tardy advance from Newcastle, and eventually it had become clear that his army would never reach the Jacobites in a position to face them in battle. Their retreat back to Newcastle allowed the prince, once he had formally received the surrender of the mayor, to enter Carlisle. King James was proclaimed, and with customary clemency the prince permitted Colonel Durand, the regular officer who had been sent to hold the town, to leave Carlisle on parole. After a few days of rest, the army resumed its march.

The Retreat

The fall of Carlisle had not been enough to energise the Jacobites of England. Those who might have stirred were as unaware of the prince's intentions as his enemies, and the failure to prepare those south of the border (however much of a security risk that would have been) prevented many from putting themselves in a position to assist him. The few attempts that had been made – some letters had been sent with vague recommendations to prepare – were either insufficient or intercepted. The lack of effective communications with the English Jacobites also meant that once the army moved beyond Carlisle, it was dependent on its own scouts for information, so it only knew what was happening within its immediate reach. It left the army vulnerable both to enemy action and, just as dangerously, to misinformation.

Before Prince Charles marched out of Carlisle, he despatched Lachlan MacLachlan, a trusted aide, back to Scotland. There, Viscount Strathallan had been left as the prince's man in Scotland to continue levying fresh men from his base at Perth. Now Charles wanted those men in England, and Strathallan was ordered to send them down. A few days later, on 22 November, the cause was at last boosted by the arrival of regular French soldiers: part of the French *Royal Scots* and pickets from their *Irish Brigade* regiments. Although some transports had been intercepted, several hundred had arrived safely on the east coast of Scotland, along with some heavy guns.[54] At their head was Lord John Drummond, younger brother of the Duke of Perth, a professional soldier with sufficient status to supersede Strathallan's command. Drummond had known Charles Edward in Paris, where the prince had found him to be tactless and antagonistic in his manner, quite unlike his more affable brother.

The Jacobite army had then progressed relatively smoothly down through north-west England, undeterred either by Marshal Wade's cautious parallel approach in the east or Sir John Ligonier's concentration of forces covering the south. Some of the heavier baggage, including much of the prince's own, was sent back to Carlisle once the quality of the roads had been assessed.[55] Discipline held, and if there was little overt support for them there was also little active resistance. To make the billeting of the army easier, Lord George Murray took one column on ahead of the main, preceded by the cavalry who were proactive in visiting villages (sometimes well off the line of march) to demand billets for extravagant numbers of men. Murray's absence ahead relieved some of the tension at headquarters, but it did little to solve the core problems and may, in fact, have exacerbated them. To avoid any jealousy, the prince alternated which regiment he accompanied on the march: 'every man had access to him, especially those yt had the least detail, so yt he enter'd into the State of every thing... He was never heard to say a rash word to any man, prais'd most graciously those yt served him well, & treated very mildly those who did not.'[56]

On the army went, through Penrith, Kendal, Lancaster and Preston. There, crossing the Ribble, the Jacobites surpassed the unfortunates of 1648 and 1715 in their progress. While there, 'the Chevalier mounted on horse back to take a view of the ground where the two former actions had happened,' and spoke with some of the veterans of the '15.[57] At Preston the army had been 'met by a great course of people and welcomed with the Loudest Shouts and acclamations of joy.'[58] The prince showed himself around the town on horseback, 'dress'd in Lowland cloaths'.[59] The reception was even warmer at Manchester, where a new regiment was formed from the English volunteers that had trickled in over the preceding days. But overall, the response had been fairly apathetic; most people neither obstructed nor aided them, although by and large the army was successful in raising the funds and supplies that it needed through the same civil means as it had in Scotland: the collection of ordinary taxes and duties supplemented with 'voluntary' contributions. It was becoming difficult, however, for the prince to maintain to his council that England was on the cusp of rising. At Manchester, therefore, Sullivan tested opinion as to the possibility of a retreat.[60] The council agreed to press on to Derby, 'that so neither the French nor the English might have it to Say, they had not marched far Enough into England to give the one Encouragement to Land and the other to join.'[61]

But if others around him were growing anxious, the prince remained outwardly confident. 'From Manchester to Derby the country seemed pretty well affected,' wrote James Maxwell, one of his aides. The roads were often lined with people 'who showed their loyalty by bonefires, acclamations, white cockades and the like.'[62] But appearances could be deceptive: one civilian witness claimed the people of Derby had lit their fires 'to prevent any resentment' and forestall hostility rather than out of zeal.[63] Reaching the handsome and industrious town of Derby was a considerable achievement for the army, however. By making a show of repairing broken bridges across the Mersey, and through a number of controlled feints, the British army gathering to the south had been deceived into expecting a south-westerly thrust. It responded by moving across to Stone, north of Stafford. By now the Jacobites knew it was commanded by William Augustus, Duke of Cumberland, who had returned to Britain from the continental front. Marshal Wade, meanwhile, had reached only as far south as Ferrybridge (between York and Doncaster), meaning the road to Derby was uncovered. The prince's army dashed along it, through Macclesfield and Leek, reaching Derby on 4 December.

When the Jacobite army entered Derby, preceded by the Lifeguards, it was 'never in better spirits.'[64] The prince was similarly so, believing that 'his fate, and the fate of the three kingdoms, must be decided in a few days.'[65] Charles Edward arrived in the evening, occupying a fine seventeenth-century riverside mansion. The arrival of the army doubled the population of the town, and while the officers resided in the larger townhouses around the market square, the soldiers crammed into every house, inn and schoolroom. After hard marches, 5 December was allocated as a day of rest. But for the prince and his council, it was to prove the most bitter day of the campaign so far.

The crisis began early that morning, perhaps even before the formal council meeting had convened. The prince seems to have been taken by surprise by Lord George Murray, who confronted him without preamble with the fact that most of the council intended to argue for a return to Scotland.[66] The prince, 'naturally bold and enterprising, and hitherto successful in every thing, was shocked with the mention of a retreat.'[67] Sullivan's account suggests Charles was close to losing his composure: 'To retire, Ld George, to retire? Why the Clans kept me quite another Language & assured me they were all resolved to pierce or to dye.'[68] The council was convened, although Tullibardine and a few others were still absent when Murray began to outline his case. It was compelling: Cumberland's army, containing veteran regiments drawn back from the continent, was within striking distance of them; Wade's army was closing in from the north, and they were no longer shielded from it by the Pennines; and London itself was surely amassing further forces. Lord George's assessment was brutal: 'there would be three armies made up of regular troops, that would surround us, being above thirty thousand men, whereas we were not above five thousand men, if so many.'[69] Even a victory on the battlefield would avail them little, as they could not replace their casualties before being forced into a second engagement. Crucially, neither the French nor the English had turned out to help them: 'Lord George concluded by saying that the Scots army had done their part'.[70]

Against these arguments, the prince's position looked rash. He simply believed that they had come so far, within 120 miles of London, that turning back was sheer madness. 'His Royal Highness had no regard for his own danger, but pressed with all the force of argument to go forward. He did not doubt but that the justice of his cause would prevail, and he could not think of retreating after coming so far.'[71] There had now been confirmation that Lord John Drummond had landed in Scotland, but although the prince argued this as proof of French commitment, others countered that the wisest course now was surely to join the two armies.[72] But Strathallan had ignored the prince's order to march south, and Drummond continued in the same vein, preferring consolidation in Scotland to throwing the reserve strength into the English gamble. No other voice was raised in support of the prince's strategy, except the Duke of Perth.[73] James Johnstone, whose decision to resign as an aide in favour of field service meant that he was further from the discussion than he might have been, heard how Perth had stood resting his head upon the fireplace in despair.[74] Sullivan concurred with Murray's assessment, but it clearly pained him to cross his prince: 'I never saw any body so concerned as he was for this disappointment.'[75]

Finding himself thwarted, Charles Edward grasped at any straw. There was a futile suggestion that they dash to Wales instead, where there was some hope of succour, but such a move hardly solved the most critical problems. Then he argued that the army would be far more vulnerable in retreat than in the advance, and that once Cumberland and Wade scented weakness they would recover the initiative. The answer was that the Jacobites had already proven they could outmarch their opponents.[76] The prince's composure completely collapsed, his frustration boiling over into an outburst of the type Sheridan might have recognised from his pupil's boyhood: 'the Prince... fell into a passion and gave most of the Gentlemen that had Spoke very Abusive Language, and said that they had a mind to betray him.'[77] Eventually, finding that neither argument nor emotion could sway the assembly, Charles Edward 'was obliged to consent' to a retreat.[78]

The meeting was over, and it seems likely that the prince stormed out and left the council behind. It had been a traumatic and protracted debate, and it is easy to imagine the uncomfortable silence which settled over the dark panelled chamber. With a scrape of chairs, the first officers rose and shuffled out of the crowded room, and eventually only Lochiel, Sheridan, Keppoch and Lord George remained. Suddenly the door burst open, and Sir John MacDonald erupted into the tense calm. He blustered his astonishment at their proposal to attempt a retreat with the enemy so close at hand, declaring that 'if we were to perish, it were better to do so with out faces to London.' Lochiel answered only that 'if you knew all, you would agree with us.' MacDonald stormed out.[79]

In Derbyshire, tradition holds that the prince then spent the rest of 5 December on a futile and humiliating mission to raise support from amongst the local gentry. Riding from country house to country house, he sought any gesture of aid which might help turn the tide back in his favour. If it is true, then the day would have been exceptionally exhausting and the mission was absolutely without success. It is more likely he remained in Derby, perhaps closeted with Broughton, whom Maxwell portrays as pouring poison into his ear. Certainly, the prince must have felt unusually isolated as he had never before been in this position. Councils had disagreed with his proposals previously, but a compromise had always been found which at least carried him part way towards his goal. This was different, and despite Elcho's attempt to frame the crisis as a Scots/Irish divide, it is notable that the council had not been split on faction lines. According to Elcho, Charles Edward still believed he could argue the others around, continuing 'all that day positive he would march to London.'[80] There was no doubt much soul-searching at All Saints' Church (now Derby Cathedral), where the officers attended divine service on that fateful evening.

The prince recalled the council later that night for one last effort. This time he was more controlled, although he remained convinced that the army should press on. His hopes were raised when Tullibardine, who had not been present in the morning, inclined to support the march on London.[81] But opinions had only hardened, and even Perth finally accepted the advice of the majority. Tullibardine seems also to have been argued down, and when Prince Charles could do no more, he gave way. Sullivan lamented that he 'never saw him take any thing after so much to heart as he did.'[82] According to Elcho, the prince 'told them he consented to go to Scotland, And at the same time he told them that for the future he would have no more Councills, for he would neither ask nor take their Advice, that he was Accountable to nobody for his Actions but to his Father.'[83] John Daniel, an English gentleman who had joined the Lifeguards, saw that 'a great alteration was afterwards seen amongst us. The brave Prince at that [decision,] out of a generous ardour and Love to his country, wished he had been twenty feet under ground!'[84] Regardless of the strategic rights and wrongs – which are still being debated today – the councils of war at Derby and the way they had been handled inflicted massive damage on the army's high command. In the presence of several officers, MacDonald recalled, the Marquis of Tullibardine called his own brother 'the most infamous of traitors.'[85]

As the retreat commenced, the prince's spirits were at rock bottom. Without the focus of his desired objective, he struggled to motivate himself. His body was probably crashing too. Charles also understood how the retreat would be seized upon by his opponents, and he was determined not to give them the satisfaction of being able to claim they had chased him out of England. As a result, Murray found his commander 'much longer in leaving his quarters, so that though the rest of the army were all on the march, the rear could not move till he went, and then he rode straight on and got to the quarters with the van.'[86] John Hay of Restalrig reported that the prince took to horse because he 'could not walk and hardly stand (as was always the way with him when he was cruelly used).'[87] Elcho noted the same: 'the Prince, who had march'd all the way to Darby on foot at the head of a Column of Infantry, now mounted on horseback and road generally after the van of the army and appear'd to be out of humour.'[88] Once the soldiers realised they were retreating, their morale sank too.

Discipline began to break down. On the way out of Derbyshire, an innkeeper was hanged after an argument. Men left the column in search of plunder, undoing their hard-won reputation for unexpected restraint. The countryfolk were emboldened by the retreat, killing stragglers sometimes in cold blood.[89] But the prince was not completely out of character: he refused to allow the execution of a woman and child who were accused of murdering a sleeping soldier, just as he had refused to hang a captured government spy. On both occasions Charles Edward's 'wonderful clemency' raised eyebrows.[90] Fortunately, the breakdown of discipline was not general – and no doubt the fate to the stragglers helped keep the regiments together. Martial discipline was still enforced, as the orderly book of Ogilvy's Regiment attests.

At Manchester, previously so welcoming, a mob gathered in the army's path and had to be dispersed, resulting in a fine being imposed. The prince halved the initial demand to £2,500, and proposed the army make a stand against Cumberland at Manchester. He was advised against it in case Wade cut across their rear at Preston, and the retreat continued.[91] The same arguments were made against his suggestion to stand at the Ribble Bridge, in case Wade cut them off at Lancaster. Finally, at Lancaster, Lord George and Lochiel agreed to scout out a possible field of battle. The prince sent the Duke of Perth north with a small force of cavalry to ride hard for Scotland, to hurry on his brother Lord John Drummond. With a potential reinforcement of several thousand men available, it now began to make more sense to avoid battle if possible until the army could be brought to its maximum strength. Unbeknownst to the prince, Drummond had declined to move any of his forces towards Carlisle, so nobody was marching to their aid. In the meantime, parties of enemy horsemen were appearing more frequently, although this at least provided the opportunity to catch some prisoners for information. With the weather deteriorating and the worst of the road still ahead, there was a real risk that part, or indeed all, of the army would be cut off.

And so it was that the Jacobite army, which remained undefeated in battle and had penetrated 200 miles into England without being intercepted, found itself lashed by rain as it staggered across the Shap fells on 17 December. There, as his army laboured desperately along the flooded and broken roads, Charles Edward Stuart's spirit had returned to him. His instincts restored, he slopped through the mud with his men, waded the swollen streams with his men, and suffered all the trials of that long and wicked march with his men. Together the prince and his column battled on to Shap, and the following morning to Penrith. Lord George and the rearguard (Glengarry's Regiment) were struggling on behind, resting that night out on the fells and reaching Shap half a day behind the rest. There it found the welcome support of John Roy Stuart's Regiment.

On Wednesday 18 December, Prince Charles formed his men for a review 'on a hill to the north of Penrith' as they awaited the safe arrival of the baggage, artillery and rearguard.[92] Growing anxious, the prince sent the Duke of Perth to discover Murray's progress. Perth had failed to get through to Carlisle with his message for Lord John Drummond, and there was an increasing fear that the army was close to being trapped. It was essential therefore that the prince await the rearguard before continuing, and all he could do was wait. By reviewing his men in the meantime, he was able at least to maintain their order and assess their strength after the previous gruelling days. It was hard to be sure, but every now and again the wind seemed to bring the drifting sound of distant musketry.

By mid-afternoon it was clear that the rearguard was in serious trouble. An 'imperfect account' reached the prince, suggesting that they had been forced to engage a party of light horse threatening to cut them off.[93] Unclear of the extent of the danger, Charles despatched Pitsligo's Horse to support them. After more waiting the prince was able to observe his baggage and artillery train trundling over the Lowther Bridge towards the safety of Penrith. Free from their encumbrance and reinforced by Pitsligo, Lord George Murray made a raid on Lowther Hall and secured one of the Duke of Cumberland's footmen, before moving the Glengarry men into the enclosures near Clifton Hall. The prisoner was conveyed to the prince by John Roy Stewart, confirming not only that it was regular forces opposing Lord George but that Cumberland himself was near at hand.[94] But the captive advised that the duke had 4,000 horse on the way, a force sufficient to threaten the whole army let alone the rearguard. Stuart's suggestion that it would make sense to 'burn the bagage' received a tart reply.[95]

Prince Charles now had a difficult decision to make. Lord George Murray's message made it clear that he believed it was possible to hold the position at Clifton, where the enclosures provided defensive cover and prevented the enemy from being able to deploy. But the position also had two swollen rivers at its back, and would require him to risk putting more men into an already uncertain situation. Accordingly, the prince made a calculated decision which, he felt, would facilitate the safe return of his rearguard without exposing the whole army. The Macphersons, the Appin Regiment and the Atholl Brigade were all despatched south to Murray's aid, to secure his successful disengagement. These regiments were already at Lowther Bridge by the time Lord George was returning from the hall raid.[96] The Atholl men remained on the Penrith side of the river ready to cover the retreat of the others, but the Appins and Macphersons crossed over to join Glengarry's and John Roy Stuart's.

The exhausted Duke of Perth, who had been sent out in the morning to link up with Murray, now returned to the prince and passed on Lord George's suggestion that the ground was favourable for a general engagement. But the prince's mind was made up that the army should continue its march to Carlisle as soon as possible. He therefore directed Sullivan to 'go towards the village of Clifton' with the Clanranald and Keppoch regiments and the fur-capped Hussars. Once Murray was safely across the river, these units would form the new rearguard to cover the retreat.[97] As this was taking place, Pitsligo's Horse returned from Clifton where the enclosed landscape had limited their value. The evening was drawing on, and the prince formed the rest of his army into column of march. In the gathering darkness of that cold winter's night, the sound of distant musket fire could now be heard. Murray's men were being attacked by Cumberland's dismounted dragoons, but the latter had met with disciplined volleys and a counter-charge that drove them off with losses.

The sounds of the firing died away, and in a short time Murray's men came safely through Sullivan's position on the north side of the river. When Lord George reached the prince, the latter was 'just taking his horse. He seemed well pleased with what had happened.'[98] And well he might, for Murray had bloodied the Duke of Cumberland's nose and ended the relentless pursuit of the army's retreat from Derby. Charles Edward set the army in motion towards Carlisle, some 20 miles distant, and as the van made its way off into the darkness, Murray's men had a brief chance to rest before they too marched off.

By noon the following day the Jacobite army was entering Carlisle. Despite what he had threatened at Derby, the prince then called a council of war 'to regulate every thing for the March & the garrison yt was to be left.'[99] Once again there were bad-tempered exchanges, this time between Perth and Murray. The former refused to let his regiment be left in garrison at Carlisle, and demanded to know 'why so many of the Atholl people were not desired to stay.'[100] Understandably, nobody was keen to be left as a garrison which was sure to soon face the might of Cumberland's army, while the rest of the army retired into Scotland. But Sullivan was sure that the castle needed to be held in order to cover the army's crossing of the Rivers Eden and Esk, both swollen from the rains.[101]

Eventually the task was given to 'the Manchester Regiment, and about two hundred more draughted ones of other corps'.[102] Their fate was a sorry one, and Prince Charles has been much criticised for leaving them behind. Sullivan's arguments are probably justifiable in cold military terms, but to many it seemed that the prince was simply unwilling to yield his last possession in England. He also hoped, assuming a successful junction with Drummond, that he would soon be marching back to the border. James Maxwell was right too in suggesting that Charles Edward 'did not know what kind of people he had to deal with,' and never therefore imagined how Cumberland would treat them.[103]

On 20 December 1745, the Jacobite army crossed the icy waters of the Esk. The swollen river was flowing rapidly, and Prince Charles 'went in himself with all the horse we had, to break the stream, yt it should not be so rapid for the foot; this of his own motion.'[104] Once again, the presence of a challenge to be surmounted had brought out the best of the prince. Behind the shield of the cavalry, the infantry entered the water in a wide column, 'holding one another by the collars'. Murray, who was wearing his philibeg that day, which meant he was less encumbered than those in the great plaid, thought 'there were two thousand men in the water at once; there was nothing seen but their heads and shoulders.'[105] Sadly, the impressive operation was not without loss as two women drowned as they crossed. On the far side of the river, in Scotland once more, pipers began to play and 'the men all danced reels, which in a moment dried them.'[106] According to the Old Style calendar then in use across Britain, this day was the prince's twenty-fifth birthday, 'so yt he was both in England & Scotland on his birth day,' noted Sullivan, 'and I hope will passe many other birthdays there, notwithstanding all yt has past.'[107]

Chapter Six

The Battle of Falkirk

As the prince walked his horse along the front of his army, he had reason to be satisfied. Most of his regiments had colours, which lifted gently in the breeze and looked fine in the winter sun. Pipers and drummers stood ready with their instruments, and the officers stood forward of their lines in their bright clothes and full panoply. The sight of the long lines drawn neatly across this scrubby moor drew an unconscious smile across the face of the Young Chevalier, who always felt better when there was the focus of meaningful activity. The campaign in England had been exhausting and demoralising, but it was far from disastrous. While he regarded the failure to press on to London with bitter regret, the army had shown itself capable of great feats of endurance and had once again confounded its enemies. Had the English risen, had the French landed, had Strathallan or Drummond marched south to aid them, who knows what might have been achieved. But all this the prince pushed from his mind as he reviewed the rank and file on the Plean Muir.

Despite the poor weather and the reluctant reception received in Dumfries and Glasgow, Charles Edward was feeling reinvigorated. On the way to Glasgow the prince had finally allowed himself a little leisure and 'gone a shooting in Duke Hamiltons Parcks.'[1] He drew the admiration of his companions by 'hitting everything he shot at, so that, without flattery, he was looked upon to be the best marksman in the army.'[2] Once at Glasgow, for the reassurance of the locals, Charles Edward had dressed less frequently in Highland habit, and for the benefit of his army he had held a review on the Green in which he 'rode through the ranks, greatly encouraging and delighting all who saw him.'[3] General reviews were rare, but it was necessary to prove that his army was just as formidable on its return to Scotland as it had been before it had left. The soldiers were also more comfortable by then, benefitting from the new shoes with which Dumfries had paid for its lack of support. Quitting Glasgow on 3 January, the revived Jacobite army marched north-west towards Stirling as the overall strategy shifted towards consolidation. At Bannockburn House, comforted by the unequivocal support of his host, the prince had even had the positive news from London that his friends were raising significant funds.

The Duke of Perth, conqueror of Carlisle, was again tasked with commanding a difficult siege. With his own regiment and that of John Roy Stuart, supported by some of the Royal Ecossais who had come across with Drummond, Perth was attempting to subdue one of Scotland's most formidable and strategically positioned fortresses: Stirling Castle. His men, on the advice of the French engineer Mirabelle de Gordon, were scratching 'trenches on a hill to the north of the castle,' Gowan Hill, where the soil was thin and the rock hard.[4] The strong garrison looked on with confidence as the Jacobite batteries were well within the range of their own guns. The town below, however, had already capitulated. Outside Stirling, Prince Charles had finally combined his army with the forces of Lord John Drummond, bringing together fresh recruits from across the Highlands and the north-east as well as the French regulars. A complex amphibious operation had brought the army's new heavy artillery across the Forth, thwarting the considerable efforts of both the army and the navy to prevent them.

The last apart, the army which Lord George and others still determinedly called 'the Highland army', had a relatively consistent appearance, with most of the men wearing tartan in some form and white cockades in their bonnets and hats. One eyewitness, avoiding the hyperbolic tendencies of some civilian reporters to diminish the appearance of the Jacobites out of prejudice, remarked that 'there is scarce any but has a gun, sword and pistol.'[5] On the muir this day, 17 January 1746, were '8,000 men, and all in very good Spirits.'[6] It was the strongest the prince's army had ever been. This was the third consecutive day on which they had formed for battle, and nervous expectation had given way to a relaxed good humour: it had taken until midday for the whole army to get into position.[7] The historic landscape encouraged those of a romantic spirit to boast how they would match the exploits of their forbears in 1314.

A strong gust of wind suddenly billowed a nearby flag, flapping it like a loose sail with a sharp snap. It made the prince turn his eyes towards the skies, where the weak but welcome winter sunshine of recent days was beginning to cloud over a little. This was no mere review: the prince had been expecting a general engagement for days and he was ready for the fight. Battle offered the opportunity to recover the strategic initiative, and victory would take the sting from the bitter news that Carlisle had been lost to the Duke of Cumberland. On hearing of it, 'the Prince was exceedingly troubled, and lamented much the loss of his subjects.'[8]

Meanwhile, the British army was marching to relieve its comrades. While Cumberland had been delayed by fears of a French landing and by the necessity of besieging Carlisle, the second army in the east had been strengthened and then sent on to Edinburgh. It was now under the command of Henry Hawley, a 60-year-old veteran with a tough, no-nonsense reputation. The removal of several regular regiments from Stirling to protect Edinburgh had unwittingly cleared the road for the Jacobites, but now Hawley was marching west to confront them. A few days before, Lord George Murray had made a dash to Linlithgow and seized Hawley's forward depot. The enemy vanguard attempted to entrap Murray's force, but the Jacobites 'made so Good an appearance & retreated in such order' that the worse the redcoats could do was exchange 'very abusive language' with them over the river.[9] The Jacobites had shown clear signs that they had recovered their confidence and remained a formidable force. On Plean Muir, they certainly looked it.

The sound of hooves drew the prince's attention away from the gathering clouds. Riders had been sent out 'to see if there was any motion in General Hawleys Camp at Falkirk,' but they now returned to confirm that the enemy showed no sign of movement.[10] This was disappointing, as 'the Prince has been this two days in choosing a field of battle and has found one so advantageous' that they could be confident of victory.[11] But Hawley had shown little urgency in the last few days, and so denied the Jacobites their preferred choice of battlefield. The size of the Jacobite army was now causing them new supply and accommodation pressures, and on each cold night the army had to disperse over a wide area before concentrating again. This made them vulnerable, so when the prince now called his senior officers together on the muir, he was ready to abandon his chosen site for a bolder course.

Prince Charles' relationship with Lord George Murray had remained strained since Derby. On 6 January, Murray had written to the prince proposing that, since so many mistakes or near-mistakes had been made in England, Charles Edward should delegate strategic planning to a standing committee. The proposed committee members would be able, he suggested, to nominate their own representatives to take their place if they could not attend meetings in person. Murray's letter was characteristically tactless and accused Charles Edward of leading them to the brink of destruction by his determination to reach London.[12]

The prince's reply had been equally hot, and revealed a fracturing temper: 'it can be no Army at all where there is no General... Every one knew before he engaged in the cause, what he was to expect in case it miscarried, and should have staid at home if he not face Death in any shape.' With considerable justification, Prince Charles had spoken in his own defence: 'I think I show every day that I do not pretend to act without taking advice, and yours oftener than any body's else, which I shall continue to do, and you know that upon more occasions than one, I have given up my own opinion to that of others.' Finally: 'my authority may be taken from me by violence, but I shall never resign it like an Idiot.'[13] The plan was rejected, but by proposing it, Murray had played into the hands of those, like Broughton and Sir John MacDonald, who remained suspicious of his motives. They, in their turn, were ever more mistrusted by those who felt they controlled access to the prince. Charles Edward could do little more than look to those he trusted most: those who had been with him the longest. But he remained far from despotic in his leadership style, and now once again he gathered his officers about him for a council.

Lord George Murray now proposed that, rather than waiting any longer for Hawley to come to them, the army should march on Falkirk instead. Charles Edward 'was much pleased with the design,' as it accorded with his own aggressive instincts and took the initiative from the enemy in much the same way the march from Edinburgh to Prestonpans had done. Another similarity was that Murray proposed racing to the high ground of 'the hill of Falkirk' over land he professed to know well.[14] Since William Boyd, the 40-year-old Earl of Kilmarnock whose residence at Callendar House was currently occupied by Henry Hawley, was one of the army's senior cavalry commanders, the Jacobites had no shortage of local knowledge. Once the decision was taken, it was put into effect with a speed which clearly surprised the men, who still thought they were being reviewed. At around midday the prince 'made the army face to the right to form a column, and immediately moved off without any person in the army being able to penetrate his design.'[15]

The army, in fact, split into two columns for this, another of the brilliant marches which so regularly distinguished this army's campaigning capacity. The first column was commanded by Lord John Drummond, comprising Lord Ogilvy's substantial regiment, Lord Lewis Gordon's Aberdeenshire men – who, in the absence of the prince's army, had fought a substantial action at Inverurie just before Christmas – and a composite battalion of Irish Picquets and Royal Ecossois amounting to around 275 men.[16] They were accompanied by the cavalry, including John Daniel, who marvelled at the infantry's ability to march 'with such celerity as kept the horse on a full trot.'[17] This column took the most direct road to Falkirk from the muir, which passed by Torwood Castle on its broad wooded ridge. As Drummond's men then marched down the long straight road towards the strategic old bridge at Larbert, he knew they would be visible to the spyglasses of the British army's patrols. But elsewhere on the Torwood hill, the British officers could see the prince's 'great White Standard,' and smoke rising from fires; their conclusion was that the Jacobites might be shuffling themselves around, or trying to tempt Hawley out into a trap, but they were coming no closer.[18]

Meanwhile, the second and much larger Jacobite column advanced undetected, coming round the eastern side of the Torwood ridge before following the track along its southern base with the Carron Water on their right. As they came round towards the river, they enjoyed a wide open view of the landscape before them, above which the skies were darkening with cloud. Their objective at the end of this 'great circuit' was the ford at Dunipace, a notoriously dangerous crossing when the river was swollen, at which even mounted travellers had been known to be swept to their deaths.[19] It was, nevertheless, a well-used crossing point and was sure to be observed by the enemy's pickets, which indeed it was.

As the march continued, Sullivan seems to have grown concerned about the wisdom of attempting the potentially difficult crossing 'in sight of an enemy, and therefore [thought] it was best delaying it till night.'[20] He rode forward to Lord George Murray at the van and made this suggestion. Murray was surprised and opined that the fords were far enough away from Falkirk that even if they were seen, they could not be opposed. Sullivan rode off to press his thoughts on the prince, whom Lord George describes as 'riding betwixt the two lines,' presumably with an escort.[21] This position – the columns were about 1.5 miles apart for most of the march – allowed him to consult with both if required.

When the prince rode up to Murray with Sullivan, he was also accompanied by Brigadier Walter Stapleton, the Franco-Irish commander of his French regulars, and without stopping the column, there was a conference over Sullivan's concerns. Stapleton was an experienced and gallant officer, and although he was a newcomer Charles Edward clearly appreciated that his opinion should carry weight. After hearing Murray's arguments and Stapleton's assessment, the prince was 'entirely satisfied' that the march should continue to Dunipace.[22] This is an interesting little episode as it shows how Charles was willing to hear concerns and consult opinions. He was prepared to disagree with Sullivan – who had himself disagreed with the prince in England – but he had heard him out and taken his concerns seriously. This incident gives a far more nuanced picture of Charles Edward's usual style of command than the accusation that he only ever listened to a handful of favourites, and one more in keeping with the openness and affability attested in other contexts.

Arriving at Dunipace, the main column was joined by Drummond's. The latter had marched to Larbert, only to then cut back west before the bridge. Some of Hawley's scouts were growing increasingly anxious as to his movement, after seeing Drummond's column approaching very obviously 'with standards and colours displayed', convincing some that they would approach the British camp directly via Larbert.[23] Others, however, including several officers perched in a tree, had seen the other column too and were undeceived.[24] A cavalry picket across the Dunipace ford 'rode off at full gallop' to give positive news of the Jacobites' obvious destination.[25] When finally confronted with this information at around 2.00 pm, General Hawley studied his map and quickly understood that the enemy was not coming straight for the camp but swinging around it towards the heights of Falkirk Muir. As the alarm went around the British camp, the skies grew ominously black and heavy.

The Jacobites now passed Dunipace House and the impressive mounds of the old castle motte before plunging into the icy waters of the challenging ford. At the ford, known as the Steps of Dunipace, the recent rains had made the road treacherous and Sullivan cursed the 'very bad sloughs & Morrasses'.[26] A gust of a strengthening wind struck the backs of the Jacobite soldiers with a quick blast of icy hail as the column passed over the rocky riverbed. On the far back, Prince Charles was 'alwaise where he was most necessary… encouraging the men, & forming them,' to ensure the army was ready to form its battle line. The atmosphere was changing, stomachs tightening with the anticipation of the coming action. Some men began to feel sick, others felt the adrenaline building within them. The strengthening wind was pushing them towards their enemy, the black skies full of menace. The prince's encouragement would have been much valued, as the column splashed on through the little Bonny Water and began to climb towards the high plateau beyond. The artillery train, already lagging, was left behind as the march turned into a race.

Lord George Murray led the vanguard on, the Clan Donald regiments rushing forward over open country cut through with little streams of black water. The sleeting rain began to blow harder, coming in sheets from their right as the wind continued to build. The column crossed the line of the Antonine Wall, climbing all the time as they cut diagonally across the muir from north-west to south-east. But off to the left of the vanguard, along the horizon-line formed by the highest part of the muir, the dark moving mass of horsemen was now visible: Hawley's dragoons had reached the summit first. Murray ignored them and kept going until he reached the edge of the moor, where the ground started to drop down into the marshy meadows of the Glen Burn: 'they marched on until they came to a bog, and then the whole army wheel'd to the left.'[27]

With this simple motion the Jacobite army formed its battleline, stretching almost half a mile from the tip of the steep-sided ravine which was torn into the moorland like a scar. The front line was composed of those 'yt were reputed to be the best troops,' with the Appins and Camerons forming the left; the Clan Donald regiments, the right; and the Frasers, MacKintoshes, Farquarsons and Cromarty's Regiment forming the centre. There seems to be little consensus on the ordering of the regiments, probably owing to the considerable confusion amongst the Jacobites themselves; although Elcho says the left of the front line was commanded by Lord John Drummond, Murray believed the latter had followed rather then led.[28] But Murray was at the far end of the line and, as is clear from other aspects of his account, had no clear picture of what was happening elsewhere, not least because he was on foot.

The second line was made up of the Lowland regiments: Gordon's on the left, Ogilvy's in the centre and the Atholl Brigade on the right behind Lord George. This line was considerably shorter than the front, but Stapleton's Picquets were stationed as a final reserve along with the various small cavalry troops, of which Elcho's was posted behind the far-right flank. This was the first time that the Jacobite cavalry had been fully deployed for battle, but they were held back as 'they were not well mounted enough to resist the choc [shock] of the enemys horse.'[29] Charles Edward Stuart was also to the rear (left of the centre) and on horseback, for an army this size could not be commanded in the manner he had led at Prestonpans.[30] His initial position has long been marked by two stones in Canada Wood, from which he had an unobstructed view over his whole army as it formed on the reverse slope facing towards the summit. But the storm had now broken in full force, driving sheets of hail and rain across the moor and making visibility difficult even from here.

As the army was still forming, and with the dark mass of the enemy dragoons hovering with menace along the distant ridge, Prince Charles sent Sullivan to check all was well on the right flank. The Irishman urged his horse through the low spreads of heather, its hooves flicking up the occasional clumps of soft, wet earth. He found Murray positioned with a stone dyke close about him, 'just at the heels of his last rank,' which was probably the enclosures beside Seafield farm that can be seen on General Roy's famous map. On Sullivan's advice, Lord George moved his line further forward so as to be unrestricted. Sullivan further proposed that, since the right flank would now be uncovered when the army advanced, Murray should bring the Atholl Brigade forward in column to cover himself. Holding the tactical reserve drawn in column rather than as a full second line was in accord with Sullivan's French training. But Murray 'wou'd not hear' of bringing up the Athollmen, presumably as he felt he had already conceded enough.[31] This would not be the last occasion on which Murray and Sullivan clashed over how to deal with stone walls on their flank. For now, the right wing moved up, creating an oblique front line which kept the lashing cold rain blowing straight into the faces of the enemy.

Sullivan then rode down the rest of the front line, dressing the regiments to match the readjustment of Murray's wing. He also 'repeated the orders to every Colonel & Major as he went along, wch was, yt the second and third rank shou'd fire only, & yt as near the enemy as possible.'[32] At the far end, Sullivan was told candidly by an officer of the Camerons that his orders would be obeyed so long as he could answer for the left flank being covered. Riding forward of the extreme left and peering beyond the ravine, Sullivan could see a mass of redcoat infantry advancing up the steep slope of the hill, 'at least four Battaillons,' he thought (Ligonier's, Barrell's, Howard's and Price's).[33] These men would be protected by the ravine and would threaten the left of the front line when it advanced, as the Camerons had clearly suspected themselves. Sullivan rode back and gave the clansmen reassurance, before sending his aide Charles Corn to warn the nearest Lowland regiment to be prepared to move up in support.

By now three regiments of British dragoons were demonstrating in front of Lord George Murray's men, hoping to induce them to discharge their muskets and invite a charge. General Hawley had thrown the dragoons up the hill in order to intercept the Jacobites who, until the last possible moment, he still believed did not seek a general engagement. Instead, he thought they intended to bypass his camp and threaten Edinburgh, and that his powerful cavalry force would be a sufficient danger to arrest their progress. Now, those horsemen were on the summit of the muir, being blasted by the full force of the weather, without the support of the infantry labouring up the hill behind them. Two of these regiments had faced the Jacobites before – Gardiner's (now Ligonier's) and Hamilton's – and had faced ridicule from their comrades for having performed so poorly at Prestonpans. It was time to discover whether their previous experience made them eager to redeem themselves with glory, or rather, as the Duke of Cumberland would put it, had encouraged the troopers to 'like safe methods' such as running away.[34]

It was now around 3.50 pm, and John Daniel gazed through the gusting sheets of rain at the 900 dragoons formed on the ridge above the Jacobite right. This 'moving cloud of horse, regularly disciplined,' was a truly formidable spectacle. The troopers' muskets were cast across their backs; their pistols remained in their embroidered saddle holsters, but their gloved hands gripped the handles of their basket-hilted blades. Rainwater ran in unnoticed streams from the gutters of their hats, and darkened their scarlet coats to dull brown. Their black horses tossed the water from their manes, jingling their bits as the tight lines began to walk towards the Jacobites. Then, shrill notes calling over the buffeting wind, the line surged on into the trot.

The Jacobites held to their rank and file with incredible discipline, although the wind was blowing so strong on their backs that the men had to brace their feet against it. Then the dragoons stopped again, and now it was the Jacobites' turn to close the gap. Mounted just behind them, Lord

Elcho looked on as 'the highlanders march'd up to them very Slowly, with their pieces presented, every man taking his aim.'[35] Then at last, the deadlock was broken. At barely ten paces' distance Murray's division unleashed a massive, devastating musket volley. The sound erupted across the muir like thunder from beneath the ground. At the same moment the dragoons charged, driving back their spurs to launch into the clansmen, 'breaking their ranks, throwing down everything before them and trampling the Highlanders under the feet of their horses.'[36] But the Jacobite volley had also done its work, ripping men from their saddles and disordering the dragoons at the critical moment.

As horses fell, their hooves lashed out indiscriminately. They shrieked with terror and pain, while men roared in terrified valour. The combat now was pell-mell, with Highlanders scrabbling for a grip on the belts and accoutrements of the riders and hauling them to the ground. Others thrust dirks into the glistening black bellies of the mounts, and in the press both sides fired pistols at point-blank range into the disorderly mass around them. A horse came crashing down, bowling and pinning Young Clanranald, who looked on helplessly as one of his clansmen wrestled in the mud with a fallen dragoon. Eventually, the Highlander overwhelmed the redcoat and came to the aid of his leader. Some troopers succeeded in breaking through the Jacobite line, but they were quickly overwhelmed. The rest, their charge failing, broke. James Johnstone called the whole spectacle 'the most singular and extraordinary combat,' and he was not wrong.[37]

From his vantage point at the rear, the prince had looked on as the right wing had closed with the enemy's horsemen. He had watched, his teeth clenched in anxiety, as his distant clansmen were shrouded in smoke. Then he heard the muted thunder rolling back across the muir, and could comprehend nothing of what happened in the brief minutes that followed. Musketry then spread across the whole of the front line from right to left as the clansmen discharged into the disordered stream of horsemen that now rode across their front.[38] The army surged forwards and the front line crested the ridge, the right disappearing completely. Behind the Clan Donald regiments went the Atholl Brigade, all pursuing the remnants of Hamilton's Dragoons beyond the ridge and smashing into the unsuspecting infantry labouring up the hill behind them. Elcho's Lifeguards rode in to join the pursuit.[39]

Closer at hand, the left wing rushed forwards too. They had spent their fire on the dragoons who crossed their front, and now the Highlanders rushed after them 'Sword in hand, & destroyed as many as they cou'd overtake.'[40] They ran straight into the volleys of the British infantry, but the storm was now raging at its greatest intensity, and as the weary redcoat foot at last reached the heights, they were struck with the full force of the weather. Powder and sparks were blown from musket pans before they could ignite, and rain soaked through paper cartridges as freezing red hands fumbled to reload. As a result, the British musketry was far less deadly than it might otherwise have proven, and the Highlanders stormed on into it with what Sullivan considered 'one of the boldest and finest actions, yt any troops of the world cou'd be capable of.'[41] The Camerons and Stewarts fell upon the British foot, smashing bayonets aside with their targes and slashing down with their broadswords: 'it seemed a total rout.'[42] Sensing victory, men from the second line began to move forward in support, to take their share in the glory. Then, from the left, came the percussive thump of rippling platoon fire.

As Sullivan had feared, the regiments on the extreme left of Hawley's line had arrived on the muir with the accidental protection of the ravine screening them from the Highland charge. Now they fired into the flank of the disordered clansmen and sent them reeling. As the Highlanders pulled back, they 'returned their fire,' but it was an unequal exchange.[43] Confusion began to spread, and a sense of desperate anxiety flooded through the Lowlanders. The second line was now barely coherent. It had advanced behind the front and then many had followed the charge when it was unleashed. Lord George had taken the whole Atholl Brigade over the ridge in support of the Clan Donald regiments, much as Sullivan had warned he might. What remained of the second line was dispersed and under strength, and apparently leaderless too. It was certainly in no position to perform its intended role, retaining its discipline to plug any potential gaps once the front was engaged. Rather, seeing some of the Highlanders repulsed and formed bodies of enemy foot on their left, the second line descended into disorder. 'There was no remedy nor succor to be given them,' cursed Sullivan.[44] Some broke and fled.

At this moment, and precisely as he should have done, Charles Edward made the critical interventions. Although he remained tactically inexperienced, it was clear to him what was required: 'happyly for us HRHs seeing this, brings up the few regular troops he had, rallys six or seven hundred men'.⁴⁵ Sullivan is not the only one to attribute the direction of the Picquets to the prince personally: 'His RH, whose attention was turned to all quarters, observing that our left wing was out-lined by the enemy, sent Brigadeer Stapleton with the pickets of the Irish Bragade and some other battalions from the second line... which recovered the disorder we were like to be put into.'⁴⁶ Lord George Murray also seems to imply he had sent orders back to move the Picquets forward on the left, but he was simply too far away from the scene for it to be plausible that he knew what was happening there at this time.⁴⁷ He may be conflating it with a later request for the general advance to resume.

The advance of the French Picquets made for a fine sight. In contrast to the confusion all around them, their ranks were tight and well-ordered. The Ecossois wore coats of dark blue and white lace over red breeches and waistcoats, while the Irish Picquets' coats were red. Their gaitered legs stepped forward in unison, the white coverings brown with mud as they trampled through the low heather. Their disciplined fire proved sufficient to deter what remained of Hawley's infantry, though the latter were given the liberty to retire in good order.

Meanwhile, a small body of dragoons had appeared round the Jacobites' extreme left flank. Lord Elcho believed they had intended to make a dash for the prince's person, but it soon became clear to the troopers that they could achieve nothing now that the Jacobite left had recovered.⁴⁸ They quickly retired when threatened, 'as fast as they cou'd drive'.⁴⁹

Now that the crisis point seemed past, the prince stiffened the resolve of the men around him: 'the presence of Charles encouraged the Highlanders: he commended their valour; made them take up the musquets which lay thick on the ground; and ordering them to follow him led them to the brow of the hill.'⁵⁰ The whole Jacobite force, except those whose panic had carried them back towards Dunipace, was now over the crest of the muir's subtle ridge and was facing towards Hawley's encampment and the adjacent town. The sounds of the battle had now slowed to sporadic distant musket shots, ever less audible over the driving rain. But the gathering darkness was adding to the terrible weather to make it almost impossible to perceive what was happening across the battlefield. Regiments were intermingled, officers missing and aides lost. The prince had to use 'all his endeavours to get his men together to make a general attack upon the camp and town'.⁵¹ Restoring

The Battle of Falkirk

order was considerably hampered by the lack of available pipers, as these gentlemen had handed their pipers to their ghillies before the charge, and the boys could not now be found.[52]

It was still unclear how much damage Hawley's army had suffered, and what fighting capacity the Jacobites still retained. For a moment, Charles Edward was 'much at a loss what to do.'[53] He could see that there was commotion on the low ground below the muir, but had no idea whether his enemy was preparing to make a further stand in either the camp or the town. The latter would present a formidable obstacle to assault in such conditions, and as the prince looked around him, he could sense the adrenaline wearing off his men and the exhaustion and misery that was replacing it. They needed food, shelter and rest, and these could only be gained by pressing on. Eventually Lord George Murray reached his prince and, after a brief conference, they agreed those regiments which could be formed should advance and secure Falkirk. Since the enemy's intentions were so unclear, Murray advised the prince to stay on the field while it was undertaken.

The prince rode across to a small hut, several of which can be seen beside the Slamannan Road on Roy's map. He stood on its north-facing side looking across towards the town, sheltered at last from the worst of the wind. A group of Lifeguards accompanied him, all staring expectantly into the darkness. Suddenly lights began to flare up at the western end of Falkirk where the British camp lay with its neat rows of tents. The retreating redcoats had attempted to set fire to it as they left, and despite the rain the wind aided some of the fires to take hold. Under the eerie illumination of these fires, Lord George entered Falkirk with the Atholl Brigade and a mixed force of Highlanders and Lowlanders, which included Lochiel, Keppoch, John Roy Stuart and Young Glengarry and Lord Ogilvy.[54] Lord John Drummond marched the French Picquets into the other end of the High Street, and between them they cleared the town. Drummond, wearing a modified version of his Royal Ecossois uniform, with shortened coat skirts and a blue bonnet, was shot in the arm as he laid his hands on a fugitive.[55] Here and there, distant shots could be heard over the rain as the Jacobites clashed with the last isolated resistance.

The Earl of Kilmarnock rode out along the road to Linlithgow, using his intimate knowledge of the area to confirm Hawley's retreat. Satisfied, he rode back up the Slamannan road to find the prince.[56] Below them the fires were already all but extinguished, the rain proving too much for the flames to overcome, and their dying light showed the shadowy figures of Murray's men as they secured the British camp. The rain continued to beat down, and combined with the darkness and the general confusion across the battlefield, it was clear that no general pursuit could be offered. Nevertheless, Kilmarnock's cavalry did as much as they could to harass Hawley's rear and round up stragglers. At around 7.30 pm, Prince Charles and his escort rode down into Falkirk before retiring at last to Callendar House. There he 'profited of General Hally's supper, which he wanted very much for he had not a bit of his own.'[57] His men filled every room and sheltered alley in Falkirk, and every farmhouse, barn and bothy across the muir.

Captain Johnstone, finding Lord Elcho and his troop at a loose end upon the muir, retired with them back to Dunipace. They re-crossed the swollen, angry ford and took sanctuary in Dunipace House. There they found Lord Lewis Gordon and 'six or seven other' officers, whose location more than 3 miles back from Falkirk did little credit to them and speaks to the extent of the confusion. It was well after 8.00 pm when Donald MacDonnell of Lochgarry, lieutenant colonel of Glengarry's Regiment, arrived at Dunipace with confirmation that the Jacobites had indeed won the battle. Johnstone wrote that 'it is impossible, without having been in our situation, to form an idea of the extreme joy which we derived from this agreeable surprise.'[58] Lochgarry had left the prince at Callendar House, where he had been ordered to ride back to Dunipace and instruct those he found there to present themselves at Falkirk by dawn. It is just possible, therefore, that the house had been identified in advance as a possible rendezvous.

The following morning, 18 January, brought no end to the relentless rain which continued to fall over Falkirk's miserable muir. There had been little opportunity for reflection during the night, and only little by little did a clearer picture of the situation appear. The fires in Hawley's camp had done little damage so the Jacobites were able to claim both the moral and material advantages of taking it. Several standards and colours were taken, to the disgrace of those who lost them, including a green guidon from Ligonier's Dragoons (formerly Gardiner's).

Several senior Jacobite officers had been wounded, including Lochiel, who had been lightly wounded in the leg, and his brother Archibald Cameron, who had been shot in the chest but saved by his targe.[59] Five or six lower-ranking officers had been killed, and brave Donald MacDonnell of Tirnadris had been taken prisoner. The hero of the skirmish at Highbridge had attempted to mount a riderless dragoon horse, but it bolted after its fleeing herd and carried him straight into the British lines. He would later be executed in Carlisle. Lord Elcho believed the army had lost 'about fifty kill'd & Sixty wounded,' although some of the injured men might have subsequently died of their wounds.[60] There might have been more wounded, but given their dispersed state many probably went unaccounted for. Despite the far greater scale of the action, and likely thanks to the difficulty of delivering effective fire in torrential rain, Jacobite casualties at Falkirk were little higher than they had been at Prestonpans. Hawley's casualties are difficult to state with certainty, although Elcho estimated 500–600 had been killed; Sullivan, 1,000; Johnstone, 600; and Maxwell, 400–500. As at Prestonpans, the British army had suffered high losses amongst its officers, with the most notable amongst the fallen being Colonel Sir Robert Monro and Lieutenant Colonel Whitney, who had survived his wounds at Prestonpans only to fall before the Clan Donald's devastating musket volley.

The Jacobites had also taken several hundred prisoners, and in the early morning Kilmarnock's Horse drove a small group of them into the grounds of Callendar House. Amongst them was John Hume, who had been captured with others from his company of Edinburgh volunteers. The earl compiled a list of their names, dismounted and entered his home. A few moments later, a large window on the first floor opened and Prince Charles himself appeared there, holding the list and examining the men while he conversed with Kilmarnock. Suddenly, the prisoners' attention was drawn to a commotion. Their guards were shouting as a redcoat soldier was walking towards them with his musket and bayonet. The prince followed the distraction of the captives and 'seemed surprised,' pointing the approaching soldier out to Kilmarnock, who flew down the stairs and out of the house. He brusquely struck the hat off the approaching soldier and stamped on its black cockade. Extraordinarily, one of the Highlanders then seized hold of the earl. The latter drew a pistol and the former a dirk, but a crowd of others rushed in to separate them. The redcoat, it turned out, was a Cameron who had turned coats after the battle and joined the Jacobites. His defender was his brother.

We can only imagine what Prince Charles made of this remarkable event.[61] He gave orders that all prisoners should be 'as well used as the circumstances would allow,' and instructed that the fallen should be decently laid to rest.[62] This order clearly took a long time to be put into effect, perhaps because those tasked with it were hoping for the rain to stop. Whatever the reason, there were many stripped bodies still lying on the field after 7.00 pm when James Johnstone was forced to wander amongst them as he tried to locate the abandoned British cannon. He had been hanging around at Callendar House when 'Mr Sullivan issued from the Prince's closet' and ordered him to lead a waiting detachment – twenty men and a sergeant – to guard the guns which the weather had prevented anyone from moving.[63] The bodies which could be identified as British officers, including Monro and Whitney, were brought into Falkirk and buried in the churchyard.[64]

During the rest of the day, the scattered Jacobites came into Falkirk 'by Showls'.[65] They had sought shelter wherever they might find it, and for many the most obvious course had been to retrace their steps to previous billets. It remained difficult, however, to assess the scale of the Jacobite army's losses; with the rain still pouring, the elation of victory began to ebb from the Jacobite commanders. Few voices were raised in favour of continuing to press Hawley back to Edinburgh, so strategic attention turned to the continuing siege at Stirling. Reflections on the battle soon gave rise to recriminations. Murray complained that Sullivan had not been active during the battle, and that Drummond had either failed to take his proper place or had never been properly instructed. Others accused Murray of having lost control on the right wing and dropping out of action. He countered that he had been given dismounted aides who had therefore been no use to him (he himself being on foot).[66]

Murray also managed to give serious offence to Arthur Elphinstone, Lord Balmerino, the gallant and learned commander of one of the Lifeguard troops. Balmerino came to the rising with both military experience and ideological zeal, but was also a hard drinker which seems to have been a trait Murray particularly objected to. John Daniel, one of Balmerino's troopers, could not discern the cause of the 'grudge' Murray seemed to have against his colonel, but complained that the whole troop suffered when Balmerino was so 'ill-used'.[67]

Against this demoralising backdrop, a tragic accident in Falkirk sent a shockwave through the army. While clearing the musket he had picked up on the battlefield, a soldier of Clanranald accidentally fired a shot from the window of his billet. The ball struck a passing officer, the brave and popular Aeneas MacDonnell, Young Glengarry. He was instantly carried into a nearby house on Burns Court and attended by surgeons, but the agonising wound would prove fatal.[68] The result was bad blood between the Clanranald and Glengarry regiments. When Young Glengarry finally died on 22 January, the regiment demanded the execution of the unfortunate shooter. To prevent further escalation, the Clanranald men performed the task themselves. The effect of the whole incident was damaging, and the prince made no intervention to limit it. When Glengarry was laid to rest in the tomb of Sir John de Graeme, hero of the first Battle of Falkirk in 1298, Charles Edward did not attend. Perhaps he did not wish to interfere in the complexities of clan rivalry – he had, after all, seen a Cameron soldier draw a dirk on the Earl of Kilmarnock over a minor affront – but it was a mistake which dampened the ardour of a substantial regiment, some of whom began to drift home.[69] Alternatively, he may just have been too far away to understand the depth of feeling: he had left Falkirk for Bannockburn on 19 January.

The prince was now determined to prosecute the Siege of Stirling Castle with more vigour. While Murray held the Highland regiments around Torwood and Falkirk, the siege lines were reinforced and the Lowland regiments billeted around the town. Walter Stapleton's arrival at the lines sped the work, the French regulars proving more willing to toil at digging the trenches than their comrades. But the outcome of the siege had been more or less decided by the decision to focus on Gowan hill, contrary to the opinion of both Sullivan and the Franco-Irish artillery officer James Grante, both of whom had played their parts in the Siege of Carlisle. Between 3.00 pm and 4.00 pm on 21 January, Prince Charles 'went to the trenches himself to encourage the men to work,' but although there were regular exchanges of small arms fire, the Jacobite battery was far from ready. Not until 28 January was it ready to open fire. Elcho believed the guns 'did the walls much damage,' and a contemporary diary records a ball smashing 'through the roof of the gaird-room,' but the garrison had been restraining its own cannon for this moment.[70] The castle battery opened fire and 'distroyed our battery & disabled our Cannon in one night, so yt there was an end to our siege.'[71] The Jacobite losses, mainly amongst the French, had been sadly futile.

In the week which followed his visit to the trenches, Prince Charles had fallen ill. He called it a cold, which is hardly to be unexpected given the weather, but he may have been struggling before the battle too. On 9 January, accounts record the purchase of expensive cinnamon, which has fed romantic tales of the prince being nursed with hot toddies. Administering the remedies was Clementina Walkinshaw, the niece of the house's owner, who would later join the prince in Europe and become his mistress. Given what Charles Edward had put his body through, and the immense mental pressures of the campaign, a physical or mental crash is hardly surprising. And while it did not stop him from facing all the challenges of the battlefield, the sickness (whether psychosomatic or not) may have contributed to the prince's relative static and unenergetic leadership during the siege. If so, its impact was significant: for the first time the prince had lost touch with the feeling in his army. The failure to pursue Hawley to Edinburgh was grumbled at, and the handling of the siege criticised. The army had lost its momentum and needed to refocus.

The spur for action came on the same day as the battery was dismounted on Gowan hill, and it provided Prince Charles with the distraction he needed from that bitter disappointment. News had come in that Hawley had been superseded in Edinburgh by the Duke of Cumberland himself, although Hawley escaped censure for his failure and was retained. The prince sent Murray of Broughton to Falkirk to advise his namesake Lord George that the army would 'go and attack the Duke of Cumberland when he advanced as far as Falkirk.'[72] Sullivan was sent too, emphasising to Murray that he must remain in Falkirk until the prince came up with the rest of the army once it was clear that Cumberland was approaching. Perhaps Sullivan should have been suspicious of the reception he had from Murray, who 'embrassd him most kindly before all the Chiefs.'[73] Shocked, the adjutant general felt as if he had just won a battle. Sullivan returned to Bannockburn with a confident report, and that night the prince 'went to bed very cheerfully'.[74]

That night, a letter arrived at the house from Lord George Murray. He had assembled a council of war with 'all the Chiefs of the Clans', at which they had drawn up a representation for them all to sign.[75] Broughton received and read the letter, and at around 11.00 pm he took it to Sullivan who recalls him saying: 'this will set him mad, for he'l see plainly yt it is a Caballe & yt Ld George has blinded all those peoples.'[76] The letter stated baldly that, as a result of desertion, they were 'in no way in a Condition to face The Dukes army.'[77] Not only would they not stand at Falkirk as requested, but they also demanded an immediate retreat into the Highlands where they could spend the rest of the winter 'by taking and mastering the forts in the north.'[78] This was not only a flat rejection of the prince's intentions, therefore, but the usurpation of the right to determine the overall strategy of the war. It was also a profoundly selfish strategy which sought to address only the issues that affected the Highland regiments.

After the prince's dismissal of Murray's proposal for a formal standing council, Murray had clearly been building a base of support within the army's senior officers. In the face of their dislike of the prince's Irish officers, especially those who had been 'so rash' as to persuade Charles Edward to come in the first place, Lord George's proposals had the comfort of coming from one of their own.[79] There were thus two different strategic approaches to the conflict within the Jacobite leadership: one more parochial and dependent on major overseas intervention, the other more ambitious and therefore (on the surface, at least) more dangerous. The prince's strategic instinct was, given the scale of the challenge and the limited time in which the advantage could be sustained, more suited to the moment. But Murray had convinced enough people that the prince, badly advised and inexperienced, was wrong. While Charles Edward had been at Bannockburn, Lord George had a free hand to make his case.

Murray knew that Charles would react badly to the chiefs' letter and in his covering letter to Broughton, he had written: 'we are sensible that it will be very unpleasant, but in the Name of God what can we do?' He also entreated that the letter's contents be kept secret from anyone who did not absolutely have to be consulted on them, perhaps because he knew there were others who would disagree.[80] Now, standing with the pages in their hands, Sullivan and Broughton chose not to wake the prince. If they waited until morning, there was perhaps still time to mollify its effects. Broughton rode out into the night and urged Murray to compromise, so far as offering Cumberland battle at the place previously chosen by the prince to receive Hawley near Plean.[81] But the entreaty was of no use and Murray knew he had the committed support of sufficient allies to hold firm.

The next morning Prince Charles awoke with the expectation that he would spend the day in making preparations for another general engagement. Perhaps this one would prove decisive: if he beat back this army a second time, it would not stand for a third. And if he beat the Duke of Cumberland, in whom George II and his ministers had placed all their faith, then who was left who might dare take the field against them? And what possible excuse could then be found for his supporters in Scotland, England and France to hold back? The conflict was surely now reaching the climax which would turn the tide once and for all, and Charles Edward Stuart had no doubt that his army could make it happen. Then, his head filled with such expectations, he was handed Murray's note and the declaration of the Highland leaders at Falkirk.

It struck Charles Edward like a thunderbolt, just as Murray's ambush before the council at Derby had done. With no warning of the sentiments of his officers, from whom the Siege of Stirling and his own weariness had kept him dislocated for a crucial week, he simply could not believe what he was reading. 'Good God,' the prince cried, 'have I lived to see this?' He was so shocked and enraged that, according to John Hay at least, he 'struck his head against the wall till he staggered.'[82] It took time for the prince to recover his composure and decide how to react. He had no arguments prepared because, to him, the correct course seemed so self-evident. His pen shook in his hand as he mustered the concentration needed to articulate his thoughts:

> Gentlemen, I have received yrs of last night and am extremely surprised at the contents of it, wch I little expected from you at this time. Is it possible that a Victory and a Defeat shou'd produce the same effects, and that the Conquerors should flie from an engagement whilst the conquer'd are seeking it? Shou'd we make the retreat you propose, how much more will that raise the spirits of our Ennemys and sink those of our own People? Can we imagin, that where we go the Ennemy will not follow, and at last oblige us to a Battle which we now decline? Can we hope to defend ourselves at Perth, or keep our Men together there better than we do here? We must therefore continue our flight to the Mountains, and soon find our selves in a worse condition than we were in at Glenfinnan. What Opinion will the French and Spaniards then have of us?... But what will become of our Lowland friends? Shall we persuade them to

retire with us to the Mountains? Or shall we abandon them to the fury of our Merciless Ennemies?...

But having told you my thoughts upon it, I am too sensible of what you have already ventured and done for me, not to yield to yr unanimous resolution if you persist in it.[83]

It is a well-reasoned response which, while full of emotion, is also weighty with foresight. The prince chose his former under-governor and trusted confidant Sir Thomas Sheridan to carry the letter, perhaps considering him a less provocative ambassador than either Sullivan or Broughton. Sheridan rode hard for Falkirk with a covering letter authorising him to speak on the prince's behalf with the chiefs. Perhaps Prince Charles should have gone himself, but that might simply have raised the temperature. Instead Keppoch and several other chiefs rode to Bannockburn for a face-to-face discussion, showing their intent to stand by their signatures rather than simply hide behind Lord George.

The meeting clearly did not go well as Prince Charles sent another letter the following day which suggests he might have lost his cool: 'I doubt not that you have been informed by Cluny and Keppoch of what passed last night and heard great complaints of my Despotick temper.' He went on to explain his reasoning once again, with much the same arguments as he had already given. Clearly the critical issue for the chiefs was the level of desertion, which they believed to be considerable. Charles rebutted that a retreat closer to the men's homes would prove a poor deterrent: 'ye nearer we come to the Forth the greater the Desertion will prove.' More to the point, retreating beyond the river abandoned everything for which they had fought so hard, and even if they proved successful at consolidating in the north, they would then have a far harder fight to receive all they had thrown away. In short, the Young Chevalier believed that the cause could not survive another retreat, and whatever the risks of the coming battle, the course being forced upon him instead would ultimately lead to their failure. 'I can see nothing,' he lamented, 'but ruin and destruction to us all in case we should think of a retreat.'[84]

On 1 February 1746, the Jacobite army retreated.

Chapter Seven

Culloden

A cold wind blew across the high open muir, and the dark clouds sent down intermittent showers of bitter rain. Prince Charles Edward Stuart wore a simple tartan coat of red, green and blue, its collar turned up against the elements, over a buff-coloured waistcoat. He urged his horse to the canter, the pounding hooves flicking up a fine spray of mud and water. As he neared his approaching troopers, the prince slowed again to the trot and then, before they closed up, drew up to a halt. He pushed back his shoulders and tossed his head in a gesture of excited impatience. Across the moor behind him, his army was drawn into its battleline much as it had been on the Plean Muir exactly three months before when it had waited in vain for Henry Hawley. The army was smaller now – there were detachments off to the north and south, and with pay fallen into arrears some of his clansmen had sought to supplement their meagre supplies by heading home for a while. But once again, battle was at hand.

The troopers of the Prince's Lifeguards looked fine even after the trials of the hard winter. Their dark coats were well-brushed, their scarlet cuffs and matching waistcoats bright against the dark of the muir. They came to a halt in front of their prince with a clatter of carbines and bits, their guns suspended from crossbelts mounted with tartan. The riders' faces were hardened from exposure and creased with weariness, but the eyes were still bright and alert. David Wemyss, Lord Elcho, raised his hand and as his men stopped their mounts, his continued to trot onwards towards the prince. Aged 24, the soft roundness of his handsome face belied the hard temper and sharp tongue which had earned him a black reputation amongst his enemies. He approached the prince with the swagger and familiarity of one who was also born to wealth and rank.

It was 15 April 1746, and that morning Elcho had been 'sent to Gett intelligence' of the enemy. He had ridden almost 8 miles north-east towards Nairn where he had spent several hours observing the army of

William Augustus, Duke of Cumberland. The army was encamped on the western side of the town, but the cavalry was off to the east on the other side of the river. Most importantly, however, they seemed to be making no preparation for a march, 'remained quiet in their Camp at Nairn, and by all appearance they did not intend to move that day.'[1] It was, after all, their commander's twenty-fifth birthday. Receiving the news, Prince Charles struck a gloved hand against his thigh in frustration. He twisted in his saddle and looked back towards his men, most of whom had their plaids drawn up around their heads and shoulders like cloaks. They hunched and huddled out of the elements as they waited for orders.

John Sullivan now caught up with the prince, his horse trotting up alongside after following in his commander's more energetic wake. At around twenty years older than Charles and Elcho, Sullivan was also a stockier build than the two youngsters. His cheeks were red from the cold, but his eyes were alert as they flashed inquisitively at Elcho. The latter showed no inclination to repeat his report. Charles Edward turned to him and said plainly, 'they'l starve us here, if we don't march to them, & not give them time to retrench themselves.'[2] Then he turned the head of his horse and began to move back towards the line. Sullivan directed Elcho where to post his troopers and then turned to follow the prince, a small escort remaining a discreet distance behind them. Charles was deep in thought as he passed through the line, but still he flashed an automatic smile at the clansmen who called an over-familiar greeting or hurriedly tugged at their bonnets. The men were in high spirits, as they always were at the prospect of a battle, and when the prince had reviewed them earlier in the day, they had cheered their huzzahs as enthusiastically as ever.

Behind the main line of Highlanders, the prince rode across to neat ranks of the Earl of Kilmarnock's Footguards. Most were Lowlanders, but their dress did not show it. They drew their muskets neatly to the shoulder as the prince arrived, showing a degree of pride in their status. The core of the regiment had once been Kilmarnock's Horse, but they had been obliged to surrender their mounts to the 130 professional troopers of the Regiment de Fitzjames who had landed at Aberdeen in late February. Sadly, they had arrived without their own horses and the rest of their regiment, which were successfully intercepted by the Royal Navy. The result had been a consolidation of the small Jacobite cavalry troops, and Kilmarnock's men had been dismounted, along with

Pitsligo's. Now these Franco-Irish horsemen, with their smart red coats with dark lapels, were also formed up ready for battle.

Once the prince reached his intended position, where a cluster of aides and secretaries waited, he gave a succession of orders. First, the men could stand easy and rest their legs as it was clear that the enemy would not oblige them with a battle this day. Second, whatever supply of biscuit was available in Inverness was to be hurried up to the muir. The commissariat was letting the army down badly, and despite the substantial supplies of food in town, little had been baked to provide easy rations and hardly any of it had been sent up to the army.[3] John Murray of Broughton, who had managed such matters fairly effectively for most of the campaign, had fallen seriously ill the previous month and was out of action. John Hay of Restalrig had taken over, but as the army concentrated with the prospect of action, it was clear Hay was not up to the task. The prince's third instruction was that the senior officers assemble for a council of war.

The muir on which the army had been formed was 'so plain a field' that the Highlanders would have no obstacle before them if the enemy had appeared in their front to receive a charge.[4] But while the lack of obstacles recommended the field's suitability to some – particularly Sullivan, who had chosen it – it unnerved others who feared there was also nothing to impede an enemy superior in number, artillery and cavalry. Chief amongst these was Lord George Murray, who had already proposed retiring to a site near Daviot on the south side of the River Nairn. This site had been rejected, however, principally because it abandoned Inverness. This was the last town in the Jacobite army's possession, the last potential access point for French aid, and the site of all the army's baggage. Without it, the army would struggle to survive even if it were not defeated. Murray had proposed another site too, a couple of miles closer towards their enemy than where they now stood, on high ground overlooking Dalcross Castle. There, a ravine promised to neutralise the enemy's cavalry, but the heights would be no salvation from the enemy's cannon, and any obstacle that impeded a redcoat attack also prevented a Highland charge.

Prince Charles was in a very similar situation to that at Plean in January. His army was formed on an open muir ready to receive the enemy when it came. That enemy was encamped to the west of a small town, preparing to march through the rain to engage. A short distance behind the prince's army was the house at which he had been lodging, although, unlike at Bannockburn, the current accommodation belonged to an avowed opponent of his cause, Duncan Forbes. In addition, a strong detachment from the army was unavailable for the battle because it was otherwise engaged. In this case, Lord Cromarty was in the north attempting to recover a critical supply of gold which had been lost in a skirmish at Tongue. And while there was some anxiety over the army's ability to concentrate rapidly, morale in the rank and file remained encouraging. But morale could now only be kept up by a decisive action: the problems of supply and the lack of pay were beginning to take their toll, and the situation would soon become unsustainable. Prince Charles needed a solution and, as he had been at Falkirk, he was now disinclined to simply wait until the enemy was ready to come to him.[5]

The upcoming council of war was the first major council for some time, although Elcho was obviously exaggerating when he claimed this was 'the first time since Derby' that the prince had sought advice.[6] For some time, however, a full gathering of all the colonels and senior officers had neither been possible nor necessary. The decision to retreat from Stirling had determined the overall strategy, and all that remained was to put it into execution. That required a dispersal of much of the army on detached operations, which then prevented any regular general consultations even if they had been deemed necessary. Prince Charles had retained overall command, the nexus-point of the army's activities, but that role required him to take no direct part in most of the action. It also meant that while others were able to distract themselves with the minutiae of their particular operation, Charles Edward could assess the full extent of the challenges the army was facing as its strategic options and financial resources dwindled. Little wonder that he relished the prospect of an imminent engagement to bring matters back to a head.

The march out of Stirling on 1 February had been bungled. As at Derby, the rank and file of the Jacobite army found themselves retreating when they had expected to advance. Elcho remembered how 'every body was Struck with amazement, for Every body that did not know of the Clans representation Expected a battle, and it appeared very Strange to run away from the very army that had been beat only a fortnight before.'[7] Believing the only explanation was the imminent arrival of the enemy, panic began to set in amongst some regiments to the extent that 'there was hardly the appearance of an army.'[8] The prince, who was up and about early in the hope that he might yet find a way to prevent the retreat altogether, tried in vain to restore order, but in the end was able only to put himself at the head of some formed bodies and lead them towards the fords at Frew. As he did, the church at St Ninian's suddenly exploded, destroying the stores of powder it contained, blowing out all the nearby windows, and killing a number of innocents. 'The Prince himself was within reach of being hurt when the thing happened,' and the detonation helped spread fear of an attack.[9] Murray, who had naturally assumed responsibility for the retreat, was not yet out of his quarters as the time appointed for the withdrawal had not yet come about.[10] A number of guns had to be abandoned and the army never looked so much like one that had been beaten. It was a punishing blow to morale, of which the surviving steeple of St Ninian's Church is a lasting memorial.

Recriminations were growing increasingly bitter. Lord George 'blamed the Prince for this retreat', but Elcho agreed only so far that the fault lay with those to whom the prince preferred to listen.[11] When the prince reached Crieff, he took pause to review the forces he had there. Although most of the horse had pushed on towards Perth along with some of the Lowland regiments, he was able to assemble most of the Highland regiments and 'found the desertion was nothing like what it had been represented'. Most of those who had appeared to be absent had simply gone off in search of better lodgings, or had simply 'indulged their restless disposition' during the idle period following the victory.[12] Once the army had moved out, they had rejoined their units. It is hard to believe that their leaders had not considered this was the case, and it is far from impossible that desertion was the pretext for causing a strategic shift.

After discovering the true strength of his army, Charles Edward was 'affected as one may imagine'.[13] At the council of war which followed, tempers boiled over on all sides. Many of the accounts move swiftly on, while Maxwell (who as an aide-de-camp was well-informed) recalled the 'heats and animosities... wrangling and altercation'.[14] Murray clearly took aim at O'Sullivan over the handling of the retreat, as it was his job to issue the necessary orders. But 'the prince did not incline to lay the blame on any body, but said he took it upon himself.'[15] Eventually this appalling council was able to conclude a plan of action, one which conveniently separated Lord George from Sullivan and the prince, as well as from the Highland officers who were so much inclined to support his part. Murray was to take one column of the army from Perth to the east coast and then up through Aberdeen, while Prince Charles led the Highland regiments directly northwards through Badenoch towards Inverness.

On his way towards the Highland capital, then occupied by a substantial body under the Earl of Loudoun, the prince had again come close to danger. He had halted at Moy Hall, around which a scattered guard of only fifty men was quartered. Loudoun attempted to seize him there with a night march in force, but several heroic messengers found their way past the column to alert the prince of the danger. Charles, woken by the voice of his footman, 'went down stairs, and his feet in his shoes, by the way of slippers, and buckled them in the close.'[16] The prince escaped into the adjacent woods where his guards assembled and shared a dram while awaiting the news. Eventually he was summoned back to the house to hear the story of how a local blacksmith and four retainers had opened fire on Loudoun's vanguard and ingeniously replicated the sounds of a large body of clansmen. The prince 'gave the smith some Guineas' for his service, and set pickets along the River Nairn to prevent another such incident.[17]

Loudoun's little army had withdrawn in disorder and remained so rattled that they abandoned Inverness at the prince's subsequent approach. As Loudoun's men withdrew, Charles Edward ordered the clans to pursue hard into the town. But the clansmen were daunted by the presence of Fort George (Inverness Castle), mounted on a high earth pile dominating the river, suspecting that Loudoun's men could make an effective stand in the streets. The prince 'assured them, yt they wou'd never defend the town… & yt the enemy wou'd never stand.'[18] Loudoun's men were ferried across to the Black Isle in the nick of time, although Sullivan was able to harass their crossing with artillery mounted on the remains of the old Cromwellian citadel.

In the weeks that followed their arrival in Inverness, the Jacobite army seemed to reinvigorate. They had already successfully secured the surrender of the tiny garrison at Ruthven Barracks, which had then been burned out to the state it remains today, completing an operation first attempted back in August. Fort George was then taken with impressive speed, the garrison surrendering on 20 February as its walls were being undermined. The prince ordered its bastions to be slighted. It was rumoured that 'men were now being raised in every direction,' in apparent vindication of the consolidation strategy.[19]

By the time Fort George surrendered, Lord George Murray had arrived with his column, which had marched with astonishing speed despite being encumbered with waggons on its long march through heavy snow. The speed of Murray's march was, however, a strategic error in that it abandoned the east coast harbour towns at the very moment that French troops and supplies were attempting to reach them. North-east Scotland was also rich recruiting ground for the Jacobites, secured for them by Lord Lewis Gordon's victory at Inverurie before Christmas, and now yielded without a fight to the Duke of Cumberland's slow but relentless advance. Nevertheless, success at Inverness had restored Prince Charles' confidence and the morale of the army had stabilised. Those who had endured Murray's hard march 'came to be greedy spectators of our dear Prince again'.[20] The prince made a tour with his Lifeguards through Nairn and Elgin to Gordon Castle, during which he ceremonially presented John Daniel with the captured green guidon of Gardiner's/Ligonier's Dragoons.[21] It bore the motto *Britons Strike Home*, lyrics from a popular Purcell opera, and the fact that Charles Edward thought it suitable for his Lifeguards gives some small insight into how he saw his mission. This flag is probably unique in having been present at all three of the major battles of the conflict, but not always on the same side.

Meanwhile a strong column had marched down the Great Glen and laid siege to Fort Augustus. Constructed with considerable expense, the fort was sited on the southern end of Loch Ness and supported by an older barrack which acted as an outwork. This the Jacobites quickly overwhelmed before James Grante turned his efforts against the main fort. Grante performed as well as he had with the batteries before Carlisle, and after successfully dropping a shell through the roof of the fort's powder magazine, the garrison surrendered. Again, it seemed the consolidation strategy might yet be vindicated. The prince then recalled the column to Inverness, but Lochiel 'came alone to beg leave of HRHs to undertake the siege of Forte William.'[22] The fort there was a challenging prospect as it could be resupplied by sea, and it was more than 60 miles from the prince's base at Inverness. But the garrison had earned the ire of the Camerons and their neighbours by launching punitive raids on their territory while the clansmen were away, adding special significance to an already obnoxious target. Although he was 'altogether against it', the prince conceded.[23]

While these sieges were under way, Lord George Murray had descended on his home territory of Atholl and taken the enemy outposts there completely by surprise. He succeeded in bottling them up into Blair Castle, by rights the home of his brother Tullibardine, which he then put to siege. Further north, the Duke of Perth was entrusted with the potentially difficult operation of pursuing the Earl of Loudoun and his force of red-coated Highlanders. At Dornoch on 20 March, he succeeded in surprising their position and taking several hundred prisoners and a cache of arms. Lord Loudoun retreated with what remained of his strength, before dispersing his companies and withdrawing to the Isle of Skye. The operation had been bloodless and impressively successful, revealing yet again the discipline and composure the Jacobite forces could deploy on a considered operation when they were well led.

But then the dark clouds had once more begun to gather over the prince's fortunes. Colonel Grante had been wounded at Fort William and his replacement, the ineffectual Mirabelle de Gordon, had mismanaged the siege. The garrison sallied and successfully overran one of the Jacobite batteries. The advance of a large force of Hessian troops towards Blair Atholl obliged Murray to quit his siege at Blair, and from Aberdeen the Duke of Cumberland's forces were threatening the Jacobite outposts along the southern coast of the Moray Firth. Confirmation also finally reached Prince Charles that the main French expedition, intended to be led by his brother Prince Henry, had long since been cancelled.

Crucially, the money to pay for the Jacobite army's activities, however successful, was running out. The prince had been putting on a brave show at Inverness so that the parlous state of the army's resources was in no way evident, appearing 'gayer even than usual' at public appearances.[24] As part of this performance, he chose to abandon the detachment from levity he had shown in Edinburgh and was seen to dance. James Maxwell believed that although some 'austere-thinking people' criticised this apparent distraction, 'the greatest part of those that saw him cheerful and easy, concluded he had resources which they did not know.'[25]

A vital lifeline appeared with the return of *Prince Charles*, a ship which had previously been captured by the Jacobites and renamed. But it was intercepted by the Royal Navy and driven aground at Tongue, losing its vital cargo of French coin. At the very moment he was attempting to consolidate his position at Inverness, the prince was obliged to detach several hundred capable fighters under Lord Cromarty in the hope of recovering the cash.

On 15 April, as Charles Edward waited for his officers to gather, Cromarty's men were rushing south as quickly as they could to rejoin him. Far nearer at hand were Keppoch's men, who at least were known to be on the road towards Drummossie Muir.[26] Sullivan had also now returned from Inverness with carts of biscuit, but the supply turned out to be woefully inadequate. With most of the meal still unbaked, there was only enough prepared for a single biscuit per man.[27] Watching the ration being distributed, the prince looked on helplessly as grumbling soldiers drifted away from the colours in small groups to search for whatever additional sustenance they might be able to find. The sight confirmed in the prince's mind that battle could no longer be avoided as Inverness and its crucial stores *must* be held. The battle must also come soon, despite the absence of a number of regiments, because once the army concentrated, the problems of paying and feeding it became increasingly acute. Besides, these men needed the prospect of imminent action to hold them together and sustain their morale. In this, the army and its commander were as one.

Once 'all the Principal officers' were assembled, Prince Charles invited their opinions. It is unclear whether he opened, as appears to have been his habit, by stating his own first. In the aftermath of what was to follow, the origin of the proposal the council adopted is variously attributed to both the prince and Lord George. It is reasonable to conclude that both men were of one mind on this fateful occasion, and if Murray was the first to articulate the plan openly, then it unquestionably appealed to Charles' own inclinations. Unusually, Lord George himself does not claim credit for the initial idea, although it is clearly credited to him by Sullivan, Elcho and Maxwell. Lochiel and Johnstone both attribute the plan to the prince, although those two might well be deflecting criticism from Lord George with the benefit of hindsight.

On balance, it seems likely that Charles Edward opened by stating his preference for an aggressive rather than defensive action, at which Murray then 'made a Speech, wherein he enlarged upon the advantages Highlanders have by Surprising their Enemy.'[28] Alternatively, as Sullivan appears to have remembered it, the prince and Murray held a conversation on the subject prior to the arrival of the others, at which Murray then presented the proposed plan of action.[29]

Murray's proposal was that the army should march towards Cumberland's camp at dusk, along the lesser road which crossed the muir on its south side parallel with the River Nairn. The darkness and the long hump of the muir itself would screen the Jacobites from the view of the Royal Navy vessels which were now visible in the Moray Firth. The vanguard, which he would lead himself, was to cross the Nairn near Cawdor and swing round to attack the town and camp from the east. The centre of the column would press on along the direct route to attack from the south and west. It was to be led by the Duke of Perth, who had continued to prove his command competence at both Dornoch and the withdrawal from the Spey. The remainder of the army would move in support of Perth's column, led by the prince himself.[30] The attack would trap the enemy in their camp with their backs to the sea, and the advantage of surprise would go a long way towards negating the disparities in number. Murray's column would also be able to sever communication between the British army's infantry and cavalry, allowing the destruction of the infantry before the cavalry could come to their aid.[31] The proposal combined elements of the two successful operations which preceded the battles at Prestonpans and Falkirk.

The plan for the march on Nairn was unanimously supported, as it appeared to be 'the best chance of getting the better of their [enemy's] numbers, their cavalry, and their cannon.'[32] Johnstone believed one of the arguments was that Cumberland's men would be 'intoxicated' on account of their general's birthday, and Sullivan attributes this naïve assumption to Murray.[33] Nevertheless, before the final decision was taken, there were 'great debates' over both the general wisdom of the plan and the detail of its implementation.[34]

There was understandable concern that a considerable part of the army's strength had not yet reached the muir, which argued for a delay. Others were concerned that, due to the Royal Navy, the departure time had to be so late in the evening that the army could not launch its attack before the dawn. On that point, according to Elcho, 'Lord George said he would Answer for it'.[35] John Sullivan, when asked his opinion, presented a considered appraisal of the plan's advantages and proposed detailed orders be given for how the assault was to be conducted. According to his own memory, 'Ld George answered yt there was no need of orders, yt every body knew what he had to do.'[36] This accords with a report in John Hume's history that Robert Anderson, who had guided the Jacobites so successfully through the marshes at Tranent, vainly entreated Murray to explain the plan to the officers. Murray refused on the grounds that any further briefing would undermine security.[37]

Once the decision was taken, it had to be kept secret for as long as possible in order not to let word seep out beyond the muir.[38] In the meantime, however, men could still be seen drifting off in search of food and shelter, 'and it was not possible to stop them.'[39] At this point Murray and others began to have doubts: 'almost every body gave it up as a thing not to be ventured.'[40] This has shades of the situation at the end of January, when Murray had first appeared to agree with the prince's plan to strike from Falkirk while in his presence, and then renege on it afterwards. But the prince was 'extremely bent upon it, and said that whenever we began the march the men would all be hearty, and those that had gone off would return and follow.'[41]

According to Maxwell, Prince Charles 'dreaded nothing so much as the appearance of fear at the approach of the Duke of Cumberland. He had too high an opinion of the bravery of his men; he thought all irresistible.'[42] Murray agreed with his aide's assessment: 'His Royal Highness had so much confidence in the bravery of his army, that he was rather too hazardous and was for fighting the enemy on all occasions. What he had seen them do, and the justice of the cause, made him too venturous.'[43] If this was recklessness or overconfidence to some, it was also the sense of belief and trust which made Charles Edward's leadership so inspiring to others. As the hours passed, the prince began to imagine the coming march to be 'the finishing stroke to restor the King.'[44] When Keppoch and his men finally arrived on the muir, the prince's spirits could only rise. He had no way of knowing that the Earl of Cromarty would never arrive, as he had already been taken prisoner along with most of his men after a running skirmish between Dunrobin and Littleferry.

As the evening grew darker, the army began to form upon Drummossie Muir. By 7.00 pm, Lord George's column was ready to head down along the 'Very Dirty Road' which led to Nairn.[45] When all was ready, the march began, preceded by MacKintosh scouts. As the column began to move, Prince Charles appeared at Lord George Murray's side. In an uncommonly warm gesture, the prince then put his arm around Murray's back and placed a hand on his shoulder, while reaching across himself to take Lord George's hand. This informal embrace was a very public gesture of both comradery and trust, showing just a hint of the prince's own insecurity and social awkwardness. Holding Murray so, he said:

> Ld George, yu cant imagine, nor I cant expresse to yu how acknowledging I am of all the services yu have rendered me, but this will Crown all. You'll restore the King by it, you'l deliver our poor Contry from Slevery, you'l have all the honr & glory of it, it is your own work, it is yu imagined it, & be assured, Dr Ld George, that the King nor I will never forget it. I speake to yu my Dr Lord George (the prince sqweesing him) from the bottom of my soul, & I am sure it is to yu we'l owe all, so Blesse yu.[46]

Prince Charles had an instinct for what was required of him at critical moments, and these words were calculated both to cut away the bad feeling which had grown between them, and to ensure Murray was marching off in the right frame of mind. But Murray 'never dained to answer one word,' perhaps not trusting in himself to choose the right ones, perhaps knowing he did not have them. For 'above a quarter of an hour' the two men walked in this posture, locked together by the prince's embrace. Eventually Charles let go, but continued to walk alongside him. Then, when it was clear that Murray would make no reply, the prince turned aside and took his leave. Lord George 'took of his Bonnet, made a stif bow, & the Prince went off.'[47]

Those who had witnessed the scene were surprised by Murray's coldness, and amongst them was the only man who recorded this affecting scene: John Sullivan. It is possible that it is a fabrication or a literary device designed to cast the two men in their intended roles for the narrative, but the small details in fact give the impression of a remarkable moment that has been lodged in the memory. Sir John MacDonald confirms that he and Sullivan were also at the head of the column, and therefore in a likely position to witness the prince's interview with Lord George.[48]

The prince returned to the rear of the column and as he walked back across the darkened muir, the figures of his soldiers were given an unearthly appearance by the flickering flames of campfires. These decoys of burning heather had been lit to convince the watching sailors that the Jacobite army remained on the high muir.[49] Once again the

Jacobites were misdirecting the attention of their enemy, just as they had done at Prestonpans and Falkirk. The fires would also help to guide in those reinforcements which might yet reach the muir, and a small party was left behind to direct them on along with any stragglers who came in after searching for food.

Leaving the comforting flames behind them, the soldiers set out into the night 'with the greatest pleasure,' hunger and discontent forgotten in the expectation of action.[50] What they were now undertaking was, according to the engraver Robert Strange, who had just completed the plates for the prince's new banknotes, 'worthy even of any of the greatest heroes of antiquity.'[51] The prince's small column set off last, in the wake of the rest of the army, along a minor track heading north-east below the ridge of the muir itself. Maxwell and Daniel both complain that the army did not use the most direct route, the good road across the muir, so evidently it had not been explained that along that road there were too many settlements to maintain secrecy.[52] The prince did not want to suffer the indignity inflicted on the Earl of Loudoun's column at Moy. As the regiments continued along the chosen road, they passed officers from units which had passed before them who had been posted as guides to keep them right.[53] After a short time, Sullivan and Sir John MacDonald appeared at the roadside, mud splashed up their horses' legs. When they spotted the prince, now mounted, they joined him on the road and informed him that Murray had asked them 'not to march with him,' as their mounts were making too much noise.[54]

The road soon became more challenging, as if it 'had scarcely been ever trode by human foot.'[55] The ground was boggy to either side, and the narrow column was squeezed further. Those who inadvertently stepped off the track itself soon found themselves wading through thick mud. Even the horses had difficulty. The road, its surface broken and saturated by the cold wet winter, had by now been churned by thousands of marching feet. As the night progressed, the prince's division began finding men who had fallen behind from regiments further ahead. The column was extending over ever greater length as men concentrated on where they were putting their own feet and less on keeping close to the man ahead. During the march, Charles Edward 'was all night in a continual motion to make every Regimt follow in their ranks, & make the straglers join.'[56] The night was black and cold, but at least it was dry. The march to Nairn combined the darkness, poor pathway and boggy ground of the march through the Tranent Meadows in September, with the far greater length of the march from Bannockburn to Falkirk in January. There were more than 8 long and difficult miles to cross on this unforgiving road, at the end of which lay either victory or defeat.

It was impossible for the individual soldiers to gauge how much progress they had made or how much time had passed, but there was little time to think on it as they focused on their footings. Gaps had opened up at irregular intervals, and the prince was amongst the officers and aides encouraging others to speed up or slow down as required to keep the column together. After several hours, Colonel Henry Ker emerged out of the darkness on horseback, passing down the line 'to give orders to the respective officers to order their men to make the attack sword in hand.'[57] Prince Charles was now riding with the Fitzjames Horse, the Franco-Irish heavy cavalry who wore armoured breastplates under their scarlet coats. He greeted his aide enthusiastically before sending him back up the line to assure Lord George that his order had been passed down to the rearmost units. The instruction sent an organic shiver of anticipation through the column, although they were barely halfway towards the destination.

But shortly afterwards came Donald Cameron of Lochiel, his boots heavy with mud and a warm red and black plaid wound tightly across his chest and shoulders. When he found the prince, he gave a very different message from Murray: 'he did not think proper to continu his march, because he cou'd never be strong enough for them, & besides it would be day.'[58] On the far side of Kilravock Castle, where the road entered the eerie black of a thick wood, Lord George had paused and assembled some of his officers. Ker, returning from the rear, had found him there 'deliberateing whether or not they should proceed, as they had about four miles to go'.[59] Those who were growing ever more concerned about the slow progress of the column began to suspect they would never reach the objective before daybreak. The choice of Lochiel to carry back these concerns shows that the message was intended to have weight. But Charles Edward was aghast and ordered Lochiel 'to tel 'em obsolutely to go on.'[60] Maxwell confirms that the prince sent 'positive orders to that purpose.'[61]

The prince continued to push on his men, who now entered the black chasm of the Kilravock woods. The difficulty of keeping the track in such an environment became ever greater, and it was critical that units held together to avoid confusion. In the early hours of the new day, Charles sent forward to check in with Murray, only to hear that the latter 'began to be missing; notwithstanding the Prince's Aides-de-Camp in riding from rank to rank asking For God's Sake, what has become of His Lordship'.[62] Anxiety began to grow, but surely it was just that too great a gap had opened up. Eventually, John Hay of Restalrig came riding hard along the line and declared to Prince Charles that 'unless he came to the front and ordered Lord George Murray to go on, nothing could be done': the prince rode forward 'pretty fast'.[63]

The prince reached the Duke of Perth at the end of the central division and fumed at the impossibility of reaching Murray, but their columns continued forward towards the enemy. Eventually, with the sky now turning from deepest black to darkest blue, the army halted 'on the brink' of reaching their destination.[64] They were close enough to hear the activity of the enemy's camp stirring. With Murray out of contact, it was unclear whether he was in position to launch the attack, and time was now desperately short. Eventually, breathlessly, confirmation was brought in that the vanguard had at last been located: 'Ld George had taken his party, & changed his march'.[65]

Convinced that the plan was doomed to fail, having covered too little ground in too long a time, Murray had turned his column off the track and begun to retreat. He turned his men off the moor road and onto the main route back, meaning that his motion was not detected by Perth's column which he presumably assumed would simply follow his wake. But Murray had progressed quicker than those behind, who had lost contact with him. The prince, 'incensed beyond expression at a retreat begun in direct contradiction to his inclination and express orders,' and declared he had been betrayed. He was overwhelmed with emotion, alternating rapidly between rage and despair.

Perth and Sullivan rode off to find Murray and turn him about, and when the latter saw the adjutant general he scoffed that 'he has nothing to say to him in particular, yt there was not a man there but had more to lose than him.'[66] There was an emotional exchange, Sullivan declaring he had only his life and honour to lose, and repeated the prince's direct orders. Victory or defeat for their cause was in Murray's hands, he declared on his master's behalf. Murray lost his temper and swore, and an officer of the Atholl Brigade shouted an insult against Sullivan's courage. Then Lord George ordered the march resumed and stomped off along the road. According to Sullivan, the whole scene was witnessed by Perth, his brother Lord John Drummond, Cameron of Lochiel and his brother Archibald, and James Hepburn of Keith. The latter, who had once escorted the prince into Holyroodhouse, 'took Sullivan in his Armes, bathed him with his tears, praying him to make another attempt on Ld George.'[67] John Hume, who was diligent in gathering evidence for his history, reports that Hepburn too had urged Murray not to retreat, supported by Johnstone.[68] But seeing there was nothing to be done, the Duke of Perth drew Sullivan away from the retreating column and spurred back towards the prince. By the time they reached him, the sky was lightening ever clearer. The coming dawn confirmed what the drum calls had warned, that Cumberland's army was already rousing and could no longer be attacked. 'We saw, as it were before us, the glorious prize; but we durst not encounter it.'[69]

The retreat back to Drummossie Muir was a shorter and easier affair than the march out had been, as the army could now use the main Inverness road and could see where it was going. There was, however, a pall of bitter disappointment draped over the column which drained the soldiers of their last reserves. As they came to the muir some began to drop out, slumping down to sleep in whatever sheltered nook they could find. They 'lay down to rest or went in quest of something to eat, according as weariness or hunger was most severely felt.'[70] Robert Strange did not even make it that far, taking sanctuary in a nearby barn.

When Charles Edward reached the muir, having recovered his composure enough to grasp the needs of his men, he made to press on to Inverness so that he could personally 'get up what provisions were there'.[71] But the Duke of Perth drew him back, sending an officer of the Fitzjames to attend to that duty. The prince gave orders to distribute whatever biscuit could be found and to 'kill Cows, wch the Prince wou'd give bills for.'[72] By the time the prince himself could finally turn to rest, it was full daylight.

The Young Chevalier rode wearily along the long straight avenue towards Culloden House, its neatly wooded parks stretching out on either side of the driveway. The unadorned simplicity of the main house, three storeys of large glazed windows flanked by two tower wings which projected slightly forward of the main façade, was topped with decorative battlements and a steepled belfry. It was a familiar sight to the prince, who had used the house intermittently as his headquarters in recent weeks. Dismounting, he entered the house and was given 'some bread and whiskie'.[73] Hot chocolate was offered too, for it had been a cold and trying night.[74] The house was full of officers, each of whom 'lay'd himself down where he Could, some on beds, others on tables, Chairs & on the floors, for the fatigue and the hunger had been felt as much amongst the officers as Soldiers.'[75] Even the most senior could not muster the energy for a consultation or a council. They all 'stared at one another with amazement; every body looked sullen and dejected.'[76] The enormity of the danger weighed heavy over the company.

When the prince took Murray to task – 'without the least anger', according to Sullivan – the latter blamed Lochiel for the decision to turn about. Lochiel was summoned and contradicted Murray's account hotly. Prince Charles ended the discussion, seeing that no good could come of deepening the wounds now. He climbed the stairs to his chamber and, without removing his boots, he dropped onto his bed. The posts were hung with fine tartan, a tight set of red, blue and yellow. Despite the thoughts and fears which tried to crowd into his head, the Chevalier fell instantly to sleep.

It was barely two hours before the prince awoke, at around 8.00 am on Wednesday 16 April 1746. The whole house was rousing and the noisiness of its motions indicated the urgency of its cause. One of Lochiel's men had fallen asleep on the roadside during the retreat, waking by the sounds of an approaching army. The Duke of Cumberland had set his men early into motion, well aware that his opponents could not yet muster their whole strength, and eager for a general engagement if they proved rash enough to offer one.[77] The sleepy Cameron, rapidly restored to his senses, flew towards Culloden with the warning. Robert Strange was woken in his barn by his hostess. He and his comrades mounted quickly and, on reaching the road, they had clearly seen the scarlet coats and black mounts of Cumberland's vanguard.[78] By the time they reached Culloden, the prince was already in motion upon the muir.

As soon as he received word of the enemy's advance, Prince Charles had ordered the pipers and drummers to call their assemblies. Officers and aides dispersed to raise the alarm and rouse their scattered men, some of whom continued to sleep throughout the gathering storm. In Inverness itself, Captain James Johnstone had finally found a bed and 'was on the point of stretching myself between the sheets' when the trumpets of the Fitzjames Horse called him back to arms. He rode back to Culloden with his 'eyes half shut'.[79] There, as they tried to shake off that weariness, the Jacobites were 'standing in clusters; and stragglers in small numbers were coming up from all quarters.'[80] Their colours flapped suddenly as a cold gust whipped them up. It was a 'dark, misty, rainy' morning, full of foreboding, and they all seemed to sense it.[81] 'Every man kept the best countenance he cou'd,' recalled John Sullivan sadly, 'it was gloriouse to fall with a falling state.'[82]

Prince Charles rode onto the muir with Lochiel's Regiment. From the faces of the clansmen, he knew what was needed of him: 'not the least concern appear'd on his face; he has yt talent superiorly, in the greatest concern or denger, its then he appears most cheerful & harty'.[83] Charles knew they were watching him, looking to him for signs that they were right to be afraid. While Sullivan set about ordering the battle line, the prince ensured he was visible and encouraging, calling out to some of the soldiers, 'here they are coming, my lads, we'l soon be wth them. They don't forget Glads-mur, nor Falkirk, & yu have the same Armes & swords.'[84] Other officers followed his lead: 'the Prince, the Duke of Perth, the Earl of Kilmarnock, Lord Ogilvy, and several other Highland and Lowland Chiefs, rode from rank to rank, animating and encouraging the soldiers by well-adapted harangues.'[85] But while their efforts succeeded in stiffening their men, the officers knew their situation was desperate. Even Sullivan admits that 'the Prince in the bottom had no great hopes.'[86] But the army was now in little state to make an orderly retreat, and to do so would probably see its break up as assuredly as a defeat. There was, from Charles Edward Stuart's perspective, no alternative to the fight.

Others, of course, disagreed. Reinforcements – whole regiments, as well as returning stragglers – were 'hourly expected,' notably Cluny's MacPhersons and Lord Cromarty's men. The latter would never arrive, no matter how long the army was waiting, though no word had yet arrived of their defeat at Littleferry.[87] Given the exhaustion of the army and this expected support, Lord George Murray advocated for a further retreat. He again argued for a position near Daviot, 'on the high ground behind the plain, having his left supported by the ruins of the castle where he could place his cannon to advantage.'[88] But this site had already been evaluated as unsuitable, forcing a defensive battle against an enemy with superior firepower.[89] Besides, the exhausted army would have had to retreat almost 3 more miles and cross the Nairn before redeploying and hoping that Cumberland obliged them with an engagement, rather than simply seizing Inverness and waiting for the Jacobite logistical crisis to force their dispersal. Even Elcho acknowledged 'it was not possible.'[90]

Instead, the Jacobite army formed for battle across the open muir, to the west of the intended position in which Sullivan had drawn them up the previous day. The choice of this new position was largely accidental, determined by the dispersal of most of the men in the western area of the muir, 'among the woods' around the headquarters at Culloden, and toward Inverness.[91] Colonel Ker, ever so reliable, was sent forward to observe the approach of the enemy, which he remembered as 'marching in three columns, with their cavalry on their left.'[92] Behind him, the Jacobite army deployed into the order of battle from the previous day, which at least meant that 'every corps knew its post and went straight to it, without waiting for fresh orders.'[93] This, however, reopened an old wound of which James Maxwell groaned: 'I cannot help observing that nothing could be more unreasonable than a dispute of that kind.'[94]

The previous day, Murray had asked that the Atholl Brigade be given the position of honour on the right. This would be the first time that these men had been posted on the front line, and remarks had been made about the comparatively low levels of risk they had been exposed to as a result.[95] As these were Murray's own men to whom he was greatly attached, he asserted his rank. The position on the right, however, was also claimed by Lochiel's men and, by an even more ancient privilege, by the Clan Donald. The issue had been raised at Prestonpans and the Camerons had conceded, but now Murray was cutting across both. The prince, who preferred not to intervene in clan matters directly, had reluctantly given way to Lord George. He had then received a delegation from the three main Clan Donald commanders. Lochgarry recalled how Prince Charles had 'intreated us for his sake we wou'd not dispute it, as he had already agreed'.[96] And while there was inevitably much grumbling about it amongst the MacDonalds, their discontent was certainly not the cause, as is commonly believed, of their failure to charge home in the coming battle. Sir John MacDonald asked some of the officers on the left and they confirmed 'they would fight wherever they were placed.'[97]

Now, as Sullivan was busy arranging the Jacobite front, Lord George rode across to him and declared 'he must change the order of battle, yt his Regimt had the right yesterday.'[98] The flustered Irishman gasped that they could not possibly change positions in the face of the approaching enemy, which Murray certainly knew already. He was just being provocative. More importantly, Lord George then protested that the ground ahead of the army had not been fully reconnoitred, which was true to the point that it had been reassessed now that it was to become the field of battle. The key features were, however, familiar enough, as this ground had lain immediately behind the previous Jacobite position.

Sullivan edged his horse forward and pointed to the features ahead: 'Yu see yt Park before you which continues to the river wth a wall of six foot high,' he said, '& them houses near it wch yu can fill wth men, & pierce the walls, yt is your right.'[99] This was Culwhiniac, a long double enclosure, the lower part of which dropped all the way down to the Nairn. The fields immediately to either side of its stone walls were cultivated, with the small farm settlement of Culchunaig standing off the enclosure's north-western corner – the 'houses' referred to by Sullivan. Close to the farm, a small burn cut a hollow as it drained down from the muir into the river. Beyond Culwhiniac was a horseshoe-shaped enclosure formed of a lower turf wall, open on its north-eastern side, which projected forward on the muir. This was the Leanach enclosure, and the low thatched roofs of a small settlement beyond it could also just be discerned.

Sullivan turned in his saddle and pointed across to the other side of the muir towards Culloden estate. There, perimeter walls enclosed two open parks and, on their north side, a plantation of woodland reaching up the avenue which approached the house from the west. 'Yu see this Park here is to be our left, & both in a direct ligne. If there be not ground enough, we'l make use of the Parks Il warrant yu my Ld,' says Sullivan, 'the horse wont come to yu there.'[100] Beyond the Culloden Park walls, the muir was watered by the forks of the Red Burn, creating an area of wet marshland which, it might be hoped, would combine with the long walls beyond them to prevent the Jacobite left from being outflanked. The Inverness-Nairn road ran across the muir, roughly diagonally from the edge of the Culloden Parks to the little settlement at Leanach. It ran along a subtle ridgeline with the ground sloping on the north-facing side towards the wetland.

After listening to Sullivan's explanation, Murray went off grumbling to attend to the Atholl Brigade on the extreme right. Forming beside them was Lochiel and his Camerons, then the Appin Regiment, the Frasers, MacKintoshes, MacLachlans and Chisholms amongst others, before finally the regiments of Keppoch, Clanranald and Glengarry. As at Falkirk, the second line was formed of mainly Lowland units, in battalion columns rather than a continuous line, ready to move forward in support of the front. The regular soldiers were split, the Irish Picquets behind the left and the Ecossois behind the right. The cavalry squadrons formed a final reserve, Strathallan's and Bagot's on the left, Elcho's and the Fitzjames' troopers on the right. In total there were about 5,500 men, far more than at Prestonpans but far fewer than Falkirk. For the first time, however, the Jacobite artillery was also deployed on the battlefield: twelve guns arranged in three batteries. Murray commanded the right, Drummond the centre and Perth the left. An icy rain was now falling, turning to sleet as a building wind began to gust it into the faces of the waiting Jacobites.

As the Jacobite army settled into its lines, the Duke of Cumberland's columns came into full view across the muir. A slow, deliberate and intimidating sight, the redcoat columns spread with precision into their battle-lines. They formed three continuous lines stretching out from the left of the road, a dark mass of cavalry advancing steadily towards Culwhiniac and the Jacobite right. Observing the enemy's lines, comprising almost 8,000 men, 'the Prince sent Sullivan' to Lord George. He advised that the flank be secured by garrisoning the houses at Culchunaig but, according to Sullivan, Murray just 'asked him huffingly if he commanded.'[101] Seeing the cavalry continuing towards the lower enclosure 'wch walls were not so high,' the two did, however, agree that two of the Gordon battalions (Stoneywood's and Avochie's) should be brought out of the second line to hold the farmstead to 'guard against any attempts that might be made on that side.'[102]

Confident that all was in hand on the right, Sullivan rode along the line to ensure everything was in order. As he did so, the line suddenly started shifting. Cumberland noticed it too, reporting that he perceived 'the Rebels at some distance making a motion towards us on the left,' and for a moment he wondered whether to expect a sudden advance.[103] Sullivan was momentarily confused, pulling up his horse as officers all along the line began shouting 'Close, close!' He turned back along the line and found 'intervals yt he had not seen before,' breaking the integrity of the front line.[104] Riding hard, he found the cause of the problem was a sudden 'changemt' in the formation of the Atholl Brigade, who had redeployed into columns of double depth. The result was, naturally enough, that the brigade took up a far narrower frontage than before, and the whole front line was now shogging to try and fill the gaps. Sullivan protested with Murray, but the latter 'wont hear him nor even answer.'[105] He could at least have taken the time to explain the reasoning of the change, which would allow his brigade to pass around the edge of the Leanach enclosure during the expected charge. Getting no help from Lord George, however, Sullivan instead rode back to the prince.

Charles Edward was in the centre-rear with Kilmarnock's Footguards, who 'had the Royal Standard', and now after a hurried consultation with his adjutant general, he set about redeploying his second line to solve the problems in his first.[106] The shift towards the right had opened a gap between the Glengarry Regiment and the park walls, leaving the flank hanging open and vulnerable. Sullivan set off to plug the gap with the Duke of Perth's and Glenbucket's regiments, while the prince himself led John Roy Stuart's men up into the front line between the Frasers and the Appin Regiment. The move brought him into the first position identified as 'ARPC' (Altesse Royale le Prince Charles) on an anonymous French officer's plan of the battle. It gave Charles the chance to further encourage the troops, assuring them that the cause depended on their boldness and reminding them not to 'amuse themselves in fireing' but to strike hard and fast.[107]

From his position just to the right of the road, Prince Charles had a clear view out across the muir. He looked out across the dark open heath towards the British army's advancing line. Cumberland had previously paused, waiting for the expected assault, but when the Jacobites remained in their place he had advanced again towards contact. To the prince, as to all his men, the long line of disciplined regulars was an intimidating sight, gaitered knees showing as brighter flashes as they rose and fell with the soldiers' steps, brick-red coats with their lapels buttoned-over and their skirt tails unhooked. 'They made a very good appearance,' noted James Maxwell of Kirkconnell.[108] The sleet stung Charles Edward's face as he watched them, thin grey veils of bitter water rolling between the two armies, bringing with them the rhythmic hum of the distant drummers. But the prince forced himself to remember, the Jacobites had beaten these men before.

Then the drums stopped. The legs stopped rising. There was a brief moment of quiet, just the background hissing of the icy rain and the muted barks of passing orders. The British line began to extend out at its right-hand end to the left from the Jacobite viewpoint, as Cumberland thinned down his third line to extend his frontage. Cobham's and Kingston's Dragoons now appeared on their extreme flank, facing over the boggy grounds around the Red Burn. And along intervals across the whole British front, the Jacobites could now see the grey carriages of the enemy cannon being wheeled up into their positions by the dark-coated figures of the Royal Artillery.

The prince's attention was snatched away by a hoarse cry from behind him, the Gaelic words lost on the wind but the defiant sentiment ringing clear. It triggered a cheer, which swelled into a roar as it spilled down the line in all directions. Across the muir, the redcoats answered with a cheer of their own, 'and there was a great many huzzahs pass'd on all sides.'[109] The prince now retired through the front line and rode towards a new post in the rear to the left of the centre, where he would have a good view of any threat to that flank from the enemy's extending line and easily direct what remained of the second line forward as required. He sent Sullivan off to the right, where the Jacobites were already being stretched thinly.

A large body of horse, commanded by Henry Hawley, was busy breaking through the far wall of Culwhiniac. Behind, Captain Colin Campbell of Ballimore was ready to push a company of Loudoun's Highlanders and three of the Argyll Militia into the enclosure. Sullivan reached the right with orders for Murray to advance immediately, and pointed out that 'now is the time to have troops in thee Park yt will take the horse in flanck when yu are marching.' But Murray, who had clearly taken to blanking Sullivan on all occasions, 'answered him no more then if he spook to a Stone.'[110] Johnstone, usually Murray's most ardent defender, says that the prince himself 'sent his aide-de-camp six or seven times, ordering Lord George to take possession' of the enclosure. But his orders were ignored, and Johnstone's criticism is that the prince should then have done it himself, rather than relying on Murray.[111] Hawley's men continued casting down the walls unimpeded, closely watched by the two Gordon battalions.

The first blast of battle thundered from the Jacobite right where the Jacobite battery opened fire on a small enemy patrol scouting towards them: 'the Princes Cannon began to fire first, and presently after they fir'd theirs.'[112] Within moments, both lines had erupted with smoke and fire. The soldiers felt the shuddering power through their legs as the guns fired, pumping orange flashes into the thickening pall of powder smoke. Most Jacobites could not see the effect of their own guns as they were firing into the smoke of the enemy's. But they saw, heard and felt the thumping of the iron balls ripping into the ground before them or whipping with a percussive hum above their heads. The sodden ground served to absorb the force of those that fell short, the gunners unable to skip the balls into the lines while the ground was so wet. Compensating, successive rounds flew over the front line without impact. Nevertheless, as the cannonade continued there came the sickening sounds of bodies ripped backwards like ragdolls, shrieks and cries cutting through above the thunder. As if the sound of the cannonade deterred the very heavens themselves, the rain finally ceased to fall. It was 1.00 pm.

The artillery duel was a new challenge for the Jacobite artillery. James Grante, who had served them so well previously, had been badly wounded at Fort William. Captain John Finlayson of Edinburgh was in command, and his centre battery was proving the most efficient. Over on the left, however, were the inexperienced gun crews drawn from the clansmen, the battery 'discontinued almost as soon as it began.'[113] On the right, where the firing had begun, the 'first volley occasioned some disorder in the left of the enemy, which was immediately repaired.'[114] But the Jacobite crews simply could not compete with the Royal Artillery for speed and effectiveness, the British guns being 'admirably well served.'[115] Along the Jacobite front, casualties were in their dozens rather than their hundreds, but an artillery bombardment is dreadful to endure and the psychological impact was huge. Some of the clansmen 'threw themselves down flatt upon the Ground' rather than stand waiting for a death they could not see coming.[116]

The cannon balls which cleared the Jacobite front line began to fall amongst the cavalry troopers behind them. John Daniel, clutching the captured green guidon of Gardiner's Dragoons, thought 'the whole fury of the enemy's Artillery seemed to be directed against us in the rear, as if they had noticed where the prince was.'[117] One of Prince Charles' grooms, 'scarcely thirty yards behind him, was killed.'[118] This is probably the same groom as Sullivan recalls as being killed later in the action, his head taken by a cannonball.[119] The prince's aides urged him to move to a less prominent position, but 'this he refused to do'.[120] As a ball struck the soft ground, 'Charles had his face bespattered with dirt.'[121]

But Balmerino's Lifeguards, clustered about their prince, were suffering casualties amongst both the men and the horses. Trooper Austin, 'a very worthy, pleasant fellow,' felt his horse suddenly slump beneath him. 'I have lost my lady!' he cried, turning to see 'one of her hind legs was shot, and hanging by the skin.' Austin managed to limp his horse out of the ranks as he dismounted, after which his mare finally crashed to the ground. Without any further word, 'he took his gun and pistols out of the holsters' and strode forward to join the infantry ranks ahead of him. Austin's comrades never saw him again.[122] Prince Charles watched these scenes with mounting discomfort, being quite unlike any of his other battlefield experiences. Eventually, the prince drew his escort off towards the right in search of a position where they were better screened from the artillery. But the criteria for such a post made it an unsuitable command position for the prince, however, so 'he himself, with his aides-de-camp, rode along the line towards the right, animating the soldiers.'[123] John Daniel was ordered back to the first position, however, lest the sight of his standard moving 'might induce others to follow.'[124]

Moving towards the right, Prince Charles was able to better comprehend the situation on the extreme flank where Hawley's cavalry was now a significant threat. They had by now broken through the near side of the enclosures and were endangering the Jacobite rear. The prince observed their position, on low ground with their backs to the river, and noted also the two Gordon battalions beside Culchunaig ready to flank them with fire should they advance. Murray had also moved up the cavalry, Elcho's and Fitzjames', who were facing down Hawley's brigade. If few in number, these men were the finest sight the Jacobite cavalry could offer, being both uniformed and well-equipped squadrons. With the ravine of a burn to their left and the enclosure walls to their right, Hawley's men took pause. For the time being, it seemed, the flank was safe.

Now was the time to attack, and Charles Edward again 'sent orders to Lord George to march to the enemy.'[125] Young Lachlan MacLachlan, who had served as one of the prince's aides since Prestonpans, was struck by a cannonball while carrying the message. When the prince tried again, he sent Walter Stapleton, but Murray seemed immoveable.[126] Colonel Ker was now sent to the left with the order for the Duke of Perth to advance as well. Crucially, Perth was not to wait for Murray to move on as the left had far more ground to cover before reaching the enemy. Although the Jacobites had aligned on the two park walls, Cumberland's army had not. As a result, the prince's army was formed obliquely across the latter's front. By the time Ker rode along the line with the order to advance, the men were crying 'aloud to be led on'.[127] To the waiting clansmen, it must have felt like an eternity since the artillery had first begun to play upon them, giving rise to stories that the artillery were firing for up to an hour, but in truth it been barely ten minutes.[128]

The whole front line lurched forward. The motion, viewed from the prince's position behind it, had a strangely organic appearance. At intervals, fractions apart, the twin crack of a musket spat out at locations along the frontage. Forward they marched, the blood coursing hot through numbed limbs and pounding loud in their ears as each man found the courage to keep stepping forwards towards the wall of fire and sound which now stood before them. The roaring rhythm of the red-coated platoons poured out 'as regular & as nurrished a fire' as could be expected of this veteran, professional army.[129] The Jacobites moved up still until, suddenly, 'we halt & fire.'[130] The thunder of volleys close thumped into the air from both left, right and centre. The smoke shrouded thick about them, enveloped them as they moved ahead, then hung over the ground where their long ranks had stood just moments before. The main fire delivered and the front surged on towards the enemy.

Cumberland watched as the Jacobites 'came running on in their wild manner'.[131] The grey guns switched from ball to canister and grape, a far more deadly foe than the long-distance musket volleys. The Highlanders rushed ahead 'in a stooping Posture, with their Targets in their left Hand, covering their Head and Breast, and their glittering Swords in their right... making a frightful Huzza.'[132] The roar of the Highlanders began a savage and meaningless howl, a show of terrifying defiance and a desperate search for the courage to endure. Out on the Jacobite left, where the distance towards the enemy was furthest, the boggy ground slowed their progress and prolonged their exposure to the enemy's fire. They were further deterred from charging fully by the presence of the dragoons, 'imagining they would be flank'd' at the critical moment.[133] The Duke of Perth ran over to Clanranald and seized hold of their colours, crying that 'from that day forth he'l call himself MccDonel if they gain the day.'[134] Keppoch was struck down beneath the enemy's fire, as was his brother Archibald. Their momentum spent, the men on the left 'came down three several time within a hundred yards of our men, fireing their Pistols and brandishin their Swords,' but could not be induced to close.[135]

In the centre, the firmer ground of the roadway made the going easier, and as the charging clansmen subconsciously followed its path they were funnelled towards the enemy's left, merging with their own right-hand division as they did. The result was a seething mass of men surging forward in such a way that none could give fire. Campbell of Ballimore had already occupied the upper Culwhiniac enclosure, which Sullivan had repeatedly asked to be defended, and the Highlanders there gave a galling fire into the flank of the Atholl Brigade as it charged. The massed attack on the Jacobite right surged past the walls and on past the turf walls of the Leanach enclosure, an unmissable target but one with terrifying momentum.

The clansmen charged forwards with their eyes down, shrouded in smoke and noise and carried onwards by the surging mass about them. Like a single body it shook and surged with the impacts of crashing fire, rolling over the fallen bodies of their comrades towards the intensifying volleys. Donald Cameron of Lochiel fell, canister fragments whipping about him, lead balls punching through his targe, his legs ripped from under him. Then a new and terrifying sound: the ear-splitting blast of mortar shells exploding close at hand, right in the heart of the dense formation, flaying men with great lumps of ragged iron. The death was all around and all that could be done was to push forwards. Then, with the noise swelling to a crescendo, the Jacobite right smashed like a wave onto the British line.

All command now was gone, the battle shrinking to the individual struggles of those who had reached the line. There was little chance to duel: bayonet tips were received on the targe and turned, smashing the lethal point aside to expose the breast and shoulders of the soldiers beyond; broadswords smashed down to slash at faces, necks, wool and leather. Others were simply driven forwards by the momentum behind them, the bayonets lunging through coats, snagging in the thick folds of tartan plaids; bodies tumbling over bodies and striking the ground in a desperate writhing thump of groping hands, unseen blades, stamping feet. The horror, funnelled mainly onto Barrell's Regiment, was irresistible. The line broke, the Jacobites surged through. But as with the wave breaking around the rocks, the charge had lost much of its force in its success, and those who pierced through faced only the sudden death offered by Cumberland's second line. The break-out was contained and while countless clansmen had fallen before the enemy's guns, 'many of the Highlanders were kill'd with bayonets.'[136]

Prince Charles looked on, able to see all this only in his mind as the front line engaged. The arcing smoke trails of the mortar shells hung over the right, which was utterly lost in the smoke and confusion of the assault. He had committed what remained of the second line – Kilmarnock's and the French, supported by the tiny squadrons of Strathallan and the Hussars – in direct support of the first. Its tactical columns advanced 'in good order' to back up the main charge.[137] These men crossed a field already littered with dead and wounded men; they kept their eyes high and their courage tight. But they marched into a turning tide: 'the flight began to become general, which spread from the right to the left of our army with the rapidity of lightning. What a spectacle of horror!'[138]

The British left had been buckled and pierced, but timely reinforcement ensured it had not shattered. Repulsed, the Jacobites had nowhere to go but back, and as they turned to flee the cannon and muskets resumed their merciless work. Ballimore's men poured in fire from the safety of the enclosures, and the battle was now a fight for survival rather than for victory. Lord George Murray was thrown from his horse, which 'reared and plunged so much that I thought he was wounded'.[139] He saw that Ecossois were up at hand, and although no such orders were needed, he urged them to cover the retreating Highlanders, who were now streaming back across the muir. They 'gave and received Several fires' and then began a fighting withdrawal as the British army began its steady advance.[140]

William Drummond, Viscount Strathallan, had his horse shot under him as he determined to hold his ground against them. He would be put to death as the line passed over him. John Daniel, 'after receiving a slight grazing ball on my left arm,' came upon Lord John Drummond and was persuaded the battle was lost. On the centre left, the Clan Donald regiments disengaged under the covering fire of both the Irish Picquets and a gallant Jacobite cannon nestled in the angle of the Culloden Park walls. Meanwhile, Hawley's cavalry had still failed to break through behind the Jacobite right, where the men of the north-east – Ogilvie's, Avochie's and Stoneywood's – had held them off with the support of the Lifeguards and Fitzjames' horse. But as the Jacobite line here shadowed Hawley's attempt to flank them, they were exposing their own backs to the advancing redcoat infantry who were following up their success against the main line. The window of opportunity for escape was narrowing.

Charles Edward Stuart was now riding amongst his fleeing men, 'endeavouring to rally the soldiers'.[141] His efforts at Falkirk during a similar, if more limited, crisis had succeeded, but now the sense of defeat was too general to be turned around. 'Horror and dismay were painted in every countenance,' recalled Robert Strange.[142] The prince's mount was 'shot in the Shoulder, kicks & cappors, he's obliged to change horses.'[143] Sullivan, who had been over towards the left during the main attack, now galloped hard over to Captain Shea of Fitzjames' and declared with despair cracking his voice: 'yu see all is going to pot. Yu can be of no great succor, so before a general deroute wch will soon be, Seize upon the Prince & take him off.'[144] By now the danger to Charles' life was becoming acute, his army disintegrating all around him. On the far left, Cobham's and Kingston's horse were moving forward to threaten the retreat of the Clan Donald, with nothing to stop them sweeping up across the muir. On the far right, the Lowlanders were now barely containing Hawley, and, in fact, one body of horse had worked around them near Culchunaig; the Royal Ecossois were fighting a desperate action to force their way free of them after covering the rout of the right. But the prince refused to retire, vowing to Sullivan that 'they wont take me alive.'[145]

> Sullivan prays him to look behind him, & yt he'd see the whole moor cover'd wth men yt were going off & yt half the Army was away. The Prince look's, sees it is true, every body presses him, in short he retirs, but does not go far, comes back again, see this Regimt of horse very near our left wch were the McDonnels yt were quit uncover'd, sees it is time & retirs. Sullivan goes to Shea & tells him to follow the Prince, yt if yt Regimnt of horse or Dragons… follow'd him, yt at least he cou'd by standing ferm a little give him time to escape.[146]

As the prince was finally crowded away from the field, yielding at last to a sense of utter powerlessness, Sullivan remained on the field. His chief concern was the threat from the cavalry on the left, and he sent Stapleton and the Picquets to extract the MacDonalds. Their disciplined volleys pushed back the threatening horse, and these brave soldiers fought their way across to the park walls. Stapleton himself was wounded as they did. As uniformed French regulars, the Picquets now needed to hold out only so long as their service could aid the escape of others. Their supporting gun would be silenced by mortars, and they would surrender as prisoners of war. On the opposite end of the line, their comrades from the Royal Ecossois fought hard to avoid complete destruction, their lieutenant colonel Lewis Drummond being wounded. In time they too were able to surrender. The Lowland battalions holding back Hawley were able to retire more or less intact, facing about several times so that the enemy horse 'durst neither attack nor pass'.[147] They left behind a field covered with up to 1,500 Jacobite casualties, although the toll would rise. Cumberland had won his victory at a cost of fifty killed outright and 259 wounded, more than the Jacobites had ever suffered in their own successes but with a far more decisive result.

Defeated, the Young Chevalier and his small escort rode south to the River Nairn where Sullivan was able to join him. Sir Thomas Sheridan was still with him, as were John Hay, Felix O'Neill, Allan MacDonald and Alexander MacLeod of Muiravonside. None of these 'knew the country well,' and no provision had been made for where the army should rendezvous in such an instance. Lochgarry, who had held the Glengarry Regiment together after the loss of Young Glengarry at Falkirk, recalled how he subsequently 'heard his RHs often regrett that a place of rendezvous had not been ordered.'[148] In the immediate term, this meant that the prince had no clear indication of where to go and no source of advice other than Sullivan and Sheridan. Sir John MacDonald had seen them go off, but knew he himself could not endure the difficulties of a retreat into the mountains so he gave himself up.[149] Others fled towards the illusory sanctuary of Inverness, while those who escaped to the south side crossed the Nairn and headed towards Badenoch. These included Lord George Murray, who came upon Cluny's MacPhersons, who were still marching *towards* the battlefield. They helped to cover the retreat and, amongst others, Murray was joined by his brother Tullibardine and the Duke of Perth.[150]

The prince crossed the Nairn at Faillie, where it is spanned by Marshal Wade's simple but charming stone bridge, and a short way beyond this he halted to take stock. As more fugitives began to assemble nearby, the prince consulted those he had with him and decided that, lacking any magazines or depots now to draw upon, it was impossible to hold what remained of the army together in the mountainous Highlands. It seemed a better course for him to seek an urgent crossing to France, where 'he still flattered himself his presence and personal application might prevail with that Court, to grant the succours that had been so long solicited in vain by his agents.'[151] Elcho saw another motive: 'as he had taken it into his head he had been betray'd and particularly by Lord George Murray, he Seemed very diffident of Every body Except the Irish officers.'[152] By contrast, however, when Colonel Ker caught up with the prince, the latter 'inquir'd particularly about Lord George, and... in the presence of all there present desired C K to find him out and to take particular care of him, which 'tis to be presumed he would not have done if he had the least suspicioun of what has been laid to his charge by his enemies.'[153]

After dismissing most of those who had gathered around him, Charles Edward and his small escort continued on a gruelling 18-mile ride heading south-west, parallel with Loch Ness. This brought them to Gorthleck House, which belonged to William Fraser, a relation of Simon, Lord Lovat. After staying his hand too long in the hope of extracting ever greater promises of reward from the prince, the Machiavellian lord had raised his men too late and too few to turn the tide. Lovat was, in fact, staying at Gorthleck and now met Charles for the first time, realising to his horror that the game was over and he had declared for the beaten party. After taking refreshment and a brief rest, the prince's party departed again at midnight. They went without the Fitzjames' troopers, who would be of little use in the mountains and would most assuredly draw unwelcome attention. Their orders were 'if thye met wth a body of the Army to joyn them, if not to give themselves up.'[154] The prince then departed 'disguised like a Servant', after exchanging clothes with their guide, Ned Burke.[155] At around 2.00 am on 17 April, they arrived at the deserted keep of Invergarry Castle where they rested into the afternoon.

It was still unclear what the best course of action might be, and information was scarce. There was a clear hope that part of the army would have assembled at Fort Augustus, as according to O'Neill there *had* been talk of the captured fort being used as a rendezvous site.[156] But on their way to Invergarry the group had waited there without 'finding a soul', and had been obliged to move on.[157] Sullivan was unsure what to advise next, and messengers crossed the Highlands in an attempt to learn the location and mood of the others.

Meanwhile, the principal remnant of the Jacobite army had gathered in the shell of Ruthven Barracks. There, the day after the battle, Lord George Murray wrote a letter to his prince. In it, he set out all his grievances and complaints, beginning with the fact that it 'was highly wrong to have set up the royal standard' without a certain commitment from France.[158] He spat bitter condemnations at Sullivan, whom he wished 'had never got any other charge in the Army than the care of the baggage which,' he added spitefully, 'I have bene told he had been brought up to.' Murray accused Sullivan of cowardice and incompetence, and lambasted John Hay for his logistical incompetence since taking over from Broughton. He ended by resigning his commission.

On 28 April, with Cumberland's patrols penetrating deep into the western Highlands and the Earl of Loudoun returning to the campaign from Skye, Prince Charles sent a last letter to those who remained in the field, which was to be shown to them by Sir Thomas Sheridan. It was dictated to John Hay at Borrodale where the prince had first arrived on the mainland and from which he now expected imminently to depart:

> When I came into this Country, it was my only view to do all in my power for your good and safety. This I will always do as long as life is in me. But alas! I see with grief, I can at present do nothing for you on this side of the water, for the only thing that can now be done, is to defend your selves till the French assist you. If not, to be able to make better terms.
>
> To effectuate this, the only way is to assemble in a body as soon as possible, and then take measures for the best, which you that know the Country are only Judges of. This makes me be of little use here, whereas by my going into France instantly, however dangerous it be, I will certainly engage the French Court either to assist us effectually and powerfully, or at least to procure you such terms as you would not obtain otherwise.
>
> My presence there, I flatter myself, will have more effect to bring this sooner to a determination than any body else,

for several reasons, one of which I will mention here, vizt. It is thought to be a Politick, tho' a false one, of the French Court, not to restore our Master but to keep a continual civil war in this Country, which renders the English government less powerful and, of consequence, themselves more. This is absolutely destroyed by my leaving this Country, which nothing else but this will persuade them that this Play cannot last, and, if not remedied, the Elector wil soon be as despotick as the French King, which I should think will oblige them to a strike the great stroke, which is always in their power, however averse they may have been to it for the time past.

Before leaving off, I must recommend to you that all things should be decided by a Council of all your Chiefs, or, in any of your absence, the next Commander of your several corps, with the assistance of the Duke of Perth and Lord George Murray, who, I am persuaded, will stick by you to the very last.

My departure should be kept as long private and concealed as possible on one pretext or other, which you will fall upon. May the Almighty bless and direct you.

The Young Chevalier had fought his last battle. The conflict, which defined the mission of his life, was over. But he did not yet know it, and retained a desperate hope that he might yet be able to rescue his tattered destiny.

Epilogue

On 10 December 1748, Prince Charles Edward Stuart stepped into his coach for the short drive across the Seine to the opera house at the Palais-Royale. The visit, against the advice of a number of friends and well-wishers who had warned that there were wild rumours circulating, was part of the prince's increasingly tense public relations conflict. For over two years now, he had been waging a futile campaign to revive the military struggle to restore the House of Stuart. But the French court, on whom the Jacobites in Scotland had come to rest all their hopes, had proved just as frustratingly ambivalent as they had since Charles' first arrival in France in 1744. And now, following the Treaty of Aix-la-Chapelle, France was at peace with Great Britain. King Louis wanted Charles gone.

All the prince's hopes of shaming the French into action in the summer of 1746 had failed, not least because it had taken him too long to reach his allies. The vigour and brutality of Cumberland's suppression of the Scottish Highlands had prevented Charles Edward from securing passage in the first critical weeks which followed Culloden, and had turned him and his followers into increasingly desperate fugitives in the heather. It is the part of the Jacobite story which is most fondly remembered today: the humble Highlanders sheltering and aiding their prince, who shared their modest meals and drank their drams in defiance of the savage soldiers who persecuted the land with fire and tyranny. The story of his time with Flora MacDonald is so poignantly affecting that it is better suited to fiction than fact and contributed greatly to his legend.

The many remarkable tales of low-key heroism and loyalty which emerged from this period were painstakingly collated and corroborated by Robert Forbes in the years following the prince's escape. They show the Young Chevalier at his lowest political and military ebb, stripped of all power and material wealth, but at his personal best. He was able to push aside defeat in order to sustain the spirits of his companions; showed courage in the face of the huge physical and mental ordeals of being on the run; and with humility and humour, earned the lasting affection of those who encountered him. Politically, Lochiel found him full of 'all the firmness of purpose that could have been wished of him,' ever sure that his return to France would restore his ability to make good his promises.[1]

But there had been a price paid in the heather too. Sullivan later reported that 'the Prince was in a terrible condition, his legs & thy's cut all over from the bryers; the mitches or flys wch are terrible in yt country devored him, & made him scratch those scares, wch made him appear as if he was cover'd wth ulsers.'[2] Although Neil MacEachain was impressed by Charles Edward's resilient constitution, there were also times when he suffered from 'a bloody flux' which he tried to hide from his companions, becoming 'so low & so peal yt Sullivan was frightend out of his witts'.[3] Food was often scarce and it was common for the fugitives to lie in the landscape exposed to the elements. The weather was often terrible, as it had been for most of the period since the march into England, although when the sun did shine it seemed to restore the prince's strength.

While Prince Charles 'always appeared very gay and cheerful, notwithstanding his crosses and misfortunes,' this disguised a mental anguish which was being suppressed rather than defeated.[4] As always, the prince found it easiest to be engaged and engaging when he had the focus of an immediate action. But while on the run, there were also times of helplessness and dependency. There were frequent and fruitless hours spent going over and over the failure of the campaign, against the backdrop not only of the party's own dangers but the constant bad news of the dreadful situation across the Highlands. More damaging in the long term was the increasing reliance on alcohol to push back the darkness: 'He took care to warm his stomach every morning with a hearty bumper of brandy, of which he always drank a vast deal; for he was seen to drink a whole bottle of a day without being in the least concerned.'[5]

Eventually, the Young Chevalier's time as a wanted fugitive had come to an end, and, on 20 September 1746, he had finally found passage out of Scotland. It was a bittersweet moment, a day short of the first anniversary of his victory at Prestonpans. James Johnstone, whose own escape had led him to that very place by then, spent the day on the battlefield: 'the spot furnished me with a most striking picture of the vicissitudes of fortune to which human nature is subject, and I compared my situation in that glorious day – when I discharged the functions of aide-de-camp to the Prince, carrying his orders everywhere and charged with the care of thirteen hundred English prisoners – to my present state, covered with rags in order to escape the scaffold, borne down with trouble and distress.'[6] He too would soon find a ship to safety, to a modest career in the French army in Canada.

When Prince Charles finally reached Roscoff in Brittany, where his ancestor Queen Mary of Scotland had arrived almost 200 years before on her way to marry the future Francis II, he immediately wrote to Paris of his need to see King Louis XV. Despite the delay of almost six months, he remained confident that the cause could be saved. As soon as word reached the French capital, Cardinal Tencin rushed the good news on to Rome: 'Je respire, Le Prince est Sauvé.'[7] King James' unimaginable 'pain of anxiety' was over, and his son was safe at last.[8] Henry Benedict rushed out from Paris to meet his brother and after almost three years, the two Stuart princes were reunited. On 17 October Henry wrote joyfully to their father of his meeting Prince Charles: 'he is not in the least altered since I saw him, except grown somewhat broader and fatter, which is incomprehensible after all the fatigues he has endured. Your Majesty may conceive it better than I can express in writing, the tenderness of our first meeting – those that were present said they never saw the like in their lives, and indeed I defy the whole world another brother so kind and so loving as he is to me.'[9] But already there were worrying signs from the French court: Henry alludes to their desire for secrecy over the prince's plan to come to Paris, and an addendum to his letter confirms that there had been difficulty in arranging an audience with Louis.

Despite the apparent reluctance of the French king or his ministers, it was agreed that Prince Charles would be immediately received if he came unofficially. There was little alternative, for the prince was on his way and attracting considerable attention already as the news spread. Ever since his expedition began, Parisians had been lapping up each new report in the *Gazette*, and the Jacobite agents in the city had helped spin the narrative to ensure that the Young Chevalier now returned as a major celebrity. King Louis made a show of leaving a council meeting to greet the prince at Fontainebleau, expressing his joy to see him safe and well, telling him: 'You have proved that all the great Qualities of the Heroes and Philosophers are united in you; and I hope, that one Day you will receive the Reward of such extraordinary Merit.'[10] As the Queen of France had once been a childhood friend of the prince's mother, there was a genuinely tender response from that quarter, and the prince's first visit went sufficiently well to permit another more official one. This took place ten days later, and must have been a surreal experience for those who took part.

Prince Charles descended the stairs of the castle, which had been prepared for his accommodation, dressed in the finest clothes he had been able to procure since his arrival, which were reported in detail by an eyewitness:

> His Coat was Rose-coloured Velvet, embroidered with Silver, and lined with Silver Tissue; his Waistcoat was a rich Gold Brocade, with a spangled Fringe set on in Scollops; the Cockade in his Hat, and the Buckles of his Shoes, were Diamonds; the George at his Bosom, and the Order of St. Andrew, which he wore also tied by a Piece of green Ribbon to one of the Buttons of his Waistcoat, were prodigiously illustrated with large Brilliants: In fine, he glittered all over like the Star which they tell you appeared at his Nativity.[11]

Outside the castle there were three coaches drawn up to receive the prince and his party, which included both those who had reached France alongside him and those who had found safety sooner. Into the first carriage went the 21-year-old David, Lord Ogilvy, son of the Earl of Airlie. Handsome and dedicated, Ogilvy would receive a senior commission in the French army to support him in exile. Not until 1783 would he return to Scotland, having received a free pardon to do so. Next came 'the venerable Glenbucket', veteran of so many Jacobite campaigns. At 73, however, his fighting days were over. He had escaped Scotland to Norway, and he would live his remaining four years in relative poverty in Paris. George Kelly entered the same coach, now restored to the prince's service after being sent to France after Prestonpans. King James continued to distrust him. He would die in Avignon in 1762. The fourth passenger in this coach was David, Lord Elcho, former commander of the Prince's Lifeguards. His aggressive conduct during the campaign ensured he was specifically excluded from any acts of clemency, and none of his powerful contacts would intervene on his behalf. Increasingly bitter about both this and the prince's inability or unwillingness to repay the money he had contributed to the campaign, Elcho blamed Charles Edward for the cause's failure. He later served in the Fitzjames' and Royal Ecossois regiments, and would die in Paris in 1787.

Prince Charles himself climbed into the second carriage, accompanied by Donald Cameron of Lochiel. Despite his initial reluctance to support an uprising, Lochiel now urged its immediate resumption in order to reverse the desperate situation he had left behind him in Lochaber. Ironically, he and the prince would soon be at odds over how best to achieve it, with Lochiel arguing for a Scottish campaign and Charles Edward insisting nothing could now be done without a French invasion of England. Elcho muttered that the prince 'never ask'd any thing for any of his people by Young Lochyell, who he Gott named to a Regiment.'[12] But Lochiel's new French unit barely got off the ground, and he would die in October 1748 of 'an inflammation within his head.' Accompanying Charles Edward and Lochiel in the carriage was Lord Lewis Gordon, four years younger than the prince, the victor of the Battle of Inverurie. His regiment had done so much at Culloden to cover the flight of others, and eventually Gordon had escaped out of Peterhead. Sadly, he would soon begin to show symptoms of mental decline, and would die at Montreuil at the age of just 30.

The third coach in the cavalcade contained John William Sullivan and a few other gentlemen of the prince's household. Sullivan and the prince had shared an emotional parting in the Highlands, after which he had reached France and spent a great deal of effort in making arrangements for the prince's rescue. He continued to enjoy Charles Edward's confidence and he was knighted for his services. Charles Edward asked Sullivan to write an account of the conflict for King James, although the resulting narrative has sometimes been neglected on account of a residual bias towards Lord George Murray's interpretation of events. The French recognised his military abilities better than subsequent histories, however, and Sullivan returned to their service as a staff officer. He was instrumental in arranging Charles' reunion with Clementina Walkinshaw, who had nursed him at Bannockburn House and later left her home country behind to become the prince's mistress.

John Sullivan seems to have died in around 1760 after returning to the relative obscurity from which he had so suddenly emerged.

Behind the three coaches was a small procession of other Jacobites on horseback. These included John Roy Stuart, veteran of Fontenoy and a loyal friend to the prince. He blamed the prince's failure on the divisions within the army caused by envy and ambition amongst his commanders.[13] An engaging personality, the epitome of the Gaelic soldier-poet, Stuart returned to French military service but would die at Boulogne within a few years. Riding alongside him this day was Dr Archibald Cameron, Lochiel's younger brother, whose tragic destiny was to be the last Jacobite leader to be executed. He was put to death in London in 1753 for his part in the 'stupid' Elibank Plot, which proved to be the prince's final clutch at the straw.[14] Betrayed, the scheme miscarried before it had even got under way. Its failure would leave Charles Edward increasingly isolated, paranoid and despondent.

There were, of course, some obvious absences from this extraordinary parade. Some, like Strathallan and Keppoch, had lost their lives on Culloden field. The Earl of Kilmarnock and Lord Balmerino, John Daniel's commander, had both been beheaded in London after their capture. The Earl of Cromarty had been sentenced with them, but received a rare mercy, thanks to his pregnant wife, and was pardoned. He was reduced to poverty, however, and forbidden from ever returning to Scotland. Lord Lovat was still awaiting his trial, and would not be executed until March 1747. William Murray, Marquis of Tullibardine and Jacobite Duke of Atholl, never made it as far as a trial. Too unwell to ride, his escape from Culloden had been fraught with difficulty and he was captured in Dumbartonshire. Tullibardine, the man who had raised the standard at Glenfinnan, died in the Tower of London on 9 July 1746.

Other Jacobite leaders, like Ewan MacPherson of Cluny, were still in hiding and would, thankfully, survive the storm which had swept away so many others. Tragically, these included amongst their number James Drummond, Duke of Perth, who had achieved in the conflict so much more than had been expected of him. He had proven himself brave, tactful, loyal and competent. Perth had also been fortunate in finding a ship out of Scotland just a few weeks after Culloden, along with his brother and Lord Elcho. But he had contracted a fever on the voyage and, his health badly impacted by the physicality of the campaigning, died before reaching France. Perth was just 33. Drummond had survived, succeeding to his brother's title and returning to French military service. He would also die of a fever, at the age of 30, at the Siege of Bergen-op-Zoom the following year.

John Murray of Broughton, the prince's Secretary of State, had been captured in the Scottish Borders on 27 June. Despite being unwell, Broughton escaped from Culloden but returned to the Highlands when the arrival of French gold at Loch Arkaig provided the brief hope that the war might be resumed. Once that hope proved illusory, he returned south but was captured before he could leave the country. By the time Broughton reached London, the fates of most Jacobite leaders had already been determined, and with that in mind he chose – to the infamy of his name – to turn King's Evidence. His reputation has never recovered, with Lochiel claiming his 'treason now horrifies all Britain', and it has blighted the record of his service to Prince Charles.[15] Although accused of fuelling the division between the prince and Lord George, Broughton had undoubtedly worked hard for the army's success, and the efficiency of the commissariat had collapsed without him prior to the final battle. His efforts to block Lord George's influence could be as easily ascribed to loyal support for the prince's natural authority as to naked personal ambition. But his decision to protect his own interests after the rising's failure has prejudiced the memory of subsequent memorialists, the damage compounded by Sir Walter Scott's colourful expansions. John Murray would live the rest of his life in comparative obscurity, dying in the south of England in 1777.

The most obvious personality missing from the procession in Paris, however, was Lord George Murray. After resigning his commission and dispersing what remained of the army at Ruthven, Murray would endure a long period in hiding before he could reach the sanctuary of the continent towards the end of the year. According to Elcho, 'the Prince talk'd very ill of Lord George' in Paris.[16] In March 1747, after meeting up with Elcho in Venice, Murray travelled to Rome and presented his own version of events to King James. The latter wrote to his son, recommending the simple but significant truth that it was possible for people to disagree with you or fail in their service to you while still being 'men of honour and honesty'. He saw no reason to believe the rumours of betrayal, and while he was right in that assessment, James was also too detached from emotional trauma of the conflict to see its events in the round. Prince Charles protested that a proper examination would identify 'severall demonstrative acts of disobedience, insolency, and creating dissension.'[17] He would later refuse to receive Murray when he came to Paris, and Murray withdrew to the Netherlands and kept his distance.

Murray's *Marches of the Highland Army* was written as a self-defence against the prince's version of events, represented by Sullivan's narrative. His straight-talking style was given support in the memoirs of Elcho and Johnstone, and all three found themselves in print long before Sullivan. History has been largely favourable to Murray, and some interpretations have gone so far as to portray him as an exceptional commander stifled into defeat by the prince and his favourites. This is too far: he was a capable and effective senior officer, whose understanding of war was well suited to leading the Highlanders; he was honest and well-intentioned. But Murray was also disruptive and overbearing, driven by confidence in his own abilities to dismiss the value of others. His strategic instincts were far less sound than his operational effectiveness, and his continuous campaign to undermine Prince Charles' military authority contributed to the rising's ultimate failure as much as his abilities had contributed to its earlier successes. Murray repeatedly observed how much he stood to lose by serving in the prince's army, much to Charles' irritation. Although he would live the rest of his life in exile, dying in the Netherlands in 1760, Lord George Murray's son would later succeed to the title and estates of the Duke of Atholl.

The Jacobite cavalcade in Paris was accompanied by two pages and ten footmen in the livery of the Prince of Wales. It 'made a very grand Appearance' and as a procession of conquered heroes, it must have drawn much curious interest. But in an environment governed by the strictest rules of etiquette and hierarchy, some French courtiers struggled to work out how to address men like Lochiel whose status was not matched by a title.[18] After the arrival of the parade, a fine state dinner was held for the noble Jacobite veterans. It was a mark of honour and a nod to the high public interest their endeavours had garnered. There was also a strong sense around Paris that the government could – should – have done more to help them. Now King Louis 'settled 40,000 livres a Year to be distributed in pensions amongst those that were not placed in Regiments,' providing a vital lifeline to the dispossessed.[19]

But amongst the pageantry of state formality, there was little room for effective diplomacy, and the reception ended without any commitment to support the continuation of the cause.

Prince Charles resorted to putting his needs in writing, appealing to Louis that Scotland 'is on the eve of annihilation, as the English government refuses to distinguish between those who remained loyal to it and those who took up arms for me'.[20] This was making the population more unhappy than ever, more ready to rise. His failure, Charles wrote, was not down to a lack of support or a faulty strategy: 'what I did lack simultaneously was money, supplies, and a handful of regular troops; with but one of these I would today still be master of Scotland and probably the whole of England.' The prince looked back on his three great battles:

> With three thousand regular soldiers, I could have penetrated England immediately after defeating General Cope, and nothing would then have opposed my arrival in London, since the Elector would have been absent and the English troops would have resisted no further.
>
> With adequate supplies, I would have been in a position to pursue General Hawley at the Battle of Falkirk and destroy his entire army, which was the flower of the English troops.
>
> If I had received two months earlier just half of the money that Your Majesty sent me, I would have fought Prince William of Hanover on equal terms, and would surely have beaten him.[21]

How much he had achieved with so little; how much might he yet do if properly resourced. If he would only be given an army of 20,000 men, Charles Edward Stuart could sweep aside his enemies and secure such a victory as would satisfy all the aims of France, as well as the restoration of the House of Stuart.

There was no answer, and the prince grew increasingly frustrated. He protested this coolness in a letter to the king on 14 January 1747: 'the current situation in which I find myself in Paris does not appear to correspond to the goodwill and welcome with which Your Majesty received me at Fontainebleau'.[22] When there was still no response forthcoming, the prince then proposed, 'as I see no evidence that you may employ me at present on the other side of the channel,' he should at least be appointed as an aide-de-camp to the king.[23] This request was declined. A lack of active purpose was always damaging to Charles Edward's state of mind, and he sensed his moment in history slipping away. Then came a hammer-blow. In April 1747 his brother slipped out of Paris without making his farewells, in fact, with an active deception. On reaching Rome, Henry was made a cardinal. Prince Charles immediately understood how poorly the move would play to public opinion in Britain, and he himself was no longer in a position to take the sorts of personal risks which had become his modus. The hopes for a Stuart succession now lay solely on him. Charles was devastated as much by the deception as by the act, and now felt betrayed by his family too. It was like a dagger in his heart, he lamented to his father.

With no obvious outlet for his energies, thwarted in all endeavours but still high in popular esteem, the prince threw himself for the first time into a passionate romance. In August 1747 he began a wild and indiscreet affair with his beautiful cousin Marie Louis de La Tour d'Auvergne, who was both immensely wealthy and well connected. When Marie Louise fell pregnant, Charles was driven to jealousy by her obligation to return to her husband's bed and there were scandalous scenes. The poor child, a boy, was born on 28 July 1748, but the prince was unable, of course, to recognise him. The infant died only a few months later.

By then, Prince Charles' political position was increasingly vulnerable. Disgusted by the attitude of the French government, he had then offended them by courting the Spanish instead. As Charles realised Louis would never give him an army, while 'he did not presently refrain going to Versailles, Fountainbleau, Choisy, or where-ever the Court was: but it was observed, he neither went so frequently, nor staid so long as he had been accustomed.'[24] Nevertheless, 'he appeared more lively, gay and spirituous, than ever,' because he knew as well, now as ever, that the court of public opinion could be just as significant.

> Whenever the young Chevalier appeared in any publick Walks, all the Company followed the Path he took, as impelled by an irresistible Attraction. When he came to the Opera or Comedy, the Attention of the whole Audience was

fixed upon him, regardless of what was presented on the Stage: The Moment of his Entrance into the Box, a general Whisper in his favour ran from one Side of the Theatre to the other; and few of the fair Sex but let fall Tears of mingled Pity and Admiration; while he alone seemed above a Sensibility of his own Misfortunes, and talked to the young Nobility, with whom he was perpetually surrounded, in the same easy, chearful, and affable Manner, he had always done.[25]

In that visible popularity he sought both to pressure the government and to protect himself from it. For the War of the Austrian Succession was drawing to a close, and peace between Britain and France would finally end the prince's hopes of a revived campaign.

On 16 July 1748, to the chagrin of the court, Charles Edward published a protest against the peace negotiations. It was a formidable piece of work. Since all Europe understood the Stuarts' hereditary right to 'the throne of Great Britain,' he argued, 'it could not without astonishment see us remain silent when the powers at war are holding an assembly for peace, which might, without regard to the justice of our cause (in which every sovereign power is interested), statute and stipulate articles prejudicial to our interests and to those of the subjects of our most honoured lord and father.'[26] Appealing to those subjects, Charles declared 'nothing shall ever alter the lively and sincere love which our birth inspires us with for them'. He closed by adding dangerously, 'we shall be always ready to spill the very last drop of our blood to deliver them from a foreign yoke.'[27]

The French government was hugely embarrassed by the protest because it was published as 'given at Paris'. At this time, the author of an account of the prince's time in France had a personal encounter with him in the Duke of Bouillon's home. When Charles heard that there was an Englishman in the house, he insisted on meeting him and spoke with a flattering ease, given their difference in station. Here once more was the Young Chevalier who had earned the affection of his soldiers: 'this was the first, and indeed the only Time I ever had the Honour of being spoke to by him; but the few Minutes I was in his Presence, served to make me cease to think it strange so many had hazarded their Lives and Fortunes in his Service.'[28] But the Treaty of Aix-la-Chapelle required

France to deny Prince Charles sanctuary within its bounds, a recognition of the danger he was still considered to pose while he was still in a position to influence affairs or make a sudden descent into Britain. After all, and despite the private concerns over his moodiness or his drinking, his tactlessness in dealing with the French government and refusal to compromise with them in his own interests, Charles was still only 28, still handsome and energetic, and still absolutely committed to his cause. When the French asked him to leave, he refused.

And so it was that, on 10 December 1748, Prince Charles Edward Stuart stepped out of his coach after a short drive across the Seine to the Palais-Royale. He had dismissed reports of his imminent arrest as idle rumour: although he had defied the French ministers' demands, he had now been told to comply by King James. If Charles was minded to obey, he would do so only after a show of doing it in his own unhurried time. As he stepped out of the coach into the empty street, all other coaches having been diverted, the prince was immediately approached by six men dressed as tradesmen, 'as if they were servants desirous to get a sight of him'.[29] He was accustomed to being crowded by the curious, but these were disguised military sergeants and, at a signal from a uniformed colleague, the prince was suddenly 'seized by the Guards'.[30]

The prince was bundled by the sergeants through a passageway and into a courtyard, where one Major Vaudreuil formally arrested him in the name of King Louis XV. The king had signed the warrant at 3.00 pm with a sigh that it was hard to be both a king and a friend. Charles replied 'without the least change in his countenance,' that the manner of the arrest was 'a little too violent.'[31] He was asked to surrender his sword, but while he agreed that they might take it, he refused to give it to them. The prince was found to be carrying 'his sword, a knife with two blades, and a brace of pistols.' Significantly, the guards asked for his assurance that he would not harm himself. Vaudreuil consulted his senior officer, who remained in an adjacent street to distance himself from what was taking place, but the colonel was unsatisfied. Taking no risks but doing themselves little honour, the guards then bound the prince's arms and legs 'to prevent him from making any attempt upon himself.'[32]

At the height of his affair with Marie Louise de La Tour, Charles Edward had fired his pistol in the streets in rage. As the Paris authorities

Epilogue

kept a close eye on him, they must have considered him unpredictable. In case he had resisted arrest, or managed to barricade himself within a house, the guards had deployed with both doctors and scaling ladders in support. To prevent any public disturbance, 'no less than 1200 of the Guards' had been deployed for the operation.[33] Prince Charles pointed out that the disgrace of it attached not to him, but to those who handled him so. He was then taken through the kitchens into a courtyard where a coach waited. From thence he was taken out through Sainte-Antoine, with mounted officers riding alongside the coach with 'a hand upon the door of each side.'

Outside the city awaited another military escort. By now, understandably enough, the prince's helplessness was feeding anxiety. He asked whether they were taking him to Hanover to be handed to his enemies. Given little reassurance, he was driven on to Vincennes where he surrendered a pair of compasses and again swore that he would not harm himself, which was clearly a serious concern. Charles did not lose his dignity nor his humour, and he enquired after the fate of his household. These, although he was not yet told it, 'were putt into the Bastille, but were soon lett out again with orders to quit Paris.'[34] After a few days as a prisoner at Vincennes, Charles was taken to Le-Pont-de-Beauvoisin and over the border into Savoy. There he was released, and after a few days in Chambéry, he proceeded to Avignon.

Thus did Charles Edward Stuart's military career come to an end, fourteen years after he had attended the Siege of Gaeta. Never again would the prince command an army or even participate in a campaign, and in that there is some regret because he had shown no small degree of ability. The prince's career in arms has been defined ever since by his defeat at Culloden, the disastrous aftermath contributing as much to the judgement as to the failure on the field itself. As the commander-in-chief of the Jacobite army, Prince Charles is, of course, responsible for that failure. But that is not to say that it was down to him that the rising failed. He demonstrated a courage and determination which was both personally commendable and stimulating to his chances of success. He had deployed his charm and rhetoric to achieve the creation of an army, and had given it the direction it needed to secure its most significant early objectives: the defeat of the enemy in the field and the capture of the Scottish capital. Contrary to later accusations, Charles had generally presided over a collaborative decision-making council, and at key moments had either compromised or yielded his own opinion. Sometimes, however, his own instincts had been better than those around him, though he lacked the experience and the practical authority to force the argument.

Charles Edward Stuart was not, therefore, a fool or a hapless novice. He was inexperienced, but so were many of those around him. Nobody was available in Scotland who possessed sufficient experience, confidence and authority to serve as the military head of the campaign in the way someone like the Duke of Berwick or the Earl Marischal might have done. Only Prince Charles was able to keep the Jacobite army together in the field, an army composed of widely differing personalities, motivations and strategic expectations. However, and not unlike his father, Prince Charles was a stubborn defender of his friends, even to the cost of his authority. He allowed factions to develop in the senior command which, by failing to adequately address them, made him appear partisan. In truth, however, he was constantly struggling to judge which of the conflicting courses to trust in, let down by the bickering of his subordinates just as much as he was well served by their hard work and sacrifice. But if he struggled to control his senior officers, Prince Charles did know how to treat his men: he held them in affection, enjoyed their company and earned their respect. He was neither selfish or cruel, nor despotic, but he could anger quickly, expressing his emotions violently, and had difficulty empathising with those who did not share his perspective. It could make him appear petulant and intolerant.

During this time, Prince Charles was a young man who faced mental and physical challenges which would be insurmountable to many of us, and if he failed to overcome them all, then that is not a personal fault. If he is to blame for the suffering of others, it is by virtue of him having drawn them into a conflict for which nobody was properly prepared. But it was one which he believed could – would – be successful, to the benefit of all. Charles understood risk, and was prepared to gamble hard for the high stakes because he saw no other way of achieving them. It is incorrect to believe, as some have asserted, that he did not care about the costs. He felt his own failure deeply and was well aware of the devastating effects it had on his country. The shock of this was felt all the more keenly because the actions of his enemies were so far from 'the moderation the Prince had shown during his prosperity, the lenity and even tenderness with which he had always treated his enemies.'[35]

The tragedy of the prince's life is that the virtues and abilities which he showed were never fully fulfilled. The pressure and strain of command and the physical intensity of the 1745–6 campaigns took an enormous toll on a young man who may already have been prone to depression. As diplomatic failure compounded military defeat, Charles Edward became ever less able to control his temperament. The alcohol, the bitterness and the violent moods which marred his later domestic life were symptoms rather than choices. They should not be excused, but they should be understood.

It is particularly regrettable that after 1748, the prince was increasingly isolated from the people he needed most: his father and brother. Returning to Rome and to his father's authority would be an admission of defeat which he could not make, and the fact that James and Henry would later clash, albeit temporarily, does show the difficulties Charles would have faced if he had gone back to the Palazzo Muti without a crown to offer the king, or a fresh focus to absorb his energies. The prince would never see his father again, and although he inherited his claim in 1766, it did not come with the political recognition that had so long sustained the Stuart cause. Charles' later marriage, like so many of his relationships, was a tempestuous failure, but in his final years he did find a degree of contentment in the company of Charlotte, his daughter by Clementina Walkinshaw.

Charles Edward Stuart died on 30 January 1788, aged 67, in the house in which he had been born. His life was complex and fascinating, too much so for its entirety to be addressed in these few pages. They have focused instead on the period of his life which defined him, which shows him at his very best, and explains how the seeds were sown for the rest. His actions touched many others, for good and ill, and continue to inspire strong responses today which can often still be distilled into arguments that Murray and Sullivan would recognise. Few presentations of Charles Edward Stuart have ever been written without bias, and if this volume is judged to be likewise, then the author hopes it is only because that is where the evidence has led it.

The final word is given to one of the prince's aides-de-camp, who served faithfully throughout the campaign and was amongst those fortunate enough, after a period in exile, to be able to return to his home.

His account of the conflict is thoughtful and moderate, and his position in the army gave him sufficient opportunity to observe the principal players closely:

> It is not to be wondered that they were beat at last, but very surprising, everything considered, they did not run away much sooner. Much the same judgement may be made of the Prince's whole expedition by any person that considers the various difficulties he had to struggle with. If he did less at Culloden than was expected from him, 'twas only because he had formerly done more than could be expected. From what he performed amidst all the disadvantages under which he laboured, it's easy to imagine what would have happened had he been supplied with money, a body of regular troops, and a few officers of rank skill and experience.
>
> James Maxwell of Kirkconnell

Bibliography

Manuscript Collections

Balfour-Melville Papers, National Records of Scotland: (NRS GD 126/30)
Caledonian Mercury
Ministère des Affaires Etrangères, Paris. MD Angleterre, Vol. 82, folios 216–21
National Library of Scotland
Royal Archive: the Cumberland Papers: (Cumberland Papers: RA CP)
Royal Archive: the Stuart Papers: (Stuart Papers: RA SP)
Scots Magazine
The York Courant
The Derby Mercury

Published Primary Works

Anon., *An Authentick Account of the Conduct of the Young Chevalier, from His First Arrival in Paris...* (London, 1749)
Anon., 'Journall and Memoirs of Prince Charles' Expedition into Scotland', in Aufrere, A. (ed.), *The Lockhart Papers*, Vol. 2, pp.479–510
Anon., *The Woodhouselee Manuscript: A Narrative Account of Events in Edinburgh...* (W. & R. Chambers, Edinburgh, 1907)
Brown, I. & Cheape, H., *Witness to Rebellion: John Maclean's Journal of the 'Forty-Five and the Penicuik Drawings* (John Donald, Edinburgh, 1996)
Burton, J., *Jacobite Correspondence of the Atholl Family* (Abbotsford Club, Edinburgh, 1860)
Carlyle, A., *Autobiography of the Rev. Dr Alexander Carlyle* (Blackwood & Sons, Edinburgh, 1860)

Chambers, R. (ed.), *Jacobite Memoirs of the Rebellion of 1745* (William & Robert Chambers, Edinburgh, 1834)

Daniel, J., 'A True Account of Mr John Daniel's Progress with Prince Charles', in Blaikie, W.B. (ed.), *Origins of the 'Forty-Five and Other Papers Relating to that Rising* (Scottish History Society, Edinburgh, 1916)

Dennistoun, J. (ed.), *Memoirs of Sir Robert Strange and his Brother-in-Law Andrew Lumisden* (Longman, Brown, Green & Longmans, London, 1855)

Elcho, Lord. See Wemyss, D.

Forbes, R. (ed.), *The Lyon in Mourning, Vol. I* (Constable, Edinburgh, 1896)

Forbes, R. (ed.), *The Lyon in Mourning, Vol. II* (Constable, Edinburgh, 1896)

Forbes, R. (ed.), *The Lyon in Mourning, Vol. III* (Constable, Edinburgh, 1896)

Grant, W., *The Occasional Writer: Containing an Answer to the Second Manifesto of the Pretender's Eldest Son* (London, 1745)

Henderson, A., *The History of the Rebellion: 1745–1746* (Edinburgh, 1748)

Home, J., *The History of the Rebellion in Scotland in 1745* (Peter Brown, Edinburgh, 1822)

Johnstone, J., *A Memoir of the 'Forty-Five* (Folio Society, London, 1958)

Kerr, H., 'Account of Events at Inverness and Culloden', in Aufrere, A. (ed.), *The Lockhart Papers*, Vol. 2, pp.513–522

Cameron of Lochiel, D., *Memoire d'un Ecossais,* available at https://www.yourphotocard.com/Ascanius/M%C3%A9moire%20d'un%20Ecossais.pdf

Lumsden, A., 'A Short Account of the Battles of Preston, Falkirk, and Culloden by a Gentleman who was in these Actions', in Blaikie, W.B. (ed.), *Origins of the 'Forty-Five and Other Papers Relating to that Rising* (Scottish History Society, Edinburgh, 1916)

MacEachain, N., 'Narrative of the Wanderings of Prince Charles in the Hebrides', in Blaikie, W.B. (ed.), *Origins of the 'Forty-Five and Other Papers Relating to that Rising* (Scottish History Society, Edinburgh, 1916)

Massie, A. & Oates, J. (eds.), *The Duke of Cumberland's Campaigns in Britain and the Low Countries, 1745–1748: A Selection of His Letters* (The History Press, Stroud, 2018)

Maxwell, J., *Narrative of Charles, Prince of Wales' Expedition to Scotland in the Year 1745* (Maitland Club, Edinburgh, 1841)

MacDonald of Clanranald, R., 'Account of the Proceedings from Prince Charles' Landing to Prestonpans', in *Miscellany of the Scottish History Society*, Vol. 9 (Constable, Edinburgh, 1958)

Marriott, P., *The Battle of Littleferry: A History and a Trail Guide* (Golspie Heritage Society, Golspie, 2022)

Micheil, M., *Young Juba, or The History of the Young Chevalier from his Birth to his Escape from Scotland...* (London, 1748)

Murray, Lord G., 'Marches of the Highland Army', in Chambers, R., *Jacobite Memoirs of the Rebellion in 1745* (Chambers, Edinburgh, 1834)

Murray, J., *Memorials of John Murray of Broughton, Sometime Secretary to Prince Charles Edward, 1740–1747* (Constable, Edinburgh, 1898)

The Orderly Book of Lord Ogilvy's Regiment, 10 October 1745 to 21 April 1746 (Society of Army Historical Research, Manchester, 1923)

Robertson, J.L., 'Log of the Dutillet', *Transactions of the Gaelic Society of Inverness*, Vol. 26 (Gaelic Society of Inverness, Inverness, 1910)

Robins, B. (ed.), *Report of the Proceedings and Opinion of the Board of General Officers on their Examination into the Conduct, Behaviour and Proceedings of Lieutenant-General Sir John Cope, Colonel Peregrine Lascelles, and Brigadier-General Thomas Fowke* (Faulkner, London, 1749)

Sullivan, J.W., see Taylor, H. & A., *The '45 and After* (Thomas Nelson, Edinburgh, 1938)

Taylor, H. & A., *The '45 and After* (Thomas Nelson, Edinburgh, 1938)

Taylor, H. & A., *The Stuart Papers at Windsor* (John Murray, London, 1939)

Taylor, H. (ed.), *A Jacobite Miscellany: Eight Original Papers on the Rising of 1745–1746* (Roxburghe Club, Oxford, 1948)

Taylor, H. (ed.), *Jacobite Epilogue: A Further Selection of Letters from Jacobites* (Thomas Nelson, London, 1941)

Warrand, D., *The Culloden Papers* (Carruthers & Sons, Inverness, 1927)

Wemyss, D., *A Short Account of the Affairs of Scotland in the Years 1744, 1745, 1746* (Douglas, Edinburgh, 1897)

Whitefoord, C., *The Whitefoord Papers* (Clarendon, Oxford, 1898)

Secondary Works

Bailey, G., *Falkirk or Paradise! The Battle of Falkirk Muir* (John Donald, Edinburgh, 2001)

Bamford, A., *The Lilies and the Thistle: French Troops in the Jacobite '45* (Helion, Solihull, 2018)

Bamford, A. (ed.), *Rebellious Scots to Crush: The Military Response to the Jacobite '45* (Helion, Solihull, 2020)

Batty, J. et al., *Culloden: The Sword and the Sorrows* (National Trust for Scotland, Edinburgh, 1996)

Beltrán, C.B., 'The Spanish Army in Italy, 1734', *War in History*, Vol. 5, No. 4, pp.401–426

Blaikie, W.B., *Itinerary of Prince Charles Edward Stuart* (Constable, Edinburgh, 1897)

Blaikie, W.B. (ed.), *Origins of the 'Forty-Five and Other Papers Relating to that Rising* (Scottish History Society, Edinburgh, 1916)

Brumfitt, J.H., 'Voltaire and Bonnie Prince Charlie: Historian and Hero', *Forum for Modern Language Studies*, Vol. 21, No. 4, pp.322–337

Cadell, General Sir R., *Sir John Cope and the Rebellion of 1745* (Prestoungrange University Press, Prestonpans, 2008)

Cameron Jacks, S., *The Last Jacobite Martyr: Dr Archibald Cameron 1707–1753* (Inverness, 2018)

Chambers, R., *A History of the Rebellion of 1745–6: New Edition* (Constable, Edinburgh, 1869)

Colletta, P., *The History of the Kingdom of Naples, 1734–1825* (Constable, Edinburgh, 1858)

Corp, E., *The Stuarts in Italy, 1719–1766: A Royal Court in Permanent Exile* (Cambridge University Press, Cambridge, 2011)

Corp, E. & Rimer, G., 'A Newly Recognised Sword of Prince Charles Edward Stuart', in *History Scotland*, Vol. 21, No. 3, May/June 2021, pp.30–34

Daiches, D., *Charles Edward Stuart: The Life and Times of Bonnie Prince Charlie* (Pan Books, London, 1975)

Douglas, H., *The Private Passions of Bonnie Prince Charlie* (Sutton, Stroud, 1998)

Duffy, C., *Fight for a Throne* (Helion, Solihull, 2015)

Duffy, C., *The '45* (London, 2003)

Ewald, A., *The Life and Times of Prince Charles Stuart* (Chapman & Hall, London, 1875)

Forster, M., *The Rash Adventurer: The Rise and Fall of Charles Edward Stuart* (Stein & Day, New York, 1973)
Forsyth, D. (ed.), *Bonnie Prince Charlie and the Jacobites* (National Museums Scotland, Edinburgh, 2017)
Gibson, J.S., *Edinburgh in The '45: Bonnie Prince Charlie at Holyrood* (Saltire Society, Edinburgh, 1995)
Gibson, J.S., *The Gentle Lochiel* (NMSE, Edinburgh, 1998)
Gibson, J.S., *The Ships of The '45: The Rescue of the Young Pretender* (Hutchinson, London, 1967)
Guiheneuf, T., 'The *Du Teillay*: fifteen months as a privateer', in *The Jacobite: Journal of the 1745 Association* (1745 Association, 2022)
Halford-MacLeod, R., *A Man whose Only Crime is being Unfortunate: Sir John Cope, Lord Loudoun and the Battle of Prestonpans: Evidence from the Loudoun Papers* (Halmac, Auchtermuchty, 2018)
Johnston, A., *On Gladsmuir Shall the Battle Be! The Battle of Prestonpans 1745* (Helion, Solihull, 2017)
Kaiser, T., 'The Drama of Charles Edward Stuart, Jacobite Propaganda, and French Political Protest, 1745–1750', in *Eighteenth-Century Studies*, Vol. 30, No. 4, pp.365–381 (Summer, 1997)
Lang, A., *Pickle the Spy; or, the Incognito Prince Charles* (Longmans, Green & Co., London, 1897)
Lang, A., *Prince Charles Edward Stuart, The Young Chevalier* (Longmans, Green & Co., London, 1903)
Linklater, E., *The Prince in the Heather* (Panther, St Albans, 1976)
Lord, S., *Walking with Charlie* (Pookus Publications, Whitney, 2003)
MacDonald, N., *The Clan Ranald of Garmoran: A History of the MacDonalds of Clanranald* (Edinburgh, 2008)
MacDonald, P., *A 1745 Era Highland Suit* (https://www.scottishtartans.co.uk/A-Jacobite-Era-Highland-Suit.pdf, 2022)
Maclean, F., *Bonnie Prince Charlie* (Guild Publishing, London, 1988)
Margulies, M., *The Battle of Prestonpans 1745* (Tempus, Stroud, 2007)
Marshall, R.K., *Bonnie Prince Charlie* (National Museums Scotland, Edinburgh, 1996)
McKenzie Annand, A., 'Lord Strathallan's Horse, or The Perthshire Squadron', in *Journal of the Society for Army Historical* Research, Vol. 57, No. 232 (1979), pp.223–236
McKenzie Annand, A., 'The Hussars of The '45', in *Journal of the Society for Army Historical* Research, Vol. 39, No. 159 (1961), pp.144–160

McKenzie Annand, A., 'The Life Guards of Prince Charles Edward 1745-6', in *Journal of the Society for Army Historical Research*, Vol. 73, No. 293 (1995), pp.10-34

McLynn, F., *The Jacobite Army in England: 1745, the Final Campaign* (John Donald, Edinburgh, 1998)

Miller, P., *James* (George Allen & Unwin, London, 1971)

Munro, K., *ARO50: "...a plantation of Scotch firs and forest-trees of considerable extent...": Locating the Parks of Culloden House at the time of the Battle of Culloden* (GUARD Archaeology, Glasgow, 2022)

Nevin, M., *Reminiscences of a Jacobite: The Untold Story of 1745* (Birlinn, Edinburgh, 2020)

Norie, W.D., *The Life and Adventures of Prince Charles Edward Stuart* (London, 1901)

Oates, J., *Battles of the Jacobite Rebellions: Killiecrankie to Culloden* (Pen & Sword, Barnsley, 2019)

Oates, J., *The Sieges of The '45: Siege Warfare during the Jacobite Rebellion of 1745–1746* (Helion, Warwick, 2021)

O'Keeffe, P., *Culloden: Battle and Aftermath* (The Bodley Head, London, 2021)

Oliphant, T., *The Jacobite Lairds of Gask* (Grampian Club, London, 1870)

Petrie, C., 'The Elibank Plot, 1752–3', in *Transactions of the Royal Historical Society*, Vol. 14, pp.175–196 (Cambridge University Press, Cambridge, 1931)

Pininski, P., *Bonnie Prince Charlie: is Life, Family, Legend* (National Museums Scotland, Edinburgh, 2022)

Pittock, M., *Great Battles: Culloden* (Oxford University Press, Oxford, 2022)

Pittock, M., *The Invention of Scotland: the Stuart Myth and Scottish Identity 1638 to the Present* (Routledge, London, 1991)

Pittock, M., *The Myth of the Jacobite Clans*: Second Edition (Edinburgh University Press, Edinburgh, 2015)

Pollard, T. (ed.), *Culloden: The History and Archaeology of Scotland's Last Clan Battle* (Pen & Sword, Barnsley, 2009)

Pollard, T. & Ferguson, N., *Prestonpans Battlefield Archaeological Project* (unpublished, Glasgow, 2008)

Reid, S., *1745: a Military History of the Last Jacobite Rising* (Spellmount, Staplehurst, 2001)

Reid, S., *Like Hungry Wolves: Culloden Moor 16 April 1746* (Windrow & Greene, London, 1994)

Royle, T., *Culloden: Scotland's Last Battle and the Forging of the British Empire* (Abacus, London, 2017)

Scott-Moncrieff, L. (ed.), *The 45: to Gather and Image Whole* (Mercat Press, Edinburgh, 1988)

Seddon, M., *The Escape of Bonnie Prince Charlie* (Spiderwize, Peterborough, 2016)

Seward, D., *The King Over the Water: a Complete History of the Jacobites* (Birlinn, Edinburgh, 2021)

Tomasson, K. & Buist, F., *Battles of The '45* (Pan, London, 1962)

Tomasson, K., *The Jacobite General* (Blackwood & Sons, Edinburgh, 1958)

Vázquez-Gestal, P., 'The System of This Court': Elizabeth Farnese, the Count of Santiesteban and the Monarchy of the Two Sicilies, 1734–1738', *The Court Historian*, Vol. 14, No. 1, pp.23–47

Wemyss, A., *Elcho of The '45* (Saltire Society, Edinburgh, 2003)

Notes

Chapter One: The Siege of Gaeta

1. Prince Charles had also lived for a few years (1726–29) in Bologna, also within the Papal States, during a low period in relations between his father and the Pope. It had not been a particularly happy time.
2. Stuart Papers: RA SP/MAIN/171 f.118–119
3. Stuart Papers: RA SP/MAIN/171 f.190–190
4. Stuart Papers: RA SP/MAIN/172 f.51–52
5. Stuart Papers: RA SP/MAIN/172 f.114–115. The incognito reduced any diplomatic awkwardness for those who wished to meet the prince without drawing the ire of the de facto British king, George II.
6. Stuart Papers: RA SP/MAIN/172 f.51–52
7. The War of the Quadruple Alliance, 1718–20.
8. Stuart Papers: RA SP/MAIN/171 f.33–34
9. I will continue to refer to the King of Naples as Parma for consistency, even after he had secured the crown. This is simply to avoid confusion amongst a cast of so many kings, dukes and Charleses.
10. Stuart Papers: RA SP/MAIN/172 f.51–52
11. Stuart Papers: RA SP/MAIN/172 f.155–156
12. Stuart Papers: RA SP/MAIN/172 f.45–46
13. Stuart Papers: RA SP/MAIN/172 f.51–52
14. 'Il est vif, et charmant,' Stuart Papers: RA SP/MAIN/172 f.51–52
15. Maclean, p.15
16. Micheil, M., *Young Juba, or the History of the Young Chevalier* (London, 1748). The 'M. Micheil' given as the Italian author was in fact Michele Vezzosi, the prince's valet at the time of The '45. His perceptions are not without bias, of course.
17. Stuart Papers: RA SP/MAIN/172 f.51–52. Dunbar's letter of 5 August is labelled as being sent from 'Mola', which is the name of the castle, with its substantial cylindrical tower, on the eastern side of the harbour at Formia.

18. Stuart Papers: RA SP/MAIN/172 f.51–52
19. Daiches, p.70
20. Stuart Papers: RA SP/MAIN/172 f.86–87
21. Stuart Papers: RA SP/MAIN/172 f.88–89
22. Stuart Papers: RA SP/MAIN/172 f.132–133
23. The twentieth-century biographer Margaret Forster speculates that Charles never even bothered reading these letters to the end. She is also scathing of the extent to which Charles' supposed display of courage had any meaning, saying 'in fact he had done nothing but have hysterics', and dismisses Berwick's reports as being over-egged (1973: 29). But her assumption that James believed the expedition had done Charles more harm than good is not borne out by the tone of his wider correspondence, and his hopes of finding him another placement in either Sicily or Lombardy.
24. Stuart Papers: RA SP/MAIN/172 f.166–167
25. Stuart Papers: RA SP/MAIN/172 f.86–87
26. Stuart Papers: RA SP/MAIN/172 f.88–89
27. The agent was Baron von Stosch. Quoted in Maclean, p.17.
28. Stuart Papers: RA SP/MAIN/173 f.82–83
29. Stuart Papers: RA SP/MAIN/172 f.149–150
30. Stuart Papers: RA SP/MAIN/172 f.156–157
31. Stuart Papers: RA SP/MAIN/172 f.85–86
32. Stuart Papers: RA SP/MAIN/173 f.68–69
33. Stuart Papers: RA SP/MAIN/173 f.68–69
34. Stuart Papers: RA SP/MAIN/173 f.68–69
35. Stuart Papers: RA SP/MAIN/177 f.2–3
36. Stuart Papers: RA SP/MAIN/177 f.23–24
37. Corp (2011), p.222
38. David was instructed to copy from an earlier original by Meytens, but was also himself very familiar with the royal family. In the final years of her life, the ascetic queen's features were showing the effects of her lifestyle, a tragic deterioration which was visible to those that knew her but not to those who saw only her portrait. From conversation with Professor Edward Corp.
39. Stuart Papers: RA SP/MAIN/207 f.65–66
40. Corp (2011), p.251
41. Stuart Papers: RA SP/MAIN/196 f.64–65
42. Stuart Papers: RA SP/MAIN/196 f.23–24
43. Stuart Papers: RA SP/MAIN/196 f.49–50

44. Stuart Papers: RA SP/MAIN/197 f.146–147
45. Stuart Papers: RA SP/MAIN/197 f.63–64
46. Stosch, quoted in Corp (2011), p.252

Chapter Two: *Du Teillay*

1. Stuart Papers: RA SP/MAIN/266 f.102–103
2. 24 metres. Guiheneuf, p.9
3. *Journal of the Prince's Imbarkation and Arrival etc*, in Forbes, Vol. I, p.285
4. Corp (2011), p.310
5. Corp (2011), p.334
6. His name is often given as O'Sullivan, although he refers to himself as Sullivan so it seems more appropriate to follow his own preference.
7. Letter from Sheridan to Edgar, 24 January 1745, quoted in Taylor, H. & A. (1938), p.15
8. Stuart Papers: RA SP/MAIN/255 f.147–148
9. Stuart Papers: RA SP/MAIN/256 f.96–97
10. Stuart Papers: RA SP/MAIN/256 f.127–128
11. Stuart Papers: RA SP/MAIN/256 f.127–128
12. Stuart Papers: RA SP/MAIN/256 f.94–95
13. Guiheneuf, p.16
14. Forbes (1895), Vol. I, p.281. Poor Buchanan does not get included in the list of the famous Seven Men of Moidart, presumably because he is counted as one of the servants rather than a protagonist in his own right. Likewise for Vezzosi.
15. He will be referred to throughout as Tullibardine to allow easy distinction between William and his youngest brother James, who was acknowledged by the British government as the Duke of Atholl.
16. Forbes (1895), Vol. I, p.285
17. Charles Edward Stuart to James Edgar, quoted in Taylor, H. & A. (1939), p.126
18. Sullivan, in Taylor, H. & A. (1938), p.47
19. There were those at court who were inclined towards a peace with Britain and therefore found the prince's presence embarrassing and potentially dangerous. It remains possible, however, that Cardinal

Tencin, a close ally of King James and now a senior French minister, may have turned a blind eye to what he suspected was going on.
20. 'Not without a little anxiety,' is how the prince put it. Stuart Papers: RA SP/MAIN/266 f.102–103
21. Durbé, *Log of the Dutillet*, Sunday 11 July 1745
22. Taylor, H. & A. (1938), p.50
23. Taylor, H. & A. (1938), p.50
24. Durbé, *Log of the Dutillet*, 19–20 July 1745
25. Taylor, H. & A. (1938), p.50
26. Stuart Papers: RA SP/MAIN/266 f.86–87
27. Bamford, p.19–20
28. Stuart Papers: RA SP/MAIN/266 f.86–87
29. Stuart Papers: RA SP/MAIN/266 f.194–195
30. Stuart Papers: RA SP/MAIN/266 f.92–93
31. Murray, p.96
32. Stuart Papers: RA SP/MAIN/266 f.194–195
33. Sir John MacDonald agrees, saying Dehau came aboard 'to receive HRH's orders'. In Taylor, H. & A. (1938), p.50
34. Forbes (1895), Vol. I, p.286. Durbé's criticism is more subtle, simply noting that *L'Elisabeth* was slower to execute the manoeuvre.
35. Forbes (1895), Vol. I, p.286
36. Taylor, H. & A. (1938), p.51
37. This part of the action is less clear from the accounts of Durbé and MacDonald, but clear from the series of illustrations produced in Britain by Samuel Scott.
38. Forbes (1895), Vol. I, p.286
39. MacDonald here gives more detail than the captain's log, which does not mention the striking of the colours. The Hinchingbrooke sketches, based on Brett's report, suggest that it was *L'Elisabeth* who first drew off.
40. *Lion* had been more badly damaged, but had lost fewer lives: 45 killed and 107 wounded. She was forced to return to England, where her officers faced a hard reception.
41. Forbes (1895), Vol. I, p.287
42. Durbé, *Log of the Dutillet*, 20–21 July 1745
43. Guiheneuf (2022), p.34
44. Forbes (1895), Vol. I, p.289
45. Forbes (1895), Vol. I, p.289
46. Taylor, H. & A. (1938), p.53

47. Home, p.32
48. Taylor, H. & A. (1938), p.57
49. MacDonald, p.201.
50. Home (p.35) says he entered 'one of the hovels', which suggests the small cluster of buildings visible on Roy's map, on the western side of the Finnan.
51. Taylor, H. & A. (1938), p.60
52. Taylor, H. & A. (1938), p.60
53. Broughton, p.168
54. Taylor, H. & A. (1938), p.60
55. Home, p.36. Duffy (2015: 85) has suggested that the nearest source of such flags or fabrics would be the signal box of *Du Teillay*.
56. Forbes (1895), Vol. I, p.292
57. Douglas, p.235
58. Broughton, p.169
59. Anon., 'Journall and Memoirs of Prince Charles' Expedition into Scotland', in *Lockhart Papers*, Vol. 2, pp.484. The author may perhaps have been Alasdair mac Mhaighstir Alasdair.
60. Taylor, H. & A. (1938), p.61

Chapter Three: Holyroodhouse

1. *Woodhouselee MS*, p.20. The account is anonymous, but was probably written by Patrick Crichton.
2. *The York Courant*, 23 September 1745
3. *Caledonian Mercury*, 25 September 1745
4. Ibid.
5. *Woodhouselee MS*, p.24
6. Home, p.71. Both Home and the Woodhouselee author (probably Crichton) were hostile witnesses, the latter vigorously prejudiced against the Highlanders.
7. Henderson, p.14
8. Elcho, p.258
9. The fraught definitions of Highlander/Lowland, and evidence of the lack of distinction between them in the army's dress and equipment, are well covered by Pittock (2015).
10. *Woodhouselee MS*, p.26

11. Home, p.75
12. Johnstone, p.36
13. Home, p.75
14. Broughton, p.185
15. Sullivan, in Taylor, H. & A. (1938), p.64
16. Broughton, p.178
17. Broughton, p.178
18. Broughton, p.179
19. *Woodhouselee MS*, p.24
20. Henderson, p.14. This might well have been the Kandler sword which is now in the collection of the National Museum of Scotland (H. LN 49), reputedly captured at Culloden. It seems most unlikely that it was in the same sword that Perth had sent to the prince in Rome, as these are still referenced in an inventory of the Palazzo del Re during his absence: Corp & Rimer (2021), pp.30–34.
21. *Woodhouselee MS*, p.24
22. Henderson, p.14
23. McKenzie Annand, p.233
24. Their positions are given in the *Woodhouselee MS*, p.24, and again by Elcho himself, p.258.
25. Taylor, H. & A. (1938), p.73
26. Elcho, p.258
27. Tomasson, p.2
28. Johnston (2017), p.78
29. Taylor, H. & A. (1938), pp.67–8
30. Taylor, H. & A. (1938), p.69
31. Johnstone, p.33
32. Taylor, H. & A. (1938), p.67
33. Johnstone, p.33
34. Johnstone, p.31
35. Murray, p.36
36. Henderson, p.14
37. Elcho, pp.258–9
38. Henderson, p.14
39. Elcho, p.259. The figure may be an overestimation, being higher than the estimated total population of Edinburgh. It does, however, provide a sense of the enormity of the reception, which is reflected consistently in other sources.

40. Taylor, H. & A. (1938), p.73
41. Broughton, p.198
42. Home, p.71
43. Henderson, p.14
44. Home, p.72
45. Elcho, p.259
46. Taylor, H. & A. (1938), p.74
47. *Woodhouselee MS*, p.27
48. *Woodhouselee MS*, p.27
49. *Woodhouselee MS*, p.29
50. Henderson, p.15
51. *Woodhouselee MS*, p.28
52. The proclamations are available in a number of places, but are conveniently collated in Henderson, pp.15–22.
53. Elcho, p.259

Chapter Four: The Battle of Prestonpans

1. Elcho, p.265
2. Home, p.72
3. Sullivan, in Taylor (1938), p.74
4. Elcho, p.262
5. Broughton, p.198
6. *Woodhouselee MS*, p.32
7. Home, p.78
8. Home, p.78
9. Broughton, p.202
10. Broughton, p.198
11. Broughton, p.199
12. Sullivan, in Taylor, H. & A. (1938), p.75
13. Broughton, p.199
14. Elcho, p.262
15. Home, p.78
16. Sullivan, in Taylor, H. & A. (1938), p.75
17. Sullivan, in Taylor, H. & A. (1938), p.75. For more about the sword, see Forsyth (2017: 84–6) and Corp & Rimer (2021): 30–31.
18. Broughton, p.200
19. Sullivan, in Taylor, H. & A. (1938), p.75

20. Sullivan, in Taylor, H. & A. (1938), p.75
21. National Library of Scotland, NLS: PDP.10/23(4)
22. Chambers, p.114
23. Broughton, p.199
24. Elcho, p.261.
25. Carlyle, p.137
26. Broughton, p.200
27. Robins (ed.), *Inquiry*, Appendix p.35
28. Elcho, p.266
29. Broughton, p.200
30. Murray, p.36. It is unclear on what grounds Murray was able to claim such intimate knowledge of the ground.
31. Broughton, p.200
32. Johnstone, p.35
33. Johnstone, p.35
34. Elcho, p.267
35. Letter from Drummore to Cope, 24 October 1745, in Robins (ed.), *Inquiry*, Appendix p.36
36. Sullivan, in Taylor, H. & A. (1938), p.77
37. Elcho, p.267
38. Cumberland Papers: RA CP/MAIN/5 f.318
39. Broughton, p.200
40. Sullivan, in Taylor, H. & A. (1938), p.77
41. Murray, p.36
42. Sullivan, in Taylor (1938), p.78
43. Broughton, p.200
44. Johnstone, p.35
45. Home, p.81
46. Murray, p.37
47. Murray, p.37
48. Henderson, p.29
49. Robins (ed.), *Inquiry*, p.87
50. Murray reports that Sullivan was in the rear but not the reason for him being there, which must be inferred from the fact that the threat to the picket seems to occur very close to the timing of Nairne's westward movement. Murray, p.37
51. Elcho, p.267
52. Murray, p.37
53. Henderson, p.29

54. Murray, p.38
55. Sullivan, in Taylor, H. & A. (1938), p.79
56. Sullivan, in Taylor, H. & A. (1938), p.78
57. Sullivan, in Taylor, H. & A. (1938), p.78
58. Sullivan, in Taylor, H. & A. (1938), p.78
59. Home, p.81
60. Sullivan, in Taylor, H. & A. (1938), p.78
61. Sullivan, in Taylor, H. & A. (1938), p.79
62. Elcho, p.268
63. Elcho, p.269
64. Murray, p.38
65. Sullivan, in Taylor, H. & A. (1938), p.80
66. Murray, p.38
67. Elcho, p.269
68. Sullivan, in Taylor, H. & A. (1938), p.80
69. Johnstone, p.36
70. Murray, p.38
71. Maxwell, p.40
72. Stuart Papers: RA SP/MAIN/268 f.42–43
73. Sullivan, in Taylor, H. & A. (1938), p.80
74. Sullivan, in Taylor, H. & A. (1938), p.79
75. Sullivan, in Taylor, H. & A. (1938), p.79
76. Murray, p.40
77. Johnstone, p.36
78. Johnstone, p.36
79. Elcho, p.270
80. Stuart Papers: RA SP/MAIN/269 f.123–124
81. Johnstone, p.36
82. *Caledonian Mercury*, 23 September 1745
83. Broughton, p.203; Johnstone, p.38
84. Elcho, p.271
85. Drummore, Robins (ed.), *Inquiry*, Appendix p.37
86. Sullivan, in Taylor H. & A. (1938), p.81.
87. Lockhart Papers, p.490
88. Murray, p.40
89. Home, p.86
90. Maxwell, p.42
91. Loudoun's written submission, Robins (ed.), *Inquiry*, Appendix p.30

92. Drummore to Cope, 24 October 1745, in Robins (ed.), *Inquiry*, Appendix, p.37
93. Sullivan, in Taylor, H. & A. (1938), p.81
94. Sir John MacDonald, in Taylor H. & A. (1938), p.82
95. Elcho, p.273; Maxwell, p.41
96. Lockhart Papers, p.491
97. Murray, p.40
98. Johnstone, p.40
99. Johnstone, p.40
100. Murray, p.42
101. Sir John MacDonald in Taylor, H. & A. (1938), pp.81–2
102. Maxwell, p.42
103. Maxwell, p.42
104. Broughton, p.205
105. Carlyle, p.142
106. Murray, p.42
107. Broughton, p.205
108. Henderson, p.32
109. Broughton, p.205
110. Home, p.89
111. Johnstone, p.40
112. Henderson, p.32
113. Stuart Papers: RA SP/MAIN/268 f.58–59
114. Stuart Papers: RA SP/MAIN/269 f.123–124. It was common for Jacobites to call the battle Gladsmuir, a place several miles to the east of Tranent. This was due to a medieval prophecy of Thomas the Rhymer, still in popular circulation, which predicted a decisive battle would be fought at a place with that name. Prestonpans seemed close enough!

Chapter Five: The Retreat

1. Sullivan, in Taylor, H. & A. (1938), p.106
2. Sullivan, in Taylor, H. & A. (1938), p.106
3. Murray, p.61
4. Murray, pp.63–4
5. Elcho, p.347

6. Elcho, p.346
7. Sullivan, in Taylor, H. & A. (1938), p.106
8. Elcho, p.347; McLynn (1998), p.176
9. Johnstone, p.66
10. Sullivan, in Taylor, H. & A. (1938), p.107
11. Blaikie, p.31
12. Maxwell, p.85
13. Sullivan, in Taylor, H. & A. (1938), p.107
14. The orderly book of Ogilvy's Regiment provides excellent insights into the army's day-to-day experience at Edinburgh.
15. Maxwell, p.54
16. Broughton, p.215
17. Broughton, p.214; 210
18. Elcho, p.290
19. Taylor (1948), p.51
20. Sullivan, in Taylor, H. & A. (1938), p.88
21. Elcho, p.297
22. Sullivan, in Taylor, H. & A. (1938), p.88
23. Broughton, p.218
24. Elcho, p.282
25. Broughton, p.211
26. Elcho, p.282
27. Maxwell, p.58
28. Sir John MacDonald, in Taylor, H. & A. (1938), p.89
29. Maxwell, p.56
30. Maxwell, p.54
31. From Elcho's diaries, in Taylor (1948), p.185
32. Murray, p.47
33. Elcho, p.290
34. Maxwell, p.53
35. Elcho, p.302
36. Sir John MacDonald, in Taylor, H. & A. (1938), p.89
37. Elcho, p.304
38. Murray, p.47
39. Sullivan, in Taylor, H. & A. (1938), p.92
40. Maxwell, p.61
41. Broughton, p.238
42. Johnstone, p.50

Notes

43. For the most part, the weather on this campaign was so poor that tents could not have been successfully erected anyway, as Marshal Wade's army learned.
44. Maxwell, p.62
45. Sullivan, in Taylor, H. & A. (1938), p.93
46. Maxwell, p.64
47. Maxwell, p.65
48. Sir John MacDonald, in Taylor, H. & A. (1938), p.93
49. Murray to Tullibardine, 15 November 1745, quoted in Murray, p.51
50. Sullivan, in Taylor, H. & A. (1938), p.95
51. Sir John MacDonald, in Taylor, H. & A. (1938), p.94–5
52. Maxwell, p.65
53. The best analysis of Perth's position is given by Maxwell, p.67.
54. Jacobite sources generally inflate these numbers, but they are carefully assessed in Bamford, p.70.
55. Sullivan, in Taylor, H. & A. (1938), p.97
56. Sullivan, in Taylor, H. & A. (1938), p.99
57. Broughton, p.246
58. Broughton, p.246
59. Elcho, p.329
60. Sullivan, in Taylor, H. & A. (1938), p.102
61. Elcho, p.333
62. Maxwell, p.72
63. *Gentleman's Magazine*, Vol. XV, pp.708–710
64. Maxwell, p.73
65. Maxwell, p.73
66. Hay of Restalrig, in Home, p.156
67. Maxwell, p.74
68. Sullivan, in Taylor, H. & A. (1938), p.102
69. Murray, p.54
70. Elcho, p.339
71. Murray, p.55
72. Johnstone, p.60
73. Murray, p.55
74. Johnstone, p.60
75. Sullivan, in Taylor, H. & A. (1938), p.103
76. Johnstone, p.61
77. Elcho, p.340

78. Sullivan, in Taylor, H. & A. (1938), p.103
79. Sir John MacDonald, in Taylor, H. & A. (1938), p.102
80. Elcho, p.341
81. Murray, p.57
82. Sullivan, in Taylor, H. & A. (1938), p.102
83. Elcho, p.341
84. Daniel, in Blaikie (1916), p.177
85. Sir John MacDonald, in Taylor, H. & A. (1938), p.102
86. Murray, p.59
87. Quoted in Elcho, p.342
88. Elcho, p.342
89. Elcho, p.343
90. Daniel, p.180
91. Elcho, p.344
92. Elcho, p.348
93. Johnstone, p.68
94. Murray, p.66
95. Sullivan, in Taylor, H. & A. (1938), p.109
96. Murray, p.66
97. Sullivan, in Taylor, H. & A. (1938), p.109
98. Murray, p.72–3
99. Sullivan, in Taylor, H. & A. (1938), p.110
100. Murray, p.73
101. Sullivan, in Taylor, H. & A. (1938), p.110
102. Maxwell, p.88; see Oates, p.87 for more detail on the composition of the Jacobite garrison.
103. Maxwell, p.88
104. Sullivan, in Taylor, H. & A. (1938), p.111
105. Murray, p.74
106. Murray, p.75
107. Sullivan, in Taylor, H. & A. (1938), p.111

Chapter Six: The Battle of Falkirk

1. Elcho, p.353
2. Daniels, p.191
3. Daniels, p.192
4. Johnstone, p.86

5. NLS MS 3736, Campbell of Mamore Letters, 'Letter concerning the rebels'
6. Elcho, p.371
7. Murray, p.80
8. Daniel, p.193–4
9. Elcho, p.370
10. Elcho, p.372
11. NRS GD 24/5/162/30, Duke of Perth to James Murray of Abercromby, quoted in Duffy (2015), p.296
12. Blaikie, p.73–4
13. Blaikie, p.74
14. Murray, p.80
15. Johnstone, p.87
16. Bamford, p.80
17. Daniel, p.194
18. NLS MS 3733, Campbell of Mamore Letters, 'Copy of... Succoth's letter', quoted in Duffy (2015), p.297
19. Johnstone, p.87. A death was reported in the *Caledonian Mercury*, 21 April 1741.
20. Murray, p.80
21. Murray, p.80
22. Murray, p.80
23. Elcho, p.373
24. Hume, p.119
25. Murray, p.82
26. Sullivan, in Taylor, H. & A. (1938), p.116
27. Elcho, p.374
28. Elcho, p.374; Murray, p.85
29. Sullivan, in Taylor, H. & A. (1938), p.117
30. Elcho (p.376) remarks that 'all the Generals and their aid de Camps were on foot,' but his wording could be understood to mean all the officers of the front line, as he is speaking primarily about Highlanders. No account mentions the prince deliberately dismounting, and we know that he had ridden to the field. Elcho himself was at the opposite end of the line.
31. Sullivan, in Taylor, H. & A. (1938), p.117
32. Sullivan, in Taylor, H. & A. (1938), p.117
33. Sullivan, in Taylor, H. & A. (1938), p.117
34. Cumberland to Hawley, 23 January 1746, in Massie & Oates, p.140

35. Elcho, p.375
36. Johnstone, p.88
37. Johnstone, p.88
38. Sullivan, in Taylor, H. & A. (1938), p.118
39. Daniel, p.197
40. Sullivan, in Taylor, H. & A. (1938), p.118
41. Sullivan, in Taylor, H. & A. (1938), p.118
42. Hume, p.124. The author was present at the battle as a volunteer in Hawley's army.
43. Hume, p.124
44. Sullivan, in Taylor, H. & A. (1938), p.118
45. Sullivan, in Taylor, H. & A. (1938), p.118
46. *Lockhart Papers*, Vol. 2, p.502
47. Murray, p.86
48. Elcho, p.376
49. Sullivan, in Taylor, H. & A. (1938), p.118
50. Hume, p.126
51. Maxwell, p.104
52. Murray, pp.87–88
53. Maxwell, p.104
54. Murray, p.88
55. Sullivan, in Taylor, H. & A. (1938), p.119
56. Johnstone, p.92
57. Sullivan, in Taylor, H. & A. (1938), p.119–20
58. Johnstone, p.93
59. Sullivan, p.120
60. Elcho, p.379
61. Hume, p.131
62. Maxwell, p.107
63. Johnstone, p.96
64. 'Prince's Household Book', in Chambers, R. (ed.), *Jacobite Memoirs of the Rebellion of 1745* (William & Robert Chambers, Edinburgh, 1834)
65. Sullivan, p.121
66. Murray, p.94
67. Daniel, p.200
68. Lockhart papers, p.503; Elcho, p.380
69. Maxwell, p.110
70. Elcho, p.382; Murray, p.98

71. Sullivan, in Taylor, H. & A. (1938), p.121
72. Maxwell, p.111
73. Sullivan, in Taylor, H. & A. (1938), p.122
74. Sullivan, in Taylor, H. & A. (1938), p.122
75. Elcho, p.384
76. Sullivan, in Taylor, H. & A. (1938), p.123
77. Elcho, p.384
78. Lord George Murray to Prince Charles: NRS GD 126/30, Balfour-Melville Papers
79. Lochiel, p.1
80. Blaikie, p.75
81. Sullivan, in Taylor, H. & A. (1938), p.123
82. Quoted in Elcho, p.384
83. Blaikie, p.76–7
84. Blaikie, p.78

Chapter Seven: The Battle of Culloden

1. Elcho, p.426
2. Sullivan, in Taylor, H. & A. (1938), p.154
3. Murray, p.121–2
4. Murray, p.121
5. Sullivan, in Taylor, H. & A. (1938), p.154
6. Elcho, p.426
7. Elcho, p.385
8. Maxwell, p.114
9. Maxwell, p.115
10. Murray, p.100
11. Elcho, p.386
12. Maxwell, p.116
13. Maxwell, p.116
14. Maxwell p.116
15. Murray, p.100
16. Alexander Stewart, quoted in Murray, p.102
17. Sullivan, in Taylor, H. & A. (1938), p.131
18. Sullivan, in Taylor, H. & A. (1938), p.131
19. Sir John MacDonald, in Taylor, H. & A. (1938), p.131
20. Daniel, p.205

21. Daniel, p.205
22. Sullivan, in Taylor, H. & A. (1938), p.136
23. Sullivan, in Taylor, H. & A. (1938), p.136
24. Maxwell, p.136
25. Maxwell, p.136
26. Maxwell, p.142
27. Sullivan, in Taylor, H. & A. (1938), p.154
28. Elcho, p.426
29. Sullivan, in Taylor, H. & A. (1938), p.154
30. Elcho, p.427
31. Sullivan, in Taylor, H. & A. (1938), p.154
32. Maxwell, p.142
33. Johnstone, p.119; Sullivan, in Taylor, H. & A. (1938), p.155
34. Lockhart Papers, Vol. 2, p.318
35. Elcho, p.427
36. Sullivan, in Taylor, H. & A. (1938), p.154
37. Hume, p.159
38. Sullivan, in Taylor, H. & A. (1938), p.155
39. Murray, p.122
40. Murray, p.122
41. Murray, p.122
42. Maxwell, p.145
43. Murray, p.122
44. Sullivan, in Taylor, H. & A. (1938), p.155
45. Maclean, p.35
46. Sullivan, in Taylor, H. & A. (1938), p.156
47. Sullivan, in Taylor, H. & A. (1938), p.156
48. Sir John MacDonald, in Taylor, H. & A. (1938), p.157
49. Elcho, p.427
50. Daniel, p.211
51. Strange, in Dennistoun (ed.), p.56
52. Maxwell, p.145
53. Sullivan, in Taylor, H. & A. (1938), p.156
54. Sir John MacDonald, in Taylor, H. & A. (1938), p.157
55. Strange, in Dennistoun (ed.), p.56
56. Sullivan, in Taylor, H. & A. (1938), p.156
57. Lockhart Papers, Vol. 2, p.519
58. Sullivan, in Taylor, H. & A. (1938), p.156
59. Lockhart Papers, Vol. 2, p.519

60. Sullivan, in Taylor, H. & A. (1938), p.157
61. Maxwell, p.146
62. Daniel, p.211
63. Hume, p.161
64. Daniel, p.211
65. Sullivan, in Taylor, H. & A. (1938), p.157
66. Sullivan, in Taylor, H. & A. (1938), p.157
67. Sullivan, in Taylor, H. & A. (1938), pp.157–8
68. Hume, p.161; Johnstone, p.120
69. Strange, in Dennistoun (ed.), p.59
70. Maxwell, p.146
71. Sullivan, in Taylor, H. & A. (1938), p.159
72. Sullivan, in Taylor, H. & A. (1938), p.159
73. Lockhart Papers, Vol. 2, p.519
74. Sullivan, in Taylor, H. & A. (1938), p.159
75. Elcho, p.429
76. Maxwell, p.147
77. Cumberland to the Duke of Newcastle, 15 April 1746, in Massie & Oates (eds.), p.182
78. Strange, in Dennistoun (ed.), p.59
79. Johnstone, p.122
80. Strange, in Dennistoun (ed.), p.61
81. Elcho, p.430
82. Sullivan, in Taylor, H. & A. (1938), p.160
83. Sullivan, in Taylor, H. & A. (1938), p.160
84. Sullivan, in Taylor, H. & A. (1938), p.160
85. Daniel, p.214
86. Sullivan, in Taylor, H. & A. (1938), p.160
87. Murray, p.123
88. Johnstone, p.123
89. For a concise appraisal of the several alternative battle sites, see Pittock (2022), pp.58–65.
90. Elcho, p.430
91. Maxwell, p.148
92. Lockhart Papers, Vol. 2, p.520
93. Maxwell, p.148
94. Maxwell, p.149
95. Sullivan, in Taylor, H. & A. (1938), p.158
96. Lochgarry's Narrative, in Blaikie, p.121

97. Sullivan, in Taylor, H. & A. (1938), pp.160–1
98. Sullivan, in Taylor, H. & A. (1938), pp.160–1
99. Sullivan, in Taylor, H. & A. (1938), p.161
100. Sir John MacDonald, in Taylor, H. & A. (1938), p.161
101. Sullivan, in Taylor, H. & A. (1938), p.162
102. Lockhart Papers, Vol. 2, p.520
103. Cumberland to Newcastle, 18 January 1746, in Massie & Oates, p.185
104. Sullivan, in Taylor, H. & A. (1938), p.163
105. Sullivan, in Taylor, H. & A. (1938), p.163
106. Maxwell, p.149
107. Sullivan, in Taylor, H. & A. (1938), p.164
108. Maxwell, p.150
109. Elcho, p.431
110. Sullivan, in Taylor, H. & A. (1938), p.163
111. Johnstone, p.127
112. Elcho, p.431
113. Maxwell, p.150
114. Maxwell, p.150
115. Maxwell, p.150
116. Elcho, p.431
117. Daniel, p.214
118. Daniel, p.214
119. Sullivan, in Taylor, H. & A. (1938), p.164
120. Daniel, p.214
121. Hume, p.167
122. Strange, in Dennistoun (ed.), p.63
123. Strange, in Dennistoun (ed.), p.63
124. Daniel, p.212
125. Maxwell, p.151
126. Sullivan, in Taylor, H. & A. (1938), p.164
127. Maxwell, p.152
128. Hume, p.167; Maclean, in Brown & Cheape, p.35
129. Sullivan, in Taylor, H. & A. (1938), p.164
130. Sullivan, in Taylor, H. & A. (1938), p.164
131. Cumberland to Newcastle, 18 January 1746, in Massie & Oates, p.185
132. Henderson, p.115
133. Lockhart Papers, Vol. 2, p.531
134. Sullivan, in Taylor, H. & A. (1938), p.164
135. Cumberland to Newcastle, 18 January 1746, in Massie & Oates, p.185

136. Elcho, p.433
137. Maxwell, p.154
138. Johnstone, p.126
139. Murray, p.124
140. Elcho, p.433
141. Strange, in Dennistoun (ed.), p.64. Elcho (p.434) denies that the prince made any effort to rally the fugitives, but this is not plausible. Elcho himself was engaged during this time and could not have seen those efforts as clearly as others who *did* report them.
142. Strange, in Dennistoun (ed.), p.64
143. Sullivan, in Taylor, H. & A. (1938), p.164; Lochgarry's Narrative, in Blaikie, p.121. Sullivan may, because he also mentions the death of the groom at this same moment, be conflating this with the earlier experience of the cannonade.
144. Sullivan, in Taylor, H. & A. (1938), p.164
145. Sullivan, in Taylor, H. & A. (1938), p.164
146. Sullivan, in Taylor, H. & A. (1938), pp.164–5
147. Maxwell, p.154
148. Lochgarry's Narrative, in Blaikie, p.122
149. Sir John MacDonald, in Taylor, H. & A. (1938), p.167
150. Murray, p.124
151. Maxwell, p.159
152. Elcho, pp.436–7
153. Lockhart Papers, Vol. 2, p.522
154. Sullivan, in Taylor, H. & A. (1938), p.167
155. Elcho, p.437
156. O'Neill, in *Lyon in Mourning*, Vol. 1, p.103
157. Sullivan, in Taylor, H. & A. (1938), p.167
158. Murray, in Blaikie, p.79

Epilogue

1. Lochiel, *Memoire d'un Ecossais,* Ministère des Affaires Etrangères, Paris: MD Angleterre, vol. 82, f. 216-21.
2. Sullivan, in Taylor, H. & A. (1938), p.193
3. Sullivan, in Taylor, H. & A. (1938), p.187
4. MacEachain, p.245
5. MacEachain, p.241

6. Johnstone, p.198
7. Stuart Papers: RA SP/MAIN/277 f.143–144
8. Stuart Papers: RA SP/MAIN/277 f.170–171
9. Stuart Papers: RA SP/MAIN/277 f.168–169
10. *Authentick Account of the Conduct of the Young Chevalier*, p.5
11. *Authentick Account of the Conduct of the Young Chevalier*, p.8
12. Elcho, p.445
13. In Taylor (1941), p.253
14. Elcho, p.448
15. Lochiel, *Memoir d'un Ecossois*
16. Elcho, p.446
17. Prince Charles to King James, 3 April 1747, in Blaikie, p.81
18. *Authentick Account of the Conduct of the Young Chevalier*, p.8
19. Elcho, p.446
20. Prince Charles to King Louis XV, 5 November 1746, in Nevin, pp.182–5
21. Prince Charles to King Louis XV, 5 November 1746, in Nevin, pp.182–5
22. Prince Charles to King Louis XV, 14 January 1747, private collection
23. Princes to the Comte d'Argenson, 23 April 1747, private collection
24. *Authentick Account of the Conduct of the Young Chevalier*, p.36
25. *Authentick Account of the Conduct of the Young Chevalier*, p.49
26. *Lyon in Mourning*, Vol. 3, p.159
27. *Lyon in Mourning*, Vol. 3, p.160
28. *Authentick Account of the Conduct of the Young Chevalier*, p.42
29. Lockhart Papers, Vol. 2, p.580
30. Elcho, p.446
31. Lockhart Papers, Vol. 2, p.581
32. Lockhart Papers, Vol. 2, p.581
33. *Authentick Account of the Conduct of the Young Chevalier*, p.60
34. Elcho, p.447
35. Maxwell, p.155

Index

Albano, 2, 14, 15, 23
Anderson, Robert, 70-2, 74, 135
Appin Regiment, 57, 102, 111,
   145, 147
artillery, 1, 6, 9, 10-11, 27, 29,
   31-2
   British, 39, 55, 64, 68-9, 70-1,
      75-6, 81, 120-21, 128,
      148-9, 150, 151
   Jacobite, 41, 42, 60, 64, 80,
      81, 83, 87, 91, 93, 101, 102,
      106, 111, 121, 131, 143,
      146, 148-9
   see also mortars
Atholl, 26, 41, 44, 133
   Brigade, 47, 54, 59, 62, 69, 71,
      73, 91-2, 102, 111-2, 114-5,
      117, 140, 144-6, 152
   James, Duke of, xviii, 48
   William, Jacobite Duke of, *see*
      Tullibardine, Marquis of
Ardsheal, Charles Stewart of, 57
Austrian Succession, War of,
   22, 167

bagpipes, 37, 51, 52, 76, 77, 78
Balmerino, Lord, 120, 164
   Regiment, 120, 150
Benedict XIV, Pope, 3, 6,
   16, 182

Berwick, Duke of, 1, 2, 7, 8, 9,
   10-13, 17, 25, 172, 183
Berwick-upon-Tweed, 55, 87, 90
Blair Castle, 41, 49, 133
Bitonto, Battle of, 7, 8, 12
Boisdale, Alexander MacDonald
   of, *see* MacDonald of
   Boisdale, Alexander
Brett, Captain Peircy, 27, 30,
   32, 185
Broughton, John Murray of,
   see Murray, John

Callendar House, 108, 118,
   119, 120
Cameron,
   clan/regiment, 37, 52, 55, 57,
      68, 69, 76, 78, 111-3, 115,
      132, 142, 144, 145
   Archibald, 118, 164
   Donald, of Lochiel,
      see Lochiel, Donald
      Cameron of
   John, of Fassefern, 35
   prisoner at Falkirk, 119
cannon, *see* artillery
Carlisle, 90, 92-5, 101-3, 106-7,
   119, 121, 132
Carlyle, Alexander, 60, 70, 79
Carriera, Rosalba, 119

Charles II, King of England, Scotland and Ireland, 46, 51, 89, 92
Charles VII, King of Naples, *see* Naples, King Charles VII of
Charles XII, King of Sweden, 39
Cisterna, 23
Clanranald,
    Ranald MacDonald, Younger of, 34-6, 57, 114
    Regiment, 35-7, 76, 103, 121, 146, 151
Clifton, xvi, 84, 102-3
Cockenzie, 62-4, 67, 76, 78
Cope, Sir John, Lieutenant General, 38, 41, 44, 48, 54-5, 57, 59-81, 85, 87, 167
Corrieyairack Pass, 42, 43
Covenanters, 89
Cromarty,
    Earl of, 129, 134, 136, 164
    Regiment, 111, 134, 136, 143
Cromlix, John Hay of, *see* Inverness, Jacobite Duke of
Culloden,
    Battle of, xi, xvi, 59, 126-58, 159, 163-4, 171, 174
    Forbes of, *see* Forbes, Duncan
    House, 129, 141-2, 144
    landscape, 128, 135, 145
    night march, 135-41
    escape from, 154-8, 165
Cumberland, William Augustus, Duke of
Cunninghame, Robert, 59, 62

Dalkeith, 60, 91
Dalrymple, Hew, *see* Drummore, Lord Hew Dalrymple
Daniel, John, 100, 109, 113, 120, 132, 138, 149, 150, 153, 164
Dehau, Captain Pierre, 27, 30-32
Dettingen, Battle of, xii
Derby, ix, xvi, 96-7, 99-100, 103, 107, 124, 129
Dolphinstone, 67, 69
Donnachaidh (clan), 58, 80
Drummond, James, *see* Perth, Duke of
Drummond, John, 95, 98, 101-2, 104, 105-6, 109-11, 117, 120, 141, 146, 153, 165
Drummond, Lewis, Lieutenant Colonel, 155
Drummond, William, *see* Strathallan, Viscount
Drummore, Lord Hew Dalrymple 60, 61, 64, 76, 77
Duddingston, 45, 53, 54, 56, 57-60, 71, 74
Dunbar, 54
    James Murray, Earl of, 4, 5, 7-13, 16, 18, 19, 23, 29
Dunipace, 109, 110, 116, 118
Dunkirk, 24, 25
Durand, Colonel, 94
Durbé, Captain Claude, 26, 27, 29-33
Du Teillay (ship), 25-33, 41, 42

Edinburgh, ix, xiii, 39, 41, 46, 49, 50, 51, 54, 67, 73, 75, 79, 86, 87, 89, 107, 108, 113, 119, 122, 133, 149
    Castle, 39, 47, 55, 66, 71, 87

204

Éguilles, Marquis d', 88, 89
Elcho, Lord David Wemyss, xvii, 40, 45-7, 50, 56, 61, 63, 64, 66, 71, 73, 76, 77, 79, 86, 87, 89, 90, 92, 99, 100, 111, 114, 116, 118, 119, 121, 126, 127, 129, 130, 134, 135, 144, 146, 156, 162-65
L'Elisabeth (ship), 25-32, 38
Elgin, 132
Eriskay, 34
Esk, River (Lothian), 60
Esk, River (Cumbria), 91, 103-4

Falkirk, 107, 117, 120, 122-5, 129, 135, 138
   Battle of, 105-120, 143, 146, 154, 167
   First Battle of (1298), 121
   landscape, 108, 109, 110
Fitzjames, Regiment de, 127, 139, 141, 142, 146, 150, 154, 156, 163
Fleury, Cardinal, 23
Fontenoy, Battle of, 164
Formia, 10
Forth, River, 58, 62, 68, 106, 125
Fox, HMS (ship), 64

Gaeta, 1-15, 17, 18, 19, 31, 42, 171
Garden, Francis, 62
Garvamore, 43, 44
Genoa, 23
George II, King of Great Britain and Ireland, xiii, 81, 84, 85, 124, 167
Gardiner, Colonel James, 62, 71, 79, 80, 113, 149

Gladsmuir, 81, 85
   see also Prestonpans, Battle of
Glasgow, 47, 85, 105
Glenbucket, John Gordon of, 35, 41, 87, 92, 147, 162
Glenfinnan, 34, 36-8, 39, 40, 41, 42, 58, 64, 124, 164
   Monument, ix, 37
Glengarry, Aeneas MacDonnell of, 57, 94, 117, 121, 155
   Regiment, 55, 101, 102, 118, 121, 146, 147, 155
Glenshiel, Battle of, 6, 26, 47
Gordon, Lord Lewis, 118, 132, 163
   Regiment, 109, 111, 146, 148, 150
   Mirabelle de, 106, 133
Grosset, Walter, 68

Haddington, 55, 65
Halkett, Lieutenant Colonel Peter, 78
Hawley, Lieutenant General Henry, 107-13, 115-25, 126, 148, 150, 153-5, 167
Hay of Cromlix, John, *see* Inverness, Jacobite Duke of
Henderson, Andrew, 40, 49, 50, 52, 66, 79, 80
Holyroodhouse, Palace of, 45, 49, 50, 53-6, 64, 72, 85-6, 141
Home, John, 37, 40, 41, 50, 53, 54, 55, 60, 70, 79

Invergarry, 43, 156-7
Inverness, 43, 128, 131-4, 141-5,
   Jacobite Duke of, 4, 16-18

Inverurie, Battle of, xvi, 109, 132, 163
Irish Picquets, 109, 111, 116, 117, 146, 153, 155

James VII & II, King of Scotland, England and Ireland, 1, 25, 51
James VIII & III, King (Jacobite), see Stuart, James Francis
Jenkinson, Beatrix and Mary, 60, 71, 80
Johnstone, Captain James, xvii, 41, 48, 49, 62, 75, 77, 84, 98, 114, 118, 119, 120, 134, 135, 141, 142, 148, 160, 166

Keith,
George, Earl Marischal, 25, 29
James Hepburn of, 50, 141
skirmish, xvi
Keppoch, Alexander MacDonald of, 38, 43, 54, 56, 57, 77, 87, 99, 117, 125, 136, 152, 164
Regiment, 83, 103, 134, 136, 146
Ker of Graden, Henry, 66-8, 86, 139, 144, 150-1, 156
Killiecrankie, Battle of, 35, 80
Kilmarnock, William Boyd, Earl of, 108, 117, 119, 121, 143, 164
Regiment, 92, 118, 119, 127, 147, 153

Lancaster, 84, 96, 100, 101
Lion, HMS (ship), 27-32, 42
Lifeguards, 87, 97, 100, 114, 117, 126, 132, 150, 154, 162
Linlithgow, 39, 51, 107, 117

Littleferry, Battle of, xvi, 136, 143
Lochiel, Cameron of, 35, 37, 43, 45, 51, 55, 67, 65, 68, 69, 72, 87, 99, 101, 117, 118, 132, 134, 139, 141, 142, 145, 152, 160, 164, 165, 166
Regiment, see Cameron, clan/ regiment
London, ix, 60, 63, 80, 92, 97, 99, 105, 108, 165, 167
Tower of, 21, 164

MacDonald, Aeneas, 25, 26, 30, 32, 33, 35, 38
MacDonald, Alexander, see Keppoch, Alexander MacDonald of
MacDonald, Sir John, xviii, 22, 32, 37, 43, 47, 65, 69, 73, 74, 78, 80, 89, 90, 93, 94, 99, 108, 137, 138, 144, 155
MacDonald of Boisdale, Alexander, 34
MacDonnell, Aeneas, see Glengarry, Aeneas MacDonnell of
MacLachlan, Lachlan, 95, 150
Regiment, 58, 145
Maillebois, Marquis de, 22
Manchester, 95, 101
Regiment, 103-4
Massa, 23
Maxwell of Kirkconnell, James, xvii, 77, 89, 93, 94, 96, 99, 104, 119, 130, 133, 134, 136, 138, 139, 144, 147, 174
Montemar, Count of, 6, 7, 8, 9
mortar(s), 64, 71, 81, 152-3, 155

Murray, James, Duke of Atholl, *see* Atholl, James, Duke of
Murray, James, Earl of Dunbar, *see* Dunbar, James Murray, Earl of
Murray, John, Lord Nairne, *see* Nairne, Lord John Murray
Murray, John, of Broughton, xvii, xviii, 29, 33, 36, 37, 42, 43, 44, 50, 51, 55, 57, 61, 65, 66, 73, 75, 79, 87, 89, 93, 99, 108, 122, 123, 125, 128, 157, 165
Murray, Lord George, xvi, xviii, 6, 26, 47, 48, 49, 57, 61, 66, 68, 69, 70, 74, 75, 76, 78, 79, 83, 84, 88, 89, 90, 91, 93, 94, 95, 97, 98, 99, 101, 102, 103, 106, 107, 108, 109, 111, 112, 113, 115, 116, 117, 122, 123, 125, 128, 130, 132, 133, 134, 135, 136, 137, 140, 143, 144-8, 150, 153, 155, 156, 157, 158, 163, 165, 166
Murray, William, *see* Tullibardine, Marquis of
Musselburgh, 55, 60, 81

Nairn, 126, 127, 128, 132, 135, 136, 138, 145
   River, 131, 135, 143, 145, 155, 156
Nairne, Lord John Murray, 54, 56, 58, 67, 69, 70, 74, 75, 77
Nantes, 25, 26
Naples, 5, 6, 10, 12, 13, 14, 17, 18
   King Charles VII of, xviii, 1-11, 13, 14, 15
Newcastle, 88, 90, 91, 92, 94
Norris, Admiral John, 24

O'Sullivan, John William, *see* Sullivan, John William
Ogilvy, Lord David, 87, 117, 143, 162
   Regiment, 92, 101, 109, 111

Parma, 3, 6, 19
   Duke of, *see* Naples, King Charles VII of
Penrith, 83-5, 96, 101, 102
Perth, 44, 45, 47, 48, 49, 55, 58, 95, 124, 130
   James Drummond, Duke of, 20, 41, 45, 47, 57, 71, 74, 75, 76, 79, 83, 84, 86, 89, 91-4, 98, 99, 101, 103, 106, 133, 135, 140, 141, 143, 146, 150, 151, 155, 158, 164-5
   Regiment, 54, 57, 92, 147
Perthshire Squadron, *see* Strathallan Regiment
Pinkie, 60, 61, 81, 90
   Battle of, 60, 61
Pitsligo's Regiment of Horse, 86, 92, 102, 103, 128
Polish Succession, War of, 1
Porto Salvo, 9
Prestonpans, 60, 144
   aftermath, 78-81, 87-88, 90, 119, 162
   Battle of, 67-78, 85, 108, 112, 135, 150, 160
   landscape, 62-72
Pringle, Magdalen, 40, 86
Purcell, Henry, 132

Ramsay, Allan, 40
Riggonhead, 72, 74
Robertson of Struan, Alexander, 80

Rome, 2, 3, 5, 6, 7, 8, 9, 13, 15, 16, 17, 18, 22, 23, 28, 29, 40, 73, 80, 161, 165, 168, 173
  Palazzo del Re, 2, 16, 18, 19, 46, 187
Ruthven Barracks, 42, 131, 157, 165
Rutledge, Walter, 25

Saint-Nazaire, 26
Santiesteban, Count of, 3, 8, 10
Saxe, Maurice de, 24, 25
Scone, 51
Scott, Sir Walter, x, 165
Shap, 83-4, 101
Sheridan, Sir Thomas, 8, 12, 13, 21, 22, 25, 34, 36, 93, 98, 99, 125, 155, 157
Sheriffmuir, Battle of, 35, 47, 80
Sobieska, Maria Clementina, xiv, 4, 15, 16, 17
Spain, 3, 5, 6, 8, 14, 22
Spanish Succession, War of, 1, 5, 47
Stirling, 44, 106, 107, 120, 121, 123, 129
Stones, Anthony, ix
Strathallan, Viscount William Drummond, 47, 95, 98, 105, 153, 164
  Regiment, 46, 57, 61, 64, 74, 78, 146, 153
Strickland, Francis, 21, 25
Stuart, Prince Henry Benedict, 4, 15, 18, 19, 23, 73, 133, 161, 168, 173
Stuart, James Francis, xvi, xviii, 2, 4, 5, 7, 12, 13, 15, 16, 18, 28, 45, 48, 52, 63, 73, 80, 94, 160, 162, 163, 165, 170

Stuart, John Roy, 59, 102, 117, 164
  Regiment, 92, 101, 102, 106, 147
Sullivan, John William, xvi, xviii, 22, 25, 26, 27, 31, 34, 36, 38, 42, 45, 48, 49, 51, 53, 54, 57, 61, 64, 65, 66-71, 73, 74, 76, 77, 79, 83, 84, 86, 88, 89, 91, 94, 96, 98, 99, 103, 104, 109, 110, 112, 115-16, 120, 121, 122, 123, 125, 127, 128, 130, 131, 134, 135, 137, 138, 140-41, 143, 144, 145, 146, 147, 152, 154, 155, 157, 160, 163-64, 166, 173

targe (shield), 20, 54, 91, 115, 119, 151, 152
Torwood, 109, 121
Tranent, 61-74, 80, 86, 136, 139
Tullibardine, William Murray, Marquis of, xviii, 6, 26, 34, 37, 41, 43, 47, 91, 93, 94, 97, 99, 100, 133, 155, 164

Venice, 19, 165
Versailles, Palace of, 24, 28, 88, 168
Vezzosi, Michele de, xii, 10, 13, 25, 53

Wade, George, Field Marshal, 90, 91, 92, 94, 95, 97, 98, 100, 156
Walkinshaw, Clementina, 122, 163, 173
Walsh, Antoine, 25, 27, 30, 31, 32, 33, 34
Wemyss, David, *see* Elcho, Lord